Injury Prevention

omit = avoid behavior
commit = perform behavior

Competencies for
Unintentional Injury Prevention Professionals

THIRD EDITION

Alton L. Thygerson, EdD, FAWM

Steven M. Thygerson, PhD, MSPH

Justin S. Thygerson, MS

JONES AND BARTLETT PUBLISHERS
Sudbury, Massachusetts

BOSTON   TORONTO   LONDON   SINGAPORE

PPt #3 Selection f Injury Interventions - ① Hadden Matrix ② 3 E's
Prioritize f choose intervention - ① Bracketology, Hanlon, Paired-comparison analysis

Education, Enforcement, Engineering
persuasion /legal req. f prohibitions/ automatic protection f environ-modifica
teach about risks, persuade to adopt safe behavior, inform policy makers
about issues (safety posters)

pass f enforce laws that require safe behavior: ① Require behavior - Tprotection, ② prohibit behavior (drunk driving, speeding) T risk/danger
→ Macro Level - car companies, elevators inspec, health f safety
→ Individual Level - wear seat belts, helmets f color f capacity f school bus,
building codes, f alcohol) smoke detectors)
EY - Enforcement = speed limit laws, wear PFD, hunter orange, building codes

Arguments used against a proposed law: ① problem is not that
important ② the proposed law won't work ③ it will cost too much
④ it is not legal (or constitutional) ⑤ it is an undue burden on personal
freedom ⑥ not feasible, or enforceable ⑦ not popular w citizens ⑧ if ppl
would only take care of themselves f families there would not be a
problem

Effectiveness d law depends on ① Likelihood f apprehension
(therefore high)
② swiftness f penalty
③ severity " " d be extreme

Engineering - make changes to environ.
product to automatically protect everyone
passive vs active
(breakaway sign posts, helmets, PFDs, detectors) etc.

Identify (cost, YPLL, mortality, news paper, NEISS, HP2010-31)

Handwritten note (top margin): Runyan criteria – Effective, Preferences, Costs, Restriction of person freedom, Stigmatizes, Feasible,

World Headquarters

Jones and Bartlett Publishers
40 Tall Pine Drive
Sudbury, MA 01776
978-443-5000
info@jbpub.com
www.jbpub.com

Jones and Bartlett Publishers
Canada
6339 Ormindale Way
Mississauga, Ontario L5V 1J2
Canada

Jones and Bartlett Publishers
International
Barb House, Barb Mews
London W6 7PA
United Kingdom

Jones and Bartlett's books and products are available through most bookstores and online booksellers. To contact Jones and Bartlett Publishers directly, call 800-832-0034, fax 978-443-8000, or visit our Web site, www.jbpub.com.

Substantial discounts on bulk quantities of Jones and Bartlett's publications are available to corporations, professional associations, and other qualified organizations. For details and specific discount information, contact the special sales department at Jones and Bartlett via the above contact information or send an email to specialsales@jbpub.com.

The procedures and protocols in this book are based on the most current recommendations of responsible medical sources. The publisher, however, makes no guarantee as to, and assumes no responsibility for, the correctness, sufficiency, or completeness of such information or recommendations. Other or additional safety measures may be required under particular circumstances.

This textbook is intended solely as a guide to the appropriate procedures to be employed when rendering emergency care to the sick and injured. It is not intended as a statement of the standards of care required in any particular situation, because circumstances and the patient's physical condition can vary widely from one emergency to another. Nor is it intended that this textbook shall in any way advise emergency personnel concerning legal authority to perform the activities or procedures discussed. Such local determination should be made only with the aid of legal counsel.

Production Credits
Acquisitions Editor: Jacqueline Ann Geraci
Associate Editor: Amy L. Flagg
Editorial Assistant: Kyle Hoover
Senior Production Editor: Julie Champagne Bolduc
Production Assistant: Jessica Steele Newfell
Marketing Manager: Wendy Thayer
Marketing Associate: Meagan Norlund
Manufacturing Buyer: Therese Connell
Cover Design: Kristin E. Ohlin
Photo Research Manager: Kimberly Potvin
Associate Photo Researcher and Photographer:
    Christine McKeen
Photo Researcher: Lee Michelsen
Photo Researcher: Timothy Renzi
Cover Image: © emily2k/ShutterStock, Inc.
Printing and Binding: Malloy, Inc.
Cover Printing: Malloy, Inc.

Library of Congress Cataloging-in-Publication Data
Thygerson, Alton L.
  Injury prevention : competencies for unintentional injury prevention professionals / Alton L. Thygerson, Steven M. Thygerson, Justin S. Thygerson. -- 3rd ed.
    p. ; cm.
  Includes bibliographical references.
  ISBN-13: 978-0-7637-5383-2 (pbk. : alk. paper)
  1. Accidents--Prevention. 2. Wounds and injuries--Prevention. I. Thygerson, Steven M. II. Thygerson, Justin S. III. Title.
  [DNLM: 1. Wounds and Injuries--prevention & control--Outlines. 2. Accident Prevention--Outlines. 3. Risk Reduction Behavior--Outlines. 4. Safety Management--Outlines. WO 18.2 T549i 2008]
  RA772.A25T49 2008
  363.1--dc22
                          2007048988
6048
Printed in the United States of America
12 11 10 09 08 10 9 8 7 6 5 4 3 2 1

Handwritten note (right margin):
P = propriety (suitable)
E = Economics
A = Acceptability
R = Resources
L = Legality

Handwritten note (bottom margin): Indian Health Service – Effectiveness, Feasible, cost, sustainable, political acceptance, social will

Human causation model = Back page

1. *punishing: ① time consuming ② uncomfortable ③ criticized*
2. *Rewarding: ① attention ③ rest, time ff ③ make or saved*
3. *Doesn't matter: ① doing it same way for years & haven't been injured ② nothing happens if act safe or unsafely*

Contents

4. *obstacles: ① deadline, pressure, in hurry ② Lack of $ to buy safety equipment ③ lack of knowledge and/or skills to be safe ③ poor lighting*

behavior change = Aimed @ masses → Education (will do right thing when only if people are motivated) They understand) Persuasion (actions take place) individual - Behavioral modification - actions are rewarded

* ⚐ abilities
*(change) ⚐
behavior
poison storage
* ⚐ use of protection

Assumptions: ① Person will retain info & take action to reduce risk skilled person less likely to have injury Educator capable of teaching info & cause attitude change training will not ↑ activity that may ↑ injuries from using a new skill

Handwritten annotations:

safety taught in: Homes, schools, colleges/universities, worksites, communities

M-V
Falls
Poisoning - Ingest
Drowning
Suffocation - Ingest
Fires, burns
Firearms
Poisoning - gas vapurs

prversed
?
poison control
learn to swim
?
learn not to burn
Hunter safety
?

El-Ed is better (than grad school)
↳ shou d tell
↳ know students
↳ methods 2
   tell me d I forget
   shou me d I remember
   Involve me d I understand
↳ small classes

Lesson Plan   ① Behavoral objectives ② concepts or content
③ learning activities

#1 learners will be able to do; observable, (what teacher is doing),
→ behavioral objectives, learning objectives, instructional, performance.

Action verb - identifies behavior to be performed (observe)
↳ explain, apply, choose, compare, develop, name, write

Φ Fuzzy verb - know, understand, appreciate

Chapter 4 ▶ Program Evaluation   95

Preface

Over the past century, we have witnessed a remarkable reduction in unintentional injuries. However, in recent years, unintentional injuries in the United States have been the number one leading cause of death in children and young adults, the fifth leading cause of death for all ages, and the leading cause of potential life lost before age 65.

The field of injury prevention professionals spans an array of disciplines such as public health, law enforcement, emergency medical services, occupational safety and health, highway and traffic safety, and education. The premise of this book is that further improvements in preventing and controlling injuries can be achieved through enlarging the pool of skilled, competent injury prevention professionals in all of these areas.

The National Training Initiative for Injury and Violence Prevention (NTI)—a joint project of the State and Territorial Injury Prevention Directors Association (STIPDA) and the Society for the Advancement of Violence and Injury Research (SAVIR)—developed a set of nine Core Competencies for Injury and Violence Prevention professionals (http://www.injuryed.org/competencies.htm). These Core Competencies outline a common understanding of the essential skills and knowledge necessary to work in the field of injury prevention. These objectives provide the foundation for this book.

While the Core Competencies focus on both violence (intentional injuries) and unintentional injuries, this book focuses solely on unintentional injuries. The first eight chapters correspond to the objectives of the first eight Core Competencies. The second half of the book addresses Core Competency 9, which requires the demonstration of knowledge, skills, and practices to address one specific injury. Chapters 9 through 15 spotlight the major unintentional injury problems (e.g., motor vehicle injuries; poisoning; fall injuries; drowning; choking, suffocation, and strangulation; residential fires; and firearm injuries), discuss the risk factors of each, and explain the appropriate interventions.

Injury Prevention: Competencies for Unintentional Injury Prevention Professionals helps readers enhance their skills in preventing and controlling unintentional injuries. Some of the key features include:

▶ Best practices and evidence-based interventions for unintentional injuries and the latest recommendations and strategies.
▶ Several methods for prioritizing injury problems and interventions, including the Hanlon Method, paired comparison analysis, and bracketology.
▶ Concise, straightforward, and essential information for the injury prevention professional.

▶ Separate chapters on the risk factors, pathophysiology, and interventions for specific injury problems such as motor vehicle injuries; poisoning; fall injuries; choking, suffocation and strangulation; drowning; residential fire injuries; and firearm injuries.

Today's injury prevention professionals must be prepared to handle many types of unintentional injuries in the scope of their practice. It is the authors' hope that each reader will enhance their skills and become a knowledgeable advocate for further improvements in unintentional injury prevention.

Acknowledgments

Appreciation is extended to those at Jones and Bartlett Publishers who helped in the development and production of this book: Jacqueline Geraci, Amy Flagg, Julie Bolduc, Jess Newfell, Kyle Hoover, Wendy Thayer, Tim Renzi, Kimberly Potvin, and Lee Michelsen. Without the support of Ardith, wife and mother, the publication of this book would not have been possible.

Note from Alton Thygerson

A book of this kind reflects an author's experience. Like everyone, I personally have been exposed to several of the injury problems discussed in this book. In addition, I have spent my professional career teaching injury prevention and emergency care courses at the university level. I have enjoyed close associations with several professional organizations and have wide consulting experience in safety. I am a medical writer who authors books and manuals in the emergency care and health fields.

I have also drawn upon long hours and decades of extensive injury-related literature research. This resulted in 25 years of authoring a weekly newspaper column devoted to safety, six years of writing a monthly emergency medical journal feature, publishing several safety books preceding this one, and authoring first aid and emergency care books and manuals for the American Academy of Orthopaedic Surgeons, American Academy of Pediatrics, American College of Emergency Physicians, American Heart Association, National Safety Council, and the Wilderness Medical Society.

By way of introduction, two of my five sons positioned themselves for involvement with this book. They accomplished this by their earning graduate degrees and working professionally in the injury prevention field.

CHAPTER 1 ▶

Magnitude and Burden of the Injury Problem

CORE COMPETENCY 1: Ability to describe and explain injury as a major social and health problem.

---

a. Define injury and describe the concepts of intentionality and mechanism as they relate to injury.

The definition of an "injury" is complicated and not easily understood. Though all of us have been injured and assume to know what an injury is, it is more difficult to define than you may think.

Injuries can be fatal or nonfatal. *Injury* is damage or harm to the body or to property. The Society for Advancement of Violence and Injury Research (SAVIR) and the State and Territorial Injury Prevention Directors Association (STIPDA) Joint Committee define *injury* as "any unintentional or intentional damage to the body resulting from acute exposure to thermal, mechanical, electrical, or chemical energy that exceeds a threshold of tolerance in the body or from the absence of such essentials as heat or oxygen" (2005). This is a good definition, but it should include the concept that injuries can include things beyond the body (e.g., property damage, lost wages, psychological effects; see Table 1-6 later in this chapter for a more complete listing). The definition also does not include ionizing radiation as a form of energy.

Injuries can be unintentional or intentional. The SAVIR-STIPDA Joint Committee defines an *unintentional injury* as one "that is judged to have occurred without anyone intending harm be done; in many settings these are termed 'accidental injuries.'" Examples of unintentional injuries include motor vehicle crashes, falls, poisoning, burns, suffocation, and drowning. This book focuses on unintentional injuries.

This committee defines *intentional injuries* as "injuries that result from purposeful human action whether directed at oneself (self-directed) or others (assaultive), sometimes referred to as violent injuries." Examples of intentional acts include homicides, suicides, assaults, and arson.

Experts and authorities in the injury field have attempted to displace the term *accident.* For example, the National Highway Traffic Safety Administration and the *British Medical Journal* (Davis and Pless, 2001) have discontinued using the term *accident.* However, most people still label unintentional injuries as *accidents* and use it in everyday speech.

There is a pattern to injuries that make injuries foreseeable and preventable—and once we know what to expect, we can begin to think about how to intervene in order to prevent injuries from happening. Changing the way people perceive injuries helps efforts to prevent them.

Before reading further about the attributes of the term *unintentional injury,* take the pretest by reading through each of the statements in Table 1-1 and following the directions as given.

There are two major attributes of unintentional injuries: (1) unintended "causes" and (2) undesirable "effects." These two factors constitute the major elements of the definition of the term unintentional injury. Two other factors essential in the definition of an unintentional injury are (1) the suddenness of the event (in seconds or minutes) and (2) the damage results from one of the forms of physical energy (e.g., mechanical, thermal, chemical, electrical, ionizing radiation) that exceeds the tolerance level or lack of physical agents (e.g., oxygen, heat).

Unintentional injuries can occur in many places, any time, and by anyone.

Table 1-1 Which Are Unintentional Injuries?

Directions: Check each item that you consider to be an unintentional injury as the term is used in the injury prevention field.

✓   1. A construction worker fractures his toe while using a jackhammer.

___   2. A construction worker is diagnosed as having tendonitis of the elbow from the chronic vibrations of using a jack hammer during the past year.

✓   3. A technician at a nuclear power plant is burned severely when a fuel rod breaks open.

___   4. Numerous residents of St. George, Utah, developed cancer 20 years after fallout from underground nuclear bomb tests in Nevada in the 1950s.

✓   5. A child is bitten by her family's dog and requires 10 stitches to her leg.

✓   6. A child dies of rabies after a bat bite.

___   7. A depressed woman dies from an overdose of aspirin. She left a note indicating her intention to commit suicide.

✓   8. An animal trainer was attacked and injured by a tiger.

✓   9. A woman fell off a trolley car with no apparent injuries, but she later sued claiming that her behavior and personality were changed because of the fall.

✓ 10. While hurrying to meet a deadline, a secretary tripped, fell, and scraped a knee.

___ 11. During an event known as "road rage," a car was run off the road and the driver died at the scene.

___ 12. Two people were trampled to death by irate soccer fans protesting by rioting over a referee's decision.

✓ 13. A professional golfer survived with only minor burns after being struck by lightning.

___ 14. A college student caught a cold from his girlfriend.

___ 15. During a bank robbery, a security guard was shot and killed.

✓ 16. The family car's right fender was bent while a teenage family member was backing the car out of the garage.

✓ 17. A 1-year-old child died after swallowing aspirin obtained from his mother's purse.

✓ 18. An elderly couple died from hypothermia after being stranded in their car during a winter blizzard.

___ 19. A 17-year-old high school football player died shortly after collapsing during a game. The boy's family reported that the boy had a heart defect that had gone undetected.

Answers: Statements 1, 3, 5, 8, 9, 10, 13, 16, 17, and 18 meet the criteria for an unintentional injury as defined in the field of injury prevention.

Unintended Causes

What is meant by an "unintended cause"? Intent is not easy to discern, such as when a young child comes to the hospital emergency department with a scald burn. Although it could be unintentional, a sizeable number of such cases are due to abuse.

The so-called "acts of God," such as being hit by lightning or drowning in a flood, are generally considered unintended causes. At the other end of the scale are "acts of man," where it is clear that the causes were due to human behavior (which could be intended or unintended).

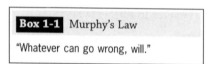

> **Box 1-1** Murphy's Law
>
> "Whatever can go wrong, will."

It is important to differentiate between events that are intentional and those that are unintentional. Unintentional events result in injuries (e.g., drowning, falls, poisoning). Intentional acts also cause injuries—some similar to those caused by unintentional events such as wounds and fractures—but are labeled as crime (e.g., homicide, assault, arson), suicide, wars, and riots. Therefore, if intent can be shown to precede the injury, the occurrence is labeled as being intentional and becomes a criminal act. This book focuses on unintentional causes that have resulted in undesirable effects (e.g., death, disability, property damage).

It is also important to note that the term unintended covers only damage from one of the forms of physical energy in the environment (e.g., mechanical, thermal, chemical, electrical, ionizing radiation) or lack of physical agents (e.g., oxygen, heat). Thus, if a person inadvertently swallows poison and is damaged, the event is called an unintentional injury. However, if that same person comes in contact with an influenza virus and become ill, the result is called a disease.

Edward Suchman (1964) indicates that the term unintentional injury is more likely to used when the event manifests the following three major characteristics:

1. Degree of expectedness—the less the event could have been anticipated, the more likely it is to be labeled an unintentional injury.
2. Degree of avoidability—the less the event could have been avoided, the more likely it is to be labeled an unintentional injury.
3. Degree of intention—the less the event was the result of a deliberate action, the more likely it is to be labeled an unintentional injury.

> **Box 1-2** Universality of Injuries
>
> "Whatever can happen to one man can happen to every man."
>
> — Seneca

These characteristics could include many daily activities such as losing things or forgetting an appointment, but within the context of the injury prevention and safety field, they result in death, disability, and/or property damage.

Undesirable Effects

What is meant by *undesirable effects*? Injury, in the medical sense, ranges from minor to severe. At any rate, the term injury usually refers to damage resulting from sudden exposure to excessive physical and/or environmental agents, while the result of long-term exposure is usually classified as disease.

Death, disability, and/or property damage—undesirable effects of an unintentional event—do not in themselves constitute the event but are the results of it. In other words, death, disability, and/or property damage indicate that an unintentional event has occurred if they result from a sudden or short-term exposure to physical and/or environmental agents.

An injury could be psychological in nature. Examples include anger, fear, and embarrassment. Such results, while a part of most injuries, would not ordinarily define an injury event.

Consequences of an injury event need not be entirely negative or undesirable. For example, though a child is burned by touching a hot pan or pot, he or she learns very quickly that pans and pots can be hot and can produce pain. Thus, the child avoids future contact with hot pans and pots (or possibly even any hot object) in an attempt to prevent being hurt again. This child's experience, though temporarily painful, has a long-term positive effect. Examples of some good things resulting from unintentional actions appears in Table 1-2.

> **Box 1-3** Unusual but True
>
> Bob Aubrey of Ottawa, Ontario, had been blind for 8 years when he tripped over his guide dog and banged his head on the floor. His sight was instantly restored.
>
> — National Safety Council, *Family Safety*

> **Box 1-4** Unusual but True
>
> Edwin Robinson, legally blind and partially deaf, was standing under a poplar tree near his Falmouth, Maine, home during an electrical storm. A bolt of lightning struck him, restoring his sight and hearing.
>
> — National Safety Council, *Family Safety*

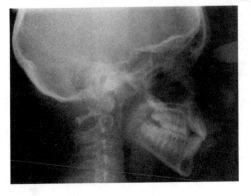

In 1895 Wilhelm Roentgen of Germany invented the X-ray.

Table 1-2 Unintentional Scientific Discoveries

Discovery	Discoverer	Year
Electrical current	Luigi Galvani of Italy	1781
Practical photograph	Louis Daguerre of France	1837
Vulcanized rubber	Charles Goodyear of the United States	1839
X-rays	Wilhelm Roentgen of Germany	1895
Radioactivity	Henri Becquerel of France	1896
Safety glass	Edouard Benedictus of France	1903
Cellophane	Jacques Brandenberger of Switzerland	1908
Popsicle	Frank Epperson of the United States	1923
Penicillin	Alexander Fleming of Scotland	1928
Teflon	Roy J. Plunkett of the United States	1938
Velcro	George de Mestral of Switzerland	1940
Superglue	Harry Coover of the United States	1942
Scotchgard	Patsy Sherman of the United States	1953
Post-it notes	Spencer Silver of the United States	1970

The after-effects of disasters offer examples of learning from bad experiences. Although human life may be taken, survivors learn that living in certain river bottoms in the springtime or being near a beach during a hurricane or tsunami should be avoided. See Table 1-3 for a list of disasters that occurred in the United States and what safety measures were put in place in reaction to those events.

Natural disasters can be devastating. This is an aerial view of an F5 tornado damage in Wichita Falls, Texas, following Red River tornado outbreak on April 10, 1978.

Table 1-3 Disasters and Their Effects on Safety Measures

Type	Location and date	Total deaths	Results
Fire	City of Chicago, IL October 9, 1871	250	Building codes prohibiting wooden structures; water reserve
Flood	Johnstown, PA May 31, 1889	2,209	Inspections
Tidal wave	Galveston, TX September 8, 1900	6,000	Sea wall built
Fire	Iroquis Theatre, Chicago, IL December 30, 1903	575	Stricter theater safety standards
Marine	*General Slocum* burned East River, NY June 15, 1904	1,021	Stricter ship inspections; revision of statutes (life preservers, experienced crew, fire extinguishers)
Earthquake and fire	San Francisco, CA April 18, 1906	452	Widened streets; limited heights of buildings; steel frame and fire-resistant buildings
Mine	Monongah, WV December 6, 1907	361	Creation of Federal Bureau of Mines; stiffened mine inspections
Fire	North Collinwood School Cleveland, OH March 8, 1908	176	Need realized for fire drills and planning of school structures
Fire	Triangle Shirt Waist Co., New York, NY March 25, 1911	145	Strengthening of laws concerning alarm signals, sprinklers, fire escapes, fire drills
Marine	*Titanic* struck iceberg Atlantic Ocean April 15, 1912	1,517	Regulation regarding number of lifeboats; all passenger ships equipped for around-the-clock radio watch; International Ice Patrol
Explosion	New London School, TX March 18, 1937	294	Odorants put in natural gas

Table 1-3 Disasters and Their Effects on Safety Measures (continued)

Type	Location and date	Total deaths	Results
Fire	Cocoanut Grove nightclub Boston, MA November 28, 1942	492	Ordinances regulating aisle space, electrical wiring, flame proofing of decorations, overcrowding, signs indicating the maximum number of occupants; administration of blood plasma to prevent shock and the use of penicillin
Plane	Two-plane air collision over Grand Canyon, AZ June 30, 1956	128	Controlled airspace expanded; use of infrared as a warning indicator
Hurricane and flood	Florida, Louisiana, and Mississippi August 25, 29–30, 2005	1,330 2,096 missing	Proposal to strengthen education, exercises, and training programs emphasizing such actions as listening to warnings, and quickly responding; space does not allow for the listing of the many lessons learned

It is not suggested that everyone should expose themselves to hazardous situations in order to learn how to avoid being damaged; rather, all people can gain from others' experiences. This is actually the basis for all education and training. They are shortcuts to experience; they teach how to avoid hazards that may have undesirable effects.

Injury replacing *accident* has created a controversy with some experts saying that a resulting injury is the outcome and does not identify the unplanned events leading to the damage or harm. Why a person is injured is a separate question from why the person was involved in the events leading to the injury.

This point-of-view says that two of the main attributes found in the definition of an unintentional injury (unintentional causes and undesirable effects) are independent of each other. It is, for example, possible for a person to trip and fall down a flight of stairs (the unintended event) without hurting him- or herself (the injury). The two factors can help in determining the appropriate interventions to be used in combating the injury problem. *Injury prevention* pertains to the efforts (e.g., education, prohibitions, licensing) to deal with the unintentional causes of injuries. *Injury control* pertains to the mitigation or lessening (e.g., rescue, safety belts, emergency medical care, helmets) of death, disability, and/ or property damage.

The term prevention has been criticized on the basis that it is not comprehensive enough to convey the idea that injury losses can be reduced even after an event (e.g., motor vehicle crash, ingesting poison). Therefore, the term injury prevention has some experts showing evidence that interventions for an injury problem should not be limited to prevention, but should include any stage of the injury-producing process. The term suggested is injury control rather than injury prevention.

Preventing injuries and their undesirable effects requires a clear concept of what an injury is. Unfortunately, even experts disagree on its definition. The common definition and fatalistic connotation of the word *accident* appears to be an obstacle because the word implies, to many people, that something unexpected and unpleasant has occurred, but it:

> **Box 1-5** Definition of Unintentional Injury
>
> *Unintentional injury* in this book is defined as events in which the injury:
> - Occurred over a short period of time (seconds or minutes)
> - Was not deliberate or intentional
> - Had undesirable effects (e.g., death, injury, property damage)
> - Resulted either from one of the forms of physical or environmental energy (e.g., mechanical, thermal, chemical, electrical, ionizing radiation) or lack of physical agents (e.g., oxygen, heat)

- ▶ · Could not be avoided, it was an accident
- ▶ Was inevitable and would have happened to anyone
- ▶ Was unforeseen, and therefore, uncontrollable
- ▶ Is not the person's fault, and therefore he or she should not be blamed
- ▶ Is bad luck, and couldn't have been prevented

As long as people view injuries as accidents, they fail to recognize that they can prevent them.

b. Describe the biomechanics that underlie how injuries occur.

Biomechanics applies engineering principles to understand how the body reacts to forces applied to it and how it is damaged. Engineering addresses the hazards by offering solutions that eliminate or control the hazards.

In order to best understand the relationship of biomechanics to injuries, it is useful to think of an injury as a mechanical event. By simulating what happens in an injury, the biomechanic expert first looks at the mechanics involved and then relates that information to various factors.

The main predicting factor for injury severity is the speed (velocity) of the collision between two objects (one being a human). Additionally, other factors include the shape of the colliding objects and their rigidity that can enhance or reduce the effects of velocity. Determining the cause of an event causing damage should be left to specially trained professionals.

An understanding of the biomechanics can improve protection against injury. Mechanical energy exceeding the body's threshold of tolerance produces about three-fourths of the human injuries. To escape injury, the energy delivered must be below the body's threshold of tolerance.

Examples of biomechanical interventions include:

▶ Crashworthy poles, fences, and motor vehicles
▶ Motorcycle and bicycle helmets
▶ Safety belts
▶ Guardrails
▶ Shoes with high-friction soles
▶ Removing and/or lowering of playground equipment
▶ Playground surfaces that reduce impact

The following is an actual example of how a biomechanical analysis helped prove or disprove a point in a court of law. In this case, a teenage wrestler sustained a neck injury during a wrestling match, and it was contended by the parents of the wrestler that the wrestling mat was not soft enough to prevent that neck injury. A lawsuit was filed both against the manufacturer of the mat as well as against the school authorities for providing a deficient wrestling mat. On the face of it, the lawsuit appears perfectly valid, and one would tend to think the parents would have no difficulty getting an exorbitant compensation. However, an analysis of the whole situation biomechanically found surprising facts. By making an appropriate biomechanical analysis of the whole situation, *the expert engineer not only proved that the mat was perfectly all right, but went ahead and proved that the softer mat which the parents had been expecting from the school, would actually have caused more severe injuries in a higher number of wrestlers!* Seems unbelievable, but the engineer proved the point scientifically through the use of biomechanics (Gomez, 2001).

c. Describe how injury compares with other leading causes of morbidity and mortality and with regard to burdens on the population (e.g., incidence, cost, years of potential life lost).

Unintentional injuries are a leading cause of death for Americans of all ages, regardless of gender, race, or economic status, but unintentional injury deaths are only part of the picture. Millions of Americans are injured each year and survive. For many of them, the injuries cause temporary pain and inconvenience, but for some, the injuries lead to disability, chronic pain, and a profound change in lifestyle.

An injury affects more than just the person injured—it affects everyone who is involved in the injured person's life. With a fatal injury, family, friends, coworkers, employers, and other members of the injured person's community feel the loss. In addition to experiencing grief, they may experience a loss of income or the loss of a primary caregiver.

✳ With a nonfatal injury, family members are often called upon to care for the injured person, which can result in stress, time away from work, and possibly lost income. They may experience a change in their relationships with the injured person and with others in the family. For instance, if a wife and mother is seriously injured, her spouse may find himself in the role of primary caregiver—not only for his wife, but also for his children. Friends of the injured person may be called on to help out and, like family members, may experience a change in their relationships with the injured person. The injured person's employer may struggle with the temporary or permanent loss of a valued employee. Others in the community—volunteer groups, religious organizations, and neighbors—also may feel the effects of the injury.

Unintentional injuries constitute a major threat to public health. This threat has been called the neglected epidemic. Table 1-4 shows injuries as a cause of death by age group and ranking compared with other causes of death. The table shows that unintentional injuries dominate the pattern of death in the United States. According to the National Center for Injury and Control (2007), for people aged 1 to 44, injury is the leading cause of death.

According to the National Safety Council, the estimated number of Americans who died from unintentional injuries in 2005 was 113,000. Of these unintentional injuries, 45,800 were from motor vehicle crashes, 4,961 occurred at work, 23,700 happened at home, and 27,699 took place in public places (National Safety Council, 2007).

Another way to understand the size of the injury problem is to look at nonfatal injuries. Many more people suffer from nonfatal injuries each year than are killed as a result of injuries. The National Safety Council (2007) reports that about one in nine people annually seek medical attention for an injury. Table 1-5 shows the leading causes of nonfatal, unintentional injury by age group in the United States.

Most people who are injured do not die of their injuries. The extent of nonfatal injuries is reflected in nonfatal injury data.

The "injury pyramid" in Figure 1-1 illustrates the relationship between death and nonfatal injury. Everyone understands the significance of injury-related deaths, but the injury pyramid helps show that the complete injury problem is much larger. Deaths from injury are only the tip of the iceberg.

Table 1-4 The 10 Leading Causes of Death in the United States for 2004, All Races, Both Sexes

Rank	<1	1-4	5-9	10-14	15-24	25-34
				Age Groups		
1	Congenital Anomalies 5,622	Unintentional Injury 1,641	Unintentional Injury 1,126	Unintentional Injury 1,540	Unintentional Injury 15,449	Unintentional Injury 13,032
2	Short Gestation 4,642	Congenital Anomalies 569	Malignant Neoplasms 526	Malignant Neoplasms 493	Homicide 5,085	Suicide 5,074
3	SIDS 2,246	Malignant Neoplasms 399	Congenital Anomalies 205	Suicide 283	Suicide 4,316	Homicide 4,495
4	Maternal Pregnancy Comp. 1,715	Homicide 377	Homicide 122	Homicide 207	Malignant Neoplasms 1,709	Malignant Neoplasms 3,633
5	Unintentional Injury 1,052	Heart Disease 187	Heart Disease 83	Congenital Anomalies 184	Heart Disease 1,038	Heart Disease 3,163
6	Placenta Cord Membranes 1,1042	Influenza & Pneumonia 119	Chronic Low Respiratory Disease 46	Heart Disease 162	Congenital Anomalies 483	HIV 1,468
7	Respiratory Distress 875	Septicemia 84	Benign Neoplasms 41	Chronic Low Respiratory Disease 74	Cerebrovascular 211	Diabetes Mellitus 599
8	Bacterial Sepsis 827	Perinatal Period 61	Septicemia 38	Influenza & Pneumonia 49	HIV 191	Cerebrovascular 567
9	Neonatal Hemorrhage 616	Benign Neoplasms 53	Cerebrovascular 34	Benign Neoplasms 43	Influenza & Pneumonia 49	Congenital Anomalies 420
10	Circulatory System Disease 593	Chronic Low Respiratory Disease 48	Influenza & Pneumonia 33	Cerebrovascular 43	Chronic Low Respiratory Disease 179	Septicemia 328

Table 1-4 The 10 Leading Causes of Death in the United States for 2004, All Races, Both Sexes (continued)

Rank	Age Groups				
	35-44	45-54	55-64	65+	All Ages
1	Unintentional Injury 16,471	Malignant Neoplasms 49,520	Malignant Neoplasms 96,956	Heart Disease 533,302	Heart Disease 652,486
2	Malignant Neoplasms 14,723	Heart Disease 37,556	Heart Disease 63,613	Malignant Neoplasms 385,847	Malignant Neoplasms 553,888
3	Heart Disease 12,925	Unintentional Injury 16,942	Chronic Low Respiratory Disease 11,754	Cerebrovasular 130,538	Cerebrovasular 150,074
4	Suicide 6,638	Liver Disease 7,496	Diabetes Mellitus 10,780	Chronic Low Respiratory Disease 105,197	Chronic Low Respiratory Disease 121,987
5	HIV 4,826	Suicide 6,906	Cerebrovascular 9,966	Alzheimer's Disease 65,313	Unintentional Injury 121,012
6	Homicide 2,984	Cerebrovascular 6,181	Unintentional Injury 9,651	Diabetes Mellitus 53,956	Diabetes Mellitus 73,138
7	Liver Disease 2,799	Diabetes Mellitus 5,567	Liver Disease 6,569	Influenza & Pneumonia 52,760	Alzheimer's Disease 65,965
8	Cerebrovascular 2,361	HIV 4,422	Suicide 4,011	Nephritis 35,105	Influenza & Pneumonia 59,664
9	Diabetes Mellitus 2,026	Chronic Low Respiratory Disease 3,511	Nephritis 3,963	Unintentional Injury 35,020	Nephritis 42,480
10	Influenza & Pneumonia 891	Septicemia 2,251	Septicemia 3,745	Septicemia 25,644	Septicemia 33,373

Source: Office of Statistics and Programming, 2007.

Table 1-5 The 10 Leading Causes of Unintentional Injury

Rank	<1	1-4	5-9	10-14	15-24	25-34
			Age Groups			
1	Unintentional Fall 118,292	Unintentional Fall 862,993	Unintentional Fall 644,546	Unintentional Fall 622,613	Unintentional Struck by/Against 984,523	Unintentional Fall 758,333
2	Unintentional Struck by/Against 31,293	Unintentional Struck by/Against 365,619	Unintentional Struck by/Against 389,048	Unintentional Struck by/Against 556,822	Unintentional Fall 889,721	Unintentional Overexertion 668,119
3	Unintentional Other Bite/Sting 13,996	Unintentional Other Bite/Sting 138,508	Unintentional Cut/Pierce 115,980	Unintentional Overexertion 276,544	Unintentional MV Occupant 869,708	Unintentional Struck by/Against 639,864
4	Unintentional Fire/Burn 12,003	Unintentional Foreign Body 118,101	Unintentional Pedal Cyclist 100,203	Unintentional Cut/Pierce 145,247	Unintentional Overexertion 747,081	Unintentional MV Occupant 596,872
5	Unintentional Foreign Body 9,440	Unintentional Cut/Pierce 87,920	Unintentional Other Bite/Sting 89,351	Unintentional Pedal Cyclist 126,468	Unintentional Cut/Pierce 510,873	Unintentional Cut/Pierce 439,800
6	Unintentional Other Specified 7,213	Unintentional Overexertion 74,345	Unintentional Overexertion 67,774	Unintentional Unknown/Unspecified 119,074	Unintentional Other Bite/Sting 198,757	Unintentional Other Bite/Sting 175,120
7	Unintentional Cut/Pierce 6,993	Unintentional Fire/Burn 59,267	Unintentional MV Occupant 67,740	Unintentional MV Occupant 92,902	Unintentional Other Specified 191,715	Unintentional Other Specified 154,178
8	Unintentional Inhalation/Suffocation 6,611	Unintentional Other Specified 59,059	Unintentional Foreign Body 55,405	Unintentional Other Bite/Sting 62,219	Unintentional Unknown/Unspecified 175,432	Unintentional Other Transport 101,938
9	Unintentional Overexertion 6,588	Unintentional Unknown/Unspecified 49,152	Unintentional Dog Bite 46,439	Unintentional Other Transport 59,209	Unintentional Other Transport 136,789	Unintentional Poisoning 95,595
10	Unintentional MV Occupant 6,547	Unintentional Poisoning 39,940	Unintentional Unknown/Unspecified 44,627	Unintentional Dog Bite 36,873	Unintentional Poisoning 115,998	Unintentional Foreign Body 92,588

Table 1-5 The 10 Leading Causes of Unintentional Injury (continued)

Rank	35–44	45–54	55–64	65+	All Ages
			Age Groups		
1	Unintentional Fall 811,860	Unintentional Fall 811,179	Unintentional Fall 617,660	Unintentional Fall 1,800,763	Unintentional Fall 7,938,467
2	Unintentional Overexertion 646,712	Unintentional Overexertion 436,517	Unintentional Struck by/Against 212,455	Unintentional Struck by/Against 205,467	Unintentional Struck by/Against 4,336,688
3	Unintentional Struck by/Against 548,619	Unintentional Struck by/Against 402,932	Unintentional Overexertion 192,284	Unintentional MV Occupant 177,515	Unintentional Overexertion 3,284,022
4	Unintentional MV Occupant 464,692	Unintentional MV Occupant 350,923	Unintentional MV Occupant 191,931	Unintentional Overexertion 167,942	Unintentional MV Occupant 2,857,722
5	Unintentional Cut/Pierce 381,872	Unintentional Cut/Pierce 278,090	Unintentional Cut/Pierce 155,344	Unintentional Cut/Pierce 114,491	Unintentional Cut/Pierce 2,236,861
6	Unintentional Other Specified 179,024	Unintentional Other Specified 142,483	Unintentional Other Bite/Sting 71,459	Unintentional Other Bite/Sting 70,903	Unintentional Other Bite Sting 1,096,234
7	Unintentional Other Bite/Sting 151,367	Unintentional Other Bite/Sting 124,531	Unintentional Other Specified 62,578	Unintentional Poisoning 59,033	Unintentional Other Specified 880,543
8	Unintentional Poisoning 131,126	Unintentional Poisoning 99,999	Unintentional Poisoning 49,445	Unintentional Other Transport 47,748	Unintentional Unknown/Unspecified 678,967
9	Unintentional Other Transport 90,675	Unintentional Other Transport 69,155	Unintentional Other Transport 34,057	Unintentional Unknown/Unspecified 42,548	Unintentional Poisoning 617,617
10	Unintentional Foreign Body 79,891	Unintentional Foreign Body 55,622	Unintentional Foreign Body 30,946	Unintentional Other Specified 38,668	Unintentional Other Transport 612,558

Source: Office of Statistics and Programming, 2005.

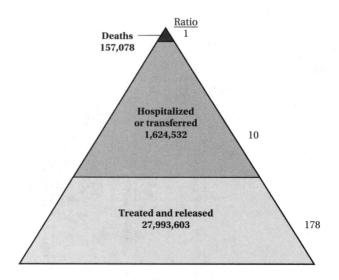

Figure 1-1 Injury Pyramid: All Causes of Injury in the United States in 2001

Source: Vyrostek SB, Annest JL, Ryan G. Surveillance for Fatal and Nonfatal Injuries—United States, 2001. *MMWR* 53(SS07):1–57.

The tragedy of the high injury death loss is that injuries kill thousands who otherwise could expect to live long and productive lives, whereas those afflicted with heart disease, cancer, stroke, and other chronic diseases usually die later in life. Calculating the years of potential life lost shows this. The calculation is based on the assumption that for most people, their productivity ends at age 65. Therefore, if someone dies at age 64 from cancer, it would be recorded as one year of potential life lost. However, if a young person dies in a motor vehicle crash at age 20, subtract 20 from 65, and there is a loss of 45 years of potential life. Comparing years of life lost from injuries to years of life lost from other public health problems shows that injury is a greater severe problem than death rates indicate.

People can be very productive past the age of 65, but determining the years of potential life lost is an indicator that injury accounts for more years of potential life lost than any other cause. (See Figure 1-2.)

Another way to measure the size of the injury problem is the costs of injury. The financial costs of injuries are staggering. Despite the difficulty in determining the overall cost of injuries, the National Safety Council estimates that injuries in the United States cost over $625 billion a year (2007). This estimate includes the economic costs of fatal and nonfatal unintentional injuries. Compare injury costs to an iceberg—only a small portion that actually can be measured appears above water. The indirect and hidden costs from the rest of the iceberg, the part below water, is not easily measured. Examples of costs are listed in Table 1-6.

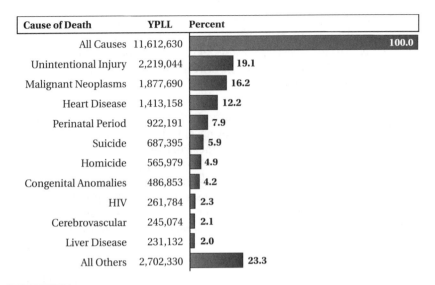

Cause of Death	YPLL	Percent
All Causes	11,612,630	100.0
Unintentional Injury	2,219,044	19.1
Malignant Neoplasms	1,877,690	16.2
Heart Disease	1,413,158	12.2
Perinatal Period	922,191	7.9
Suicide	687,395	5.9
Homicide	565,979	4.9
Congenital Anomalies	486,853	4.2
HIV	261,784	2.3
Cerebrovascular	245,074	2.1
Liver Disease	231,132	2.0
All Others	2,702,330	23.3

Figure 1-2 Years of Potential Life Lost

Source: Office of Statistics and Programming, National Center for Injury Prevention and Control, Centers for Disease Control and Prevention (2004). Available at http://webapp.cdc.gov/sasweb/ncipc/ypll10.html.

Table 1-6 Some Social and Economic Consequences of Injuries

Social	Economic
1. Grief over the loss of loved ones	1. Costs of rescue equipment required
2. Loss of public confidence	2. Injury investigation and reporting
3. Loss of prestige	3. Fees for legal actions
4. Deterioration of morale	4. Time of personnel involved in rescue
5. Denial of education	5. Medical fees (physicians, hospitals, etc.)
6. Lack of guidance for children	6. Disability costs of severely injured persons
7. Psychological effects of a change in standard of living	7. Replacement cost of property damaged or lost
8. Psychic damages affecting behavior	8. Slowdown in operations while injury causes are determined and corrective actions taken
9. Embarrassment	9. Loss of income
10. Lost pride	10. Loss of earning capability
11. Inconvenience	11. Rehabilitation costs for those who have lost limbs, mental abilities, or physical skills
12. Adversely affected interpersonal relationships (anger, resentment, etc.)	12. Funeral expenses for those killed
	13. Financial support for injured persons or for dependents of those killed
	14. Training costs and lower output of replacements
	15. Production loss for employer

The economic impact of fatal and nonfatal unintentional injuries of over $625 billion in a recent year was equivalent to about $2,100 per capita or about $5,500 per household. These are costs that every individual and household pays, whether directly out of pocket, through higher priced goods and services, or through higher taxes (National Safety Council, 2007).

Not all costs can be measured in dollars. Perhaps the greatest cost of injuries is measured in terms of the human pain and suffering that cannot be quantified. Therefore, the actual cost of injuries may never be known. The costs of a family's or an individual's pain and suffering are incalculable.

Box 1-6 Injuries Affect Everyone
"The risk of injury is so great that most persons sustain a significant injury at some time during their lives."
— U.S. Department of Health and Human Services, 2000

The human suffering and financial loss from preventable injuries constitute a public health problem second only to the ravages of ancient plagues or world wars. From the American Revolution (1775–1783) through the Gulf War (1990–1991), 650,954 battle deaths occurred involving the United States (National Safety Council, 2004). In making comparisons of fatal unintentional injuries with war, it must be kept in mind that nearly everyone is exposed to the potential of being injured, but relatively few are exposed to war. The point is that Americans are very much concerned about war and its effects, but to be unconcerned about a domestic problem that causes as much or even more damage betrays a paradox in human thought and values.

The injury picture in the United States is grim, yet it is fair to assume that without organized efforts, the United States' injury record would be even more shocking than it is. The National Safety Council (2007) reports that unintentional injury death per 100,000 were reduced 51 percent from 82.4 to 38.1 between 1912 and 2005. The reduction in the overall rate during a period when the nation's population tripled has resulted in 5,100,000 fewer people being killed due to unintentional injuries than there would have been if the rate had not been reduced.

Frederick Rivara and colleagues provide three factors for the decline in injury deaths over the past century (2001):

1. The reduction in the exposure to hazards capable of causing injury. Examples include safer transportation, safer occupations, and better housing.
2. Improved emergency medical care. The interval between the time of an injury to definitive medical care has decreased dramatically. Also, transfusions, antibiotics, new surgical techniques, and effective organ support, among other advances, have made a difference.
3. Increased use of injury prevention and control interventions based on scientific evidence of their effectiveness. This book focuses and presents

information on evidence-based interventions and strategies for injury prevention and control.

Injuries often are considered only when they are catastrophes because these events make newspaper headlines and television newscasts. It is significant that relatively few lives are lost as a result of natural or manmade disasters when contrasted with the total number of deaths resulting from other types of unspectacular, unpublished injuries.

d. Explain how injuries are preventable.

Injuries can be studied just as diseases are. By charting their occurrence, identifying those at risk, and intervening to prevent injury, death and disability can be reduced. Just as the occurrence of an injury requires the interaction of several factors, preventing one may require a mixture of interventions. Injuries are understandable, predictable, and preventable.

Injury prevention consists of interventions that include educational or persuasive appeals designed to motivate people to change behaviors that put them at risk, laws and regulations that require changes in behavior, and changes in products and environmental characteristics that provide automatic protection from injury.

The science of injury prevention is incomplete; there is much more still to be learned. This book contains the "best practices" or "evidence-based interventions" that can be put into place to save lives and resources.

e. Describe an approach to prevention that includes the following steps: (1) problem detection/assessment, (2) identification of risk and protective factors, (3) development of interventions, and (4) evaluation of the effectiveness of interventions.

To solve public health problems, including injuries, the public health model can be used. The model has four steps: define the problem, identify risk and protective factors, develop interventions, and evaluate interventions.

Problem Detection/Assessment

Before implementing an intervention to prevent injuries, an accurate description of the problem is needed. This is accomplished by gathering and analyzing data—often called *surveillance.* This description helps identify who is affected most by the problem and where the problem occurs most frequently. It guides in developing realistic objectives for the intervention and provides a baseline against which to measure progress. A clear definition of the problem is needed to convince community leaders, parents, volunteers, and potential funders.

The information needed to describe the problem can be obtained from several sources. Quantitative data is available from a number of agencies and organizations that collect statistics on injuries, and surveying or interviewing community members to get qualitative information (e.g., opinions, attitudes).

Identify Risk and Protective Factors

A *risk factor* is a characteristic that increases the likelihood of a person becoming a victim of an unintentional injury. A *protective factor* is a characteristic that decreases the likelihood of a person becoming a victim of an unintentional injury.

It is not enough to simply know that a certain type of injury is affecting a certain group of people in a certain area—researchers also need to know why. What factors put people at risk for that injury? What factors protect people from it? Programs then can be implemented to eliminate or reduce risk factors for injuries and to capitalize on or increase factors that protect people from being injured.

Develop and Implement Interventions

With so many interventions to choose from, start by reviewing the characteristics of the community and the intended participants. Also consider the most appropriate settings for the intervention, based on research about the intended participants. Review the goals and objectives. The selected intervention should best suit all of these factors. It also should be appropriate for the resources available.

Build on the experience of others. Other interventions that have worked serve as models. Later sections of this book offer many examples of interventions and which ones work (known as an *evidence-based approach* or *best practices*). Nevertheless, modification of an intervention may be necessary to make it appropriate for a situation.

Once materials and activities are developed, after resources and personnel have be secured, and the staff trained, it is time to implement the intervention. Implementation varies greatly from intervention to intervention in terms of duration (how long the intervention lasts), frequency (how many times in a given period activities occur), and intensity (how much material is covered and how much time is spent during each activity). With all interventions, supervising and support of the staff, maintenance of a consistent level of participation, and keeping the community interested in the intervention are needed.

Evaluate Interventions

The interventions are studied and evaluated to determine whether and how well they are working. This information is used to identify any elements needing changing to eliminate difficulties or increase effectiveness.

Throughout the intervention, it should be monitored for progress to make sure it is on track and on schedule. At the end of the intervention, a final (or summative) evaluation to determine how well the goals and objectives were achieved should take place. Assessing how well the intervention reached the intended participants and whether the outcomes were obtained according to what was planned is essential. A comparison of the costs of the programs to the benefits of the program should take place. In addition, planning a follow-up study to assess the long-term effects of the intervention is wise.

Many organizations have limited resources and may be tempted to skip evaluation, instead dedicating that money to intervention activities. However, evaluation is a critical step. It can demonstrate to funders, community leaders, and intervention staff that the effort was a success. If the intervention fell short of expectations, evaluation helps to identify what went wrong so necessary changes can be made.

If an organization does not have the expertise needed to evaluate the intervention but has resources to devote to it, a consultant can be hired. If resources for evaluation are lacking, partner with an area university that would be willing to design and carry out an evaluation by either a faculty member or capable graduate student.

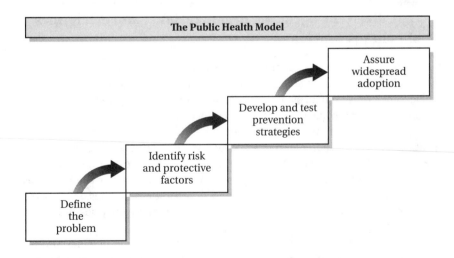

Figure 1-3 Public Health Approach

Source: Centers for Disease Control and Prevention, National Center for Injury Prevention and Control, 2007b.

f. Explain the continuum of injury from primary prevention to acute care and rehabilitation.

Various classification schemes of interventions have been developed. The most common classification in public health is primary, secondary, and tertiary prevention:

- ▶ Primary prevention measures attempt to stop or hinder an event (e.g., motor vehicle crash) that might result in injuries.
- ▶ Secondary prevention attempts to modify the consequences of such events to either prevent or reduce the severity of an injury (e.g., air bag inflating upon impact).
- ▶ Tertiary prevention—also called acute medical care and rehabilitation—focuses on returning the injured victim to the fullest physical, psychological, social, vocational, avocational, and educational level of functioning society after an injury.

The Haddon matrix (see Table 1-7) shows a continuum matching the three levels of preventive measures and provides another way of explaining these three measures. The preevent phase is the primary phase, the event phase is the secondary phase, and the postevent phase is the tertiary measures.

g. Explain the importance of collaboration and the role that different agencies, organizations, and disciplines play in prevention.

Many opportunities for collaboration across the spectrum of injury prevention exist. Stakeholders wanting to reduce the incidence of injuries exist at local, state, and federal government agencies and organizations. Nonprofit organizations and for-profit businesses have contributed to injury prevention efforts.

Multiagency collaboration within the different parts of the local and state health departments along with other local and state agencies (e.g., education, fire services, law enforcement, emergency medical services) can access more of the population and can use their various expertises to better use resources and data sharing. Competition for local and state monies often has discouraged collaboration. However, some states are conducting interagency coalitions and task forces.

At the local level, injury prevention falls under numerous agencies and organizations. Because of the stakeholders' diversity, coalitions have been formed and proven helpful in focusing on specific injury problems, educating target populations, and combining resources. Coalition building plays a major role for preventing injuries.

h. Describe how conceptual models (e.g., Haddon matrix, social ecological model, etc.) are used to portray the multiple factors underlying injury.

Injury Epidemiology

Epidemic literally means "affecting many individuals within a population, community, or region at the same time" (Merriam-Webster Dictionary, 2003). Formerly, epidemiology was defined as the medical science dealing with epidemics. It was most often found in public health programs that dealt with infectious and communicable diseases. However, chronic diseases (e.g., heart disease, cancer) and injuries also have been studied by the epidemiological method. In relation to injuries, epidemiology is the study of why some get injured and some do not. John Gordon probably was the first to use the epidemiological approach for an injury problem (see Gordon, 1949). He and others stressed the fact that injury problems can be treated in the same way, with the same methods used in the epidemiological approach to other public health problems. This model is central to uncovering multiple causes and devising multiple solutions to prevent injuries.

The epidemiological model includes the interaction of hosts, agents, and environmental factors. The host is the person injured. The agents of injury are the various forms of energy in excessive amounts. Mechanical energy is the usual agent for injuries involving motor vehicle crashes, falls, and gunshots. Thermal energy is the agent of burns. Chemical, electrical, and ionizing radiation are other forms of energy accounting for injuries. The lack of oxygen is the agent for drowning, choking, suffocation, and strangulation. James Gibson (1964) originated the idea of classifying agents of injury in terms of various forms of energy (e.g., thermal, chemical, electrical, mechanical).

In epidemiological usage, the term *vehicle* refers to any inanimate (nonliving) carrier that conveys damaging agents. The term *vector* is used to refer to animate

William Haddon, Jr., M.D. developed the Haddon matrix, which portrays both causal factors and all options available to reduce injuries.

(living) carriers. With unintentional injuries, most of the carriers of excessive energy are vehicles (e.g., motor vehicles, firearms). A few are vectors (e.g., dogs, poison ivy).

The environment is both the physical and social environment. Physical environment can be how highways are built and whether homes contain fire-proof materials. Social environment refers to the informal practices and formal laws that influence how our society functions and how it encourages or discourages certain behaviors.

Haddon Matrix

William Haddon, Jr. (1999; 1980) developed a strategy system to aid in the identification of interventions. Though originally developed to cope with the motor vehicle injury problem, the concept and matrix can be applied to any type of injury problem. The strategy is to reduce losses due to injuries rather than merely focus on prevention. Haddon states that even when an injury event cannot be prevented, there are many ways to prevent or reduce the frequency and severity of injuries resulting from an injury event.

Haddon suggests approaching the problem of reducing injuries by considering the three major phases that determine the final outcomes. These three phases are shown in Table 1-7 with examples of interventions related to crashes, poisoning, and drowning.

The *first phase*, or preevent phase, consists of many factors that determine whether an injury event will take place. Elements that cause people and physical forces to move into undesirable interaction are included here. For example, probably the most important human factor in the preevent phase is alcohol intoxication in almost all injury types.

In the past, the emphasis in injury prevention has been on human behavior and attempts to change it. Injuries usually are regarded as someone's fault, rather than as a failure that could have been prevented by some change in the environment. For example, if a boy, while cutting the grass with a power rotary

Table 1-7 Examples of Haddon's Three Phases

Injury type	Preevent	Event	Postevent
Motor vehicle crashes	Drinking and driving legislation	Safety belt use	Fast EMS response
Poisoning	Labeling of toxic products	Packing poisons in small, nonlethal amounts	National poison control telephone number
Drowning	Constructing fences around backyard swimming pools	Wearing personal floatation devices (PFDs)	Cardiopulmonary resuscitation (CPR)

lawn mower, ejects a stone from the mower that cuts a bystander, the resulting injury (the cut from the stone) is likely to be blamed on the boy operating the mower, rather than being attributed to the fact that a rotary mower may have no protective device to prevent the ejection of stones and debris. Such devices are now required, but are often taken off.

Thus, the mower can contribute to the initiation of the injury, either by placing excessive demands or restrictions on the operator or through mechanical inadequacies or failure. For example, in motor vehicle crashes, steering, tire, and brake failures sometimes initiate crashes but seldom are searched for after the crash.

Other preevent interventions relate to the environment, and the principle of separation plays an important role. For example, children can be separated from cleaning agents containing caustic ingredients through the use of child-resistant containers and by storing containers in locked compartments out of reach of children.

The *second phase*, or event phase, begins when physical forces exert themselves unfavorably on people and/or property. Interventions preventing harmful effects even when excessive energy (e.g., mechanical, chemical, thermal, electrical, ionizing radiation) is contacted are part of this second phase. Examples of event phase interventions for motor vehicle injuries include "packaging people" for crashes through the use of safety belts, padded dashes, and collapsible steering wheel columns. Nontraffic examples are boxing gloves, safety shoes, hard hats, helmets, lead X-ray shields, nets for acrobats, and gloves for laborers.

This second phase is to soften contact regardless of the cause. Stressing this phase follows the idea that because injury events will happen, let's protect humans and property the best way possible.

The *third phase*, or postevent phase, involves salvaging people and/or property after contact with excessive amounts of energy (e.g., mechanical, chemical, thermal, electrical, ionizing radiation) has taken place. Early detection of aircraft crashes through transducers that start broadcasting a special signal at the time of a crash is an example of the third phase, as are fire detection systems (heat and smoke), SOS and MAYDAY signals, and the use of cell phones to call the emergency medical services.

In case of severe injury, it is important to provide expert medical care as quickly as possible. Transportation of the injured, trained emergency medical technicians and paramedics, hospital emergency departments, and trauma centers are appropriate interventions of this third phase.

Haddon's other matrix consists of putting the three phases (preevent, event, and postevent) and the three epidemiological factors (human or host, agent, and environment) together in a matrix that provides a greater practical and theoretical utility in categorizing intervention options. See Table 1-8. Chapter 3 also contains more detailed information on the Haddon matrix.

It should be clear that both of the Haddon matrices still encompass injury prevention efforts aimed at changing or influencing human behavior. Traditionally,

Table 1-8 Haddon Matrix for Motor Vehicle Crashes

	Preevent	Event	Postevent
Host factors (human)	Driver education	Wear safety belt	Victim's health status
Agent factors (vehicle)	Vehicle inspections	Type and height of bumpers	Gas tank protection against fire
Physical environment	Type of roadway	Guardrails	Fast EMS response
Sociocultural environment	Attitudes about drinking and driving	Level of law enforcement	Funding for EMS and rehabilitation

using education and persuasion dominated the injury prevention scene—that is, until Haddon developed his matrices. During the 1960s and 1970s, Haddon and others felt that health education was ineffective against injuries. A strong emphasis on environmental intervention and passive protection evolved along with criticism of education and persuasion. In recent years, advances in knowing how humans make decisions and how to influence or change their behavior brought credibility back to attempting to prevent injuries through education and persuasion (Gielen, Sleet, DeClemente, 2006). Past and present attempts were made to change individual behavior, but those efforts now include influencing legislators and the media.

Haddon's 10 Strategies

There are additional ways to sort out options and tactics for reducing injuries. Haddon identified 10 logically based strategies that serve as a guideline in formulating interventions (Haddon, 1973). All 10 strategies may be used for reducing the damage from all types of injury events.

These 10 basic strategies, each with illustrative interventions, are to:

1. *Prevent the creation of the hazard.* Examples: prevent the production of boats, handguns, snowmobiles, or poisons
2. *Reduce the amount of the hazard.* Examples: reduce the speed of vehicles; reduce the height of hospital beds and child high chairs; make fewer amounts of alcoholic beverages
3. *Prevent the release of the hazard that already exists.* Examples: bolting or timbering mine roofs; impounding dangerous toys; make bathtubs less slippery
4. *Modify the rate of spatial distribution of release of the hazard.* Examples: packing medications in individual units instead of in bottles; creating flame-retardant materials that smolder and go out instead of bursting into flames; release bindings on skis
5. *Separate, in time or space, the hazard from that which is to be protected.*

Examples: walkways over or around hazards; evacuation; the banning of vehicles carrying explosives from areas where they and their cargoes are not needed

6. *Separate the hazard from that which is to be protected by a material barrier.* Examples: gloves; child-proof the closures of containers holding poison; vehicle air bags; electrical cord insulation

7. *Modify relevant basic qualities of the hazard.* Examples: using breakaway roadside poles; make crib slat spacing too narrow to strangle a child; padded vehicle dashboards; rounding sharp surfaces on vehicle interiors and exteriors

8. *Make what is to be protected more resistant to damage from the hazard.* Examples: making structures more fire- and earthquake-resistant; making motor-vehicles more crash resistant; strengthening human bones against fracture

9. *Begin to counter the damage already done by the hazard.* Examples: rescuing the shipwrecked; reattaching severed limbs; extricating trapped miners

10. *Stabilize, repair, and rehabilitate the object of the damage.* Examples: post-trauma cosmetic surgery; physical rehabilitation for amputees and others with disabling injuries; rebuilding after fires and natural disasters

Two points should be kept in mind in using these strategies: (1) they provide guidelines for possible injury control programs and (2) the strategies do not center on causation but instead on the entire realm of how to reduce damages. These strategies do not provide a formula or guide for specific cases, but rather should be dealt with on an individual basis.

These 10 strategies and examples suggest that a variety of interventions can reduce the likelihood and severity of injuries, as well as the severity of the consequences of injury once it has occurred. In choosing among potentially useful interventions, priority should be given to the ones most likely to effectively reduce injuries. Those with built-in automatic protection minimize the amount and frequency of effort required of the individuals involved.

Social Ecological Model*

Sustained improvements in injury prevention often benefit from long-term, repeated exposure to behaviorally focused injury education/promotion efforts through a variety of channels. The social ecological model provides a conceptual framework that can assist in the planning and evaluation of multiple-component injury prevention education/promotion programs.

Prevention requires understanding the factors that influence behavior. A four-level social ecological model helps to better understand injuries and the effect of .

---

*Adapted from Centers for Disease Control and Prevention, National Center for Injury Prevention and Control. The Social-Ecological Model. Available at www.cdc.gov/ncipc/dvp/Social-Ecological-Model_DVP.htm. Accessed April 27, 2007.

potential prevention strategies. This model takes into consideration the complex interplay between individual, relationship, community, and societal factors. It allows injury prevention professionals to address the factors that put people at risk for experiencing injuries.

Prevention strategies should include a continuum of activities that address multiple levels of the model. This approach is more likely to sustain prevention efforts over time than any single strategy.

Ecological models specific to injury prevention education/promotion are multifaceted, targeting environmental, behavioral, and social policy changes that help individuals make choices in their daily lives. Ecological models are unique in that they take into account the physical environment and its relationship to people at various levels. This perspective is based on the major focus of the social ecological model—behavior does not occur in a vacuum.

> **Individual.** The first level identifies biological and personal history factors that influence how individuals behave and increase their likelihood of becoming injured. Some examples include age, education, income, attitudes, and values. Strategies to intervene at this level include mass media campaigns, social marketing, and skills development.
>
> **Relationship.** This level looks at close relationships such as those with family, friends, and peers. Intervention strategies at this level include enhancement of social supports and social networks.

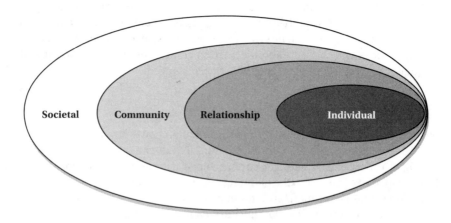

Figure 1-4 Social Ecological Model

Source: Centers for Disease Control and Prevention, National Center for Injury Prevention and Control, 2007a.

Community. The third level explores the community contexts in which social relationships occur such as schools, workplaces, and neighborhoods. This level identifies the characteristics of these settings that increase the risk of injury. Strategies to intervene at this level include incentive programs, coalition development, and mass media campaigns.

Societal. The fourth level looks at the broad societal factors that help create a climate in which injuries receive little attention. Strategies to intervene at this level include mass media campaigns, political change, and lobbying.

Social ecology engages the social processes and agencies that have a major influence on the desired behaviors. The goal is to establish an injury-free environment within the social space.

Ecological models address multiple layers of influence on behavior. This provides a comprehensive approach for injury prevention promotion initiatives. Many of the predominant theories and models of behavior focus on one dimension of health promotion, such as knowledge, attitudes, or skills. Ecological models link intervention strategies that target individual behaviors and environmental influences to behavior.

No single intervention is likely to eliminate injuries, but it is expected that a comprehensive, multilevel prevention approach would be most effective.

i. Describe the disparity in the risks of injury and the influence of a variety of factors (e.g., differences by age, gender, race, ethnicity, education, location, access to economic resources, access to health care services, sexual orientation, creed, community norms, the environment).*

Injuries affect everyone, but some injuries are a bigger problem for some groups of people. The U.S. population can be split along many different lines—racial, ethnic, gender, age, socioeconomic, and geographic. When determining who is affected by a particular type of injury, it is important to consider all of these factors. They shape a person's beliefs, values, preferences, and life experiences. Those factors, in turn, strongly affect how a person responds to prevention efforts.

Two things can be done by focusing on a small segment of the population— the segment affected most by a particular type of injury: (1) design a prevention program tailored to the needs, preferences, and life circumstances of that group, and (2) maximize the use of resources by targeting efforts where they will have

---

*Adapted from the National Center for Injury Prevention and Control. (2001). *Injury Fact Book.* Atlanta: Centers for Disease Control and Prevention; and McKenzie, James F., et al. (2002). *An Introduction to Community Health*, Sudbury, MA: Jones and Bartlett Publishers.

the greatest impact. Simply stated, the people with the most needs are those who must be reached by the programs to get the best results. The following is a look at how injuries affect different groups.

Age

Age is one of the most important factors in injury occurrence. After the first few months of life, unintentional injuries become the leading cause of death in children. They are the leading cause of death in those 1 through 44 years of age and the third leading cause of death in the 45 to 54 year age group (National Safety Council, 2007). Over 70 percent of all adolescent deaths were caused by an injury. About half of the millions of hospital emergency department visits are by 15- to 24-year-old males (National Safety Council, 2007).

Motor vehicle crashes are the leading cause of unintentional injury deaths for all age groups except for those 80 years of age and older. Falls are the leading cause of unintentional injury deaths for those 75 years of age and older (National Safety Council, 2007).

Some injuries occur almost exclusively in one particular age group, while other injuries occur over a much wider age span but tend to be more prevalent at certain ages than others. The time of life at which an injury predominates is influenced by such factors as the degree of exposure at various ages and variations in susceptibility with age. Many injuries, such as in fatally injured adult pedestrians, show a progressive increase in prevalence with increasing age.

Infants and Young Children

Infants and young children are at greater risk for many injuries. This increased risk may be attributable to many factors. Children are curious and like to explore their environment. This characteristic may lead children to sample the pills in the medicine cabinet, play with matches, or venture into the family pool. Young

Small children are curious and like to explore their environment, which attributes to an increased risk for injury.

children have limited physical coordination and cognitive abilities. This factor can lead to a greater risk for falls from bicycles and playground equipment and make it difficult for them to escape from a fire. In addition, their small size and developing bones and muscles may make them more susceptible to injury in car crashes if they are not properly restrained.

Children and Adolescents

Children and adolescents are at a higher risk for injuries for many reasons. Because of their stage of cognitive development, they often are impulsive and unable to judge the safety of a situation. For example, they may dart out into a busy street to retrieve a ball, fail to follow the rules of the road while riding a bike, or assume that an unfamiliar dog is friendly. Their size also may put them at risk. Because they are small, they are hard to see when walking in traffic, they may be seen as an easy target for a dog prone to attack, and they are not well protected by adult seat belts in motor vehicles.

Teens and Young Adults

Teens and young adults are at higher risk for many types of injuries. For many reasons, teens are at increased risk for motor vehicle–related injuries and deaths.

Children are often unable to judge the safety of a situation.

Motor vehicle injuries are the leading cause of death for teens and young adults.

Teens are more likely than older drivers to speed, run red lights, make illegal turns, ride with an intoxicated driver, and drive after using alcohol or drugs. Teens also are more likely than older drivers to underestimate the dangers in hazardous situations, and they have less experience coping with such situations. Additionally, nearly two-thirds of high-school age students do not consistently wear seat belts (National Center for Injury Prevention and Control, 2001). Driving behaviors, such as not wearing a seat belt and speeding, may be linked to teens' impulsiveness and tendency to take risks. These factors also are likely linked to teens' and young adults' higher risk for spinal cord injuries and drowning and to the reluctance to wear bicycle helmets.

Older Persons

Americans ages 65 and older are at higher risk for many types of unintentional injuries. Older adult drivers are at a greater risk of dying in a car crash than younger and middle-age drivers. This risk may be due to vision problems, slower reflexes, and impaired thinking due to aging. Older adults also are at greater risk than any other age group for pedestrian deaths.

The same risk factors that apply to motor vehicle–related deaths may also lead to pedestrian deaths. Decreased bone density and medical conditions that can complicate injuries may contribute to deaths among older pedestrians. These same conditions are linked to this age groups' high risk of fall- and fire-related injuries and deaths.

Gender

Men and women differ in many ways, including habits, social relationships, environmental exposures, and other aspects of daily living. The higher male prevalence of traffic fatalities is at least partly related to the fact that, on the

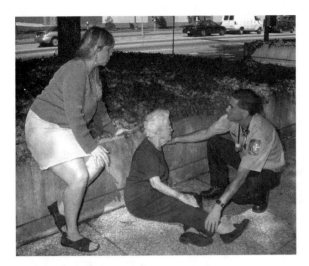

People 65 and older are at an increased risk for falling.

average, men drive motor vehicles more often than women (National Safety Council, 2007).

The National Safety Council (2007) reports that males incur more deaths due to unintentional injuries than females at all ages from birth to age 82. Overall, the rate of male deaths to female deaths is nearly two to one (Doll et al., 2007). The excess number of deaths for males compared to females is most evident from the late teenage years to the late forties where the gap begins to narrow.

Unintentional injury deaths are at their lowest level for both sexes from about age 4 to about age 13. For males, the highest number of deaths occurs at age 43, including another peak for those aged 22. For females, however, the highest totals occur among the elderly. from about age 78 and older. The greatest number of female deaths occurs at age 85 (National Safety Council, 2007).

Several factors may account for these differences. For instance, males are more likely than females to engage in behaviors that put them at risk, such as driving or boating after drinking alcohol, failing to wear seat belts, and participating in potentially dangerous sports and leisure activities (Doll et al., 2007).

Although females are less at risk for many injuries when compared with males, in several injury areas (e.g., falls, fires, poisoning), the risk to women is much greater. Among older women, for example, the risk of falling and fracturing a hip is much higher than among men in the same age group (Doll et al., 2007). Bone loss is a contributing factor for this increased risk. Many more women than men suffer from osteoporosis, a condition that makes bones brittle and susceptible to fractures.

The type of unintentional fatality with the widest disparity is firearm injuries. Most injuries occur more frequently in males, others more frequently in females. A gender difference in injury incidence initially brings to mind the possibility of hormonal or reproductive factors that either predispose or protect. For example, premenstrual syndrome (PMS) can be a significant factor affecting women's susceptibility to injuries.

Race and Ethnicity

AFRICAN AMERICANS

The injury rate for African Americans is higher than that for nearly all other racial and ethnic groups. This disparity may be due in part to the fact that a greater percentage of African Americans have lower education levels and higher poverty levels. Such characteristics have been shown to increase risk for injury. They are associated with higher pedestrian fatality rates and higher fatality rates from residential fires.

HISPANIC AMERICANS

Overall, the injury rate for Hispanic Americans is lower than for non-Hispanics. However, for some injury problems, Hispanics are at a higher risk than other racial or ethnic groups. Among this group, pedestrian fatalities are nearly twice as high as for whites (National Center for Injury Prevention and Control, 2001). This disparity may be explained largely by the fact that Hispanics make 55 percent more walking trips than do non-Hispanics, according to the U.S. Department of Transportation (National Center for Injury Prevention and Control, 2001). This difference may be attributable to a lower vehicle ownership rate among Hispanics.

AMERICAN INDIANS AND ALASKA NATIVES

This group has a higher rate than many racial and ethnic groups for injuries resulting from fires in their homes. This disparity may be attributable to a higher percentage of American Indians and Alaska Natives living in rural areas and in manufactured housing, a known risk for fire-related injuries and deaths.

Burden of Injuries

Despite the fact that injuries have declined during the past century, ample data provides sobering evidence of their large health and financial burden. Injuries are one of the major public health problems in the United States as well as globally. Unlike other leading causes of death (e.g., heart disease, cancer), injury deaths affect the young and the old.

j. Describe the influence of a variety of factors (e.g., age, gender, race, ethnicity, education, access to economic resources, sexual orientation, creed, community norms, access to health care services, the environment) on injury prevention.

Injury rates and causes vary according to age, gender, race, ethnicity, education, access to economic resources, creed, community norms, access to health care services, and the environment. Identifying factors such as those listed is essential for developing targeted, efficient prevention strategies. Young, inexperienced drivers are most likely to be involved in motor vehicle crashes. Thus, graduated driver licensing focuses on these drivers. In most injuries, males have higher death and disability rates than females. Parental counseling by the family physician focusing on boys could be conducted. As noted, residential fires impact certain racial and ethnicity groups (e.g., American Indians, Alaska Natives). Requiring smoke alarm installation in all residences decreases fire-related deaths. Those with little education and economic resources experience a greater number of injuries. Loan or give-away programs for smoke alarms and child restraint seats are available.

Where unintentional injuries occur is a matter of great importance. The availability of data for states in the United States has permitted the discovery of interesting place-to-place variations in unintentional injury occurrence. Differences in death rates between urban and rural areas are a common finding. The higher fatality rate from motor vehicle crashes in rural than in urban areas is consistent with the fact that faster driving occurs in rural areas, and it is the speed of the vehicle that is a major factor in death causation. Types and condition of roads and highways, the availability of quick responding emergency medical services, and distance from definitive medical care all play a part in having more unintentional injury deaths in rural areas.

Despite the deficiencies of the available research, enough information is available for identifying how the named factors affect the outcome of an unintentional injury. Prevention efforts focusing upon these named factors can involve providing information and motivation. Examples include media campaigns, education, incentives or punishment, and enhancing people's perception of the hazards.

Conclusion

Unintentional injuries represent one of the most serious public health problems. This chapter identified unintentional injuries as an enormous impact and burden on society. This impact of injuries can be portrayed by several ways: economic, value of lost productivity, death, and disability. Difficult to measure but nevertheless real are the psychological effects.

Tracking deaths represents one way to show the size of the injury problem. Unintentional injuries rank as the fifth leading cause of death in the United States (National Safety Council, 2007) and is the leading cause of death for people aged 1 through 44 years.

Nonfatal injuries represent another way to show the magnitude of the injury problem. Although death information is more accurate than nonfatal injury information, these nonfatal injuries far exceed those who have died.

Another way of showing the impact of injuries involves calculating years of potential life lost. By comparing years of life lost from injuries to years of life lost from other public health problems, injuries exceed those of any other health problem.

Unintentional injuries impose a significant financial burden. For some injuries, the cost are minimal; however, for other injuries, medical treatment, lost wages, and other variables may persist for years or even decades after the initial injury.

References

Centers for Disease Control and Prevention, National Center for Injury Prevention and Control. (2007a). The social-ecological model. Available at www.cdc.gov/ncipc/dvp/Social-Ecological-Model_DVP.htm. Accessed April 27, 2007.

Centers for Disease Control and Prevention, National Center for Injury Prevention and Control. (2007b). The public health model. Available at www.cdc.gov/ncipc/dvp/PublicHealthApproachToViolencePrevention.htm. Accessed May 2, 2007.

Davis, R.M. and I.B. Pless. (2001). BMJ bans accidents: Accidents are not unpredictable. *British Medical Journal* 322, 1320–1321.

Doll, L.S., S.E. Bonzo, D.A. Sleet, and J.A. Mercy. (2007). Handbook of injury prevention and violence prevention. New York, NY: Springer Science and Business Media.

Gibson, J.J. (1964). The contribution of experimental psychology to the formulation of the problem of safety—A brief for basic research. In: Haddon W., E.A. Suchman, D. Klein, eds. *Accident Research: Methods and Approaches.* New York: Harper & Row.

Gielen, A.C., D.A. Sleet, and R. DiClemente. (2006). Injury and violence prevention: Behavioral science theories, methods and applications. San Francisco: Jossey-Bass.

Gomez, M. (2001). Biomechanics of soft-tissue injury. Tucson, AZ: Lawyers and Judges Publishing Company.

Gordon, J.E. (1949). The epidemiology of accidents. *American Journal of Public Health* 39:504–515.

Haddon, W. (1999). The changing approach to the epidemiology, prevention, and amelioration of trauma: The transition to approaches etiologically rather than descriptively based. *Injury Prevention* 5:231–235.

Haddon, W. (1980). Advances in the epidemiology of injuries as a basis for public policy. *Public Health Reports* 95:411–421.

Haddon, W. (1973). Energy damage and the ten countermeasure strategies. *Journal of Trauma* 13:321–331.

McKenzie, J.F., P.R. Pinger, and J.E. Kotecki. (2002). An Introduction to Community Health. Sudbury, MA: Jones and Bartlett Publishers.

Merriam-Webster Dictionary. (2003). Springfield, MA: Merriam-Webster, Inc. Publishers.

National Center for Injury Prevention and Control. (2001). Injury fact book 2001–2002, 41. Atlanta: Centers for Disease Control and Prevention.

National Safety Council. (2007). Injury facts. Itasca, IL: National Safety Council.

National Safety Council. (2004). Injury facts. Itasca, IL: National Safety Council.

Office of Statistics and Programming, National Center for Injury Prevention and Control, Centers for Disease Control and Prevention. (2005). 10 leading causes of nonfatal unintentional injury, United States. Available at: www.cdc.gov/ncipc/wisqars/nonfatal/quickpicks/quickpicks_2005/uninstall.htm.

Office of Statistics and Programming, National Center for Injury Prevention and Control, Centers for Disease Control and Prevention. (2004). 10 leading causes of death, United States. Available at: http://webapp.cdc.gov/sasweb/ncipc/leadcaus10.html.

Rivara, F.P., P. Cummings, T.D. Koepsell, D.C. Grossman, and R.V. Maier. (2001). Injury control: A guide for research and program evaluation. Cambridge, England: Cambridge University Press.

Society for the Advancement of Violence and Injury Research and the State and Territorial Injury Prevention Directors Association. (2005). Core competencies for injury and violence prevention. Available at: www.InjuryEd.org.

Suchman, E.A. (1964). A conceptual analysis of the accident phenomenon. In: Haddon, W., E.A. Suchman, and D. Klein (editors). *Accident Research: Methods and Approaches*. New York: Harper & Row Publishers, Inc.

Thygerson, A.L. (1992). Safety, 2nd edition. Sudbury, MA: Jones and Bartlett Publishers.

U.S. Department of Health and Human Services. (2000). Healthy People 2010: Understanding and improving health, 2nd edition. Washington, D.C.: U.S. Government Printing Office.

Vyrostek, S.B., J.L. Annest, and G. Ryan. Surveillance for fatal and nonfatal injuries—United States, 2001. *MMWR* 53 (SS07): 1–57.

CHAPTER 2 ▶

Injury Data Use

CORE COMPETENCY 2: **Ability to access, interpret, use, and present injury data.**

Having good injury data makes it possible to identify and understand an injury problem. It also helps prioritize among a list of problems and determine the size of specific problems. It identifies patterns of when and how injuries occur and to monitor trends (have injuries increased or decreased over time?).

Data helps to answer the 5W and H questions (who, what, where, why, when, and how) necessary in selecting an appropriate intervention. The key questions are:

- ▶ Who is being injured? (age, gender, ethnicity, physical attributes)
- ▶ What happened? (description of the injury incident)
- ▶ Where are the injuries taking place? (countries, regions within a country, areas within a community)   .
- ▶ Why did the injury occur? (causes, circumstances)
- ▶ When are the injuries occurring? (time trends)
- ▶ How is the person injured? (mechanism of injury)

It is very important to look at both fatal and nonfatal injuries. The injury pyramid on page 16 shows that deaths are just the tip of the iceberg, and the farther down on the pyramid, the greater the number of injuries. Far more people suffer nonfatal injuries than those suffering fatalities.

a. Describe key sources of data at the national, state, and community levels, and describe their strengths and weaknesses.

National Injury Data Systems

The following is a list of national data systems compiled by the Centers for Disease Control and Prevention's (CDC) National Center for Injury Prevention and Control (www.cdc.gov/ncipc/osp/InventoryInjuryDataSys.htm) that provides nationwide injury-related data. Each data system is listed along with the agency or organization and associated Web sites. You can get additional information about survey or surveillance methods and findings by clicking on the agency's URL on a computer. Data systems are organized according to topic. Some data systems are listed more than once if relevant to different injury-related topics. Data systems that have state-based data are noted with an asterisk.

Behavioral Risk Factors/Injury Incidence

▶ Behavioral Risk Factor Survey System (BRFSS)*, Centers for Disease Control and Prevention—National Center for Chronic Disease Prevention and Health Promotion (CDC-NCCDPHP) annual survey
Web site: www.cdc.gov/brfss

▶ Youth Risk Behavior Survey (YRBS)*, CDC-NCCDPHP, biennual school-based survey for state/local, occasional national survey
Web site: www.cdc.gov/nccdphp/dash/yrbs/index.htm

▶ Injury Control and Risk of Injury Survey (ICARIS I, II, II½), Centers for Disease Control and Prevention—National Center for Injury Prevention and Control (CDC-NCIPC) periodic survey conducted by NCIPC
Web site: None available.

Good data is essential in identifying injury problems.

▶ National Health Interview Survey (NHIS), Centers for Disease Control and Prevention—National Center for Health Statistics (CDC-NCHS) annual household survey
Web site: www.cdc.gov/nchs/nhis.htm

Injury Morbidity Data

▶ National Electronic Injury Surveillance System (NEISS), Consumer Product Safety Commission (CPSC), NEISS All Injury Program, CPSC/CDC-NCIPC, and NEISS-work-related injury, CPSC/CDC-National Institute for Occupational Safety and Health (NIOSH), ongoing
Web site: www.cpsc.gov/epidemiology
Web site: www.cpsc.gov/library/neiss.html
Web site: www.cdc.gov/ncipc/wisqars (nonfatal injury data)
Web site: www2a.cdc.gov/risqs/default.asp (work-related injury)

▶ National Hospital Ambulatory Medical Care Survey (NHAMCS), CDC-NCHS, annual survey
Web site: www.cdc.gov/nchs/about/major/ahcd/ahcd1.htm

▶ National Ambulatory Medical Care Survey (NAMCS), CDC-NCHS, annual survey
Web site: www.cdc.gov/nchs/about/major/ahcd/ahcd1.htm

▶ National EMS Information System (NEMSIS), National Highway Traffic Safety Administration (NHTSA), prehospital care data base
Web site: www.nemsis.org

▶ National Hospital Discharge Survey (NHDS), CDC-NCHS, annual survey
Web site: www.cdc.gov/nchs/about/major/hdasd/nhds.htm

▶ Healthcare Cost & Utilization Project (HCUP), Agency for Healthcare Research and Qualty (AHRQ)
Web site: www.ahrq.gov/data/hcup

▶ Medical Expenditure Panel Survey (MEPS), AHRQ/CDC-NCHS
Web site: www.meps.ahrq.gov/WhatIsMEPS/Overview.HTM

▶ Indian Health Service (IHS)—Ambulatory Care & Inpatient Care Systems, ongoing
Web site: www.ihs.gov/nonmedicalprograms/ihs%5Fstats

▶ Outcome and Assessment Information Set (OASIS), Centers for Medicare and Medicare (CMS), Home Health Care System, ongoing
Web site: www.cms.hhs.gov/oasis

▶ Minimum Data Set for Nursing Home Resident Assessment and Care Screening (MDS-Nursing Homes), CMS
Web site: www.cms.hhs.gov/states/mdsreports

Injury Deaths: Death Certificates

▶ National Vital Statistics System (NVSS)*, CDC-NCHS, ongoing
   Web site: www.cdc.gov/nchs/nvss.htm

▶ National Mortality Follow-back Survey: 1993 (NMFS93), CDC-NCHS,
   periodic
   Web site: www.cdc.gov/nchs/about/major/nmfs/nmfs.htm

Automotive/Transport Injury Data

▶ Fatality Analysis Reporting System (FARS)*, NHTSA, ongoing, motor vehicle
   crash deaths
   Web site: www-fars.nhtsa.dot.gov

▶ National Automotive Sampling System—General Estimates System (NASS-
   GES), NHTSA, annual
   Web site: www-nrd.nhtsa.dot.gov/departments/nrd-30/ncsa/ges.html

▶ National Automotive Sampling System—Crashworthiness Data System
   (NASS-CDS), NHTSA, annual
   Web site: www-nrd.nhtsa.dot.gov/departments/nrd-30/ncsa/cds.html

▶ NHTSA Special Crash Investigation (SCI), NHTSA, (includes air-bag–related
   injuries), ongoing
   Air-bag fatality summary report and tables
   Web site: www-nrd.nhtsa.dot.gov/departments/nrd-30/ncsa/sci.html
   Cases shown as having a case status of "Available" can be found at:
   Web site: www-nass.nhtsa.dot.gov/BIN/logon.exe/airmislogon

The National Institute of Occupational Safety and Health makes recommendations to the federal OSHA.

► Department of Transportation (DOT) Federal Railroad Administration, Railway Safety Statistics*, annual (includes statistics on fatal and nonfatal injuries associated with train collisions)
Web site: http://safetydata.fra.dot.gov/OfficeofSafety/Default.asp

Automotive Behavioral Injury Data

► National Occupant Protection Use Survey (NOPUS), NHTSA, periodic
Web site: www-nrd.nhtsa.dot.gov/departments/nrd-01/summaries/4313ga.html

► Motor Vehicle Occupant Safety Survey, NHTSA, biennial
Web site: www.nhtsa.dot.gov/people/injury/research

► National Survey of (Drinking and Driving)/(Distracted and Drowsy Driving)/(Speeding and Unsafe Driving) Attitudes and Behaviors, NHTSA, periodic
Web site: www.nhtsa.dot.gov/people/injury/research

Occupational Injury Data

► National Traumatic Occupational Fatality Surveillance System (NTOF)*, CDC-NIOSH
Web site: www.cdc.gov/niosh/injury

► National Electronic Injury Surveillance System—Work RISQ—Nonfatal work-related injuries, CDC-NIOSH
Web site: www2a.cdc.gov/risqs/default.asp

► Census of Fatal Occupational Injuries (CFOI)*, Bureau of Labor Statistics (BLS), ongoing
Web site: www.bls.gov/iif/oshfat1.htm

Several key sources collect motor vehicle injury data.

▶ Survey of Occupational Injuries and Illnesses (SOII)*, BLS, annual survey
Web site: www.bls.gov/iif/home.htm

▶ Census of Agriculture (COA)*, Department of Commerce (DOC), periodic
Web site: www.nass.usda.gov/Census_of_Agriculture/index.asp
Note: Although available reports do not provide injury statistics, the 1992 Census of Agriculture (COA) did ask questions about the number of work-related injuries. More recent COAs do not ask about injury.

Other Injury Data

▶ National Fire Incident Reporting System (NFIRS), United States Fire Administration (USFA), ongoing
Web site: www.usfa.fema.gov/inside-usfa/nfirs.cfm

Private Injury Data System Trauma Care/Poisoning Data

▶ National Trauma Data Bank (NTDB)—American College of Surgeons, ongoing
Web site: www.facs.org/trauma/ntdb.html

▶ Toxic Exposure Surveillance System (TESS)—American Association of Poison Control Centers, annual
Web site: www.aapcc.org/poison1.htm

▶ United States Eye Injury Registry—American Society of Ocular Trauma
Web site: www.useironline.org

State and Community Data Sources

Data for fatalities is common, but few state or community nonfatal injury surveillance systems exist. Unfortunately, state and community data is often not readily available nor complete. State and community data sources vary among the localities but may include:

▶ Vital Statistics and Death Certificate Data
▶ Medical Examiner and Coroner Reports
▶ Hospital Discharge Data
▶ Trauma Registries
▶ Emergency Medical Services Data
▶ Emergency Department Data
▶ Police Reports
▶ Fire Reports
▶ Poison Control Center Data
▶ Child Death Review Teams
▶ Newspaper archives

b. Describe the strengths and weaknesses of the International Classification of Diseases system and its use.

The International Classification of Diseases (ICD) is designed to promote comparability in the collection, processing, classification, and presentation of mortality statistics. This includes providing a format for reporting causes of death on death certificates. The reported conditions then are translated into medical codes through the use of the classification structure and the selection and modification rules contained in the ICD, published by the World Health Organization (WHO). These coding rules improve the usefulness of mortality statistics by giving preference to certain categories, by consolidating conditions, and by systematically selecting a single cause of death from a reported sequence of conditions.

Weaknesses of the ICD

Because there is no single cause of an injury, contributory causes that play a part in causing an injury go unidentified. Revisions of the ICD produce problems when comparing one year against another year or tracking trends of a particular injury type. The National Safety Council (2007) found that the external cause categories were affected by the revisions for unintentional injuries. For example, for firearms, the older ICD-9 had separate codes to identify rifles, shotguns, and larger firearms while the ICD-10 combines them into one code. For motor vehicle crashes, falls, fires, and drownings, there were fewer deaths assigned to a cause under ICD-10 than under ICD-9.

The accuracy of data depends on the documentation available on the accuracy of information obtained from death certificates, coroners' reports, and other relevant documentation. It often is difficult to obtain enough details to use the most specific codes in the ICD-10. In addition, alerting users of the ICD of the changes and revisions can be absent or difficult to disperse.

The ICD-9, in some cases, offered more detail, but, in other cases, less than the newer ICD-10. The ICD-9 used E codes for external cause of injury. The newer ICD-10 replaced E codes with V, W, X, and Y codes that can be more specific about external causes of injury. These are used for mortality data while the ICD-9-CM and E codes are still being used for morbidity data.

In the ICD-9, the nature of injury codes was known as N codes but, in the ICD-10, they have become S and T codes. One main difference is that body part (e.g., arm, leg) now is the major classification while the type of injury (e.g., fracture, dislocation) is a subcategory under body part. Epidemiologists and others using health statistics need to be sure to utilize the newer V, W, X, and Y codes when analyzing data for injury programs.

The ICD-10, like its predecessor the ICD-9, contains so many detailed codes that it centers on details and fails to focus on the larger injury problem. Another weakness of ICD-10 coded data is the heavy reliance on "multiple" and "unspecified" categories that are of little use to researchers.

Reliable injury data provides the foundation for prevention efforts. Although numerous state and national data sources monitor injuries and their consequences, most include data only on serious injuries that result in death. A major impediment to injury prevention efforts today is the lack of detailed information in many data systems on the external cause of nonfatal injuries (e.g., fall from stairs; suffocation by plastic bag). For all injury-related deaths that occur in the United States, coding of the external cause is recorded on the death certificate, but such coding for nonfatal injuries that lead to a hospitalization or emergency department visit is not universal.

Despite the benefits of external caused coded data and the low cost of their collection, only about half of the states require hospitals to report external cause of injury codes. The required use of external caused codes in hospital discharge records would greatly add to the knowledge needed for effective injury prevention programs.

Efforts by the WHO led to a more detailed classification of external causes compatible with the ICD classification. Known as the International Classification of External Causes of Injury (ICECI), it is based on best practices of injury surveillance and on international consensus about how external causes may be described. The ICECI helps researchers and prevention practitioners to:

▶ Define more precisely the domain of injuries they are studying
▶ Answer questions on the circumstances of the injuries
▶ Provide more detailed information about specific injury categories, like home and leisure injuries or traffic crashes

The U.S. Centers for Disease Control and Prevention (CDC) has developed a short version of the ICECI to capture external causes of injury data from hospital emergency departments.

c. Describe the differences between primary data ("self-collected") and secondary data ("existing") and provide examples of appropriate uses of each method.

Primary data refers to data that is collected directly from people. For example, if a researcher were putting together a data collection plan for getting information about injury-related behaviors, he or she might administer anonymous and confidential surveys or have people complete a health risk appraisal.

Secondary data refers to data that someone else has collected and is being used for a purpose that is secondary to their original purpose. Vital records, such as death certificates, are a major source of secondary data for injury program evaluators. Medical records may contain information desired for an evaluation.

However, data abstraction from these sources must address several issues. First is the quality of the data as recorded and its availability for abstraction. Because the data in records is for clinical rather than evaluation purposes, the information can be inconsistent and vary by the practitioner recording the data.

Another source of secondary data is national surveys, such as the National Health Interview Survey. This and several others are conducted periodically by various federal agencies with a health and safety focus. These data sets have been used for community assessment. Data from some surveys are publicly accessible through the Internet and can be used to evaluate population-level programs. Some data sets have restrictions or stipulations on their use. A drawback to using some of these surveys is that the most recent data can be 2 years old. Also, as secondary data sets, they may be of limited value in determining the effect of small-scale programs. However, they may be useful for evaluating a population-level program, such as a state program. Large secondary data sets for the evaluation of programs face the challenge of determining the reliability and validity of the data. In addition, data from some national surveys may not generate results applicable to rural populations, while other data may be at the individual rather than the aggregate level. Overall, the user of the data needs to be cautious and have a specific rationale for using large secondary data sets for evaluation purposes.

State and local health departments may have information from the Youth Risk Behavior Surveillance (YRBS) or the Behavioral Risk Factor Surveillance Survey (BRFSS) that was administered in a specific area. This is an example of secondary data collection. There are a number of sources of secondary data. Once members of a program planning committee or evaluation committee have determined what information they are seeking, they will need to contact appropriate sources to see if they have data that are helpful.

d. Describe how data can be used to identify disparate populations.

Disparity is a term for the important differences in health status among racial and ethnic groups. Well-documented injury disparities exist. For example, African Americans—in all age groups—have higher rates of injury-related visits to emergency departments than whites (National Safety Council, 2007).

Race is based on the idea that some human populations are distinct from others, according to external physical characteristics or places of origin. Because of the similarity between race and ethnicity, in that both are determined mainly by their group association and distinction, there is an increasing trend toward use of the term *race/ethnicity*.

A problem is that broad categories of racial/ethnic groups may be inadequate to capture unique cultural differences. For example, about 52 different tribes of Native Americans are registered in the United States today, representing 52 different cultures, backgrounds, and possible genetic make-ups. A similar situation is also true for African Americans, Hispanics, and whites.

Epidemiology attempts to discover explanations for rate differences among groups by identifying unique behaviors or characteristics in a racial/ethnic group. Associating risk behaviors and injuries with a particular group can then provide insights about injury causes and appropriate interventions.

e. Explain how data can be used to identify emerging issues in injury.

Which injury problems affect the most people? Which ones are on the rise? Which ones are decreasing in incidence and prevalence? How does one target population relate on various injury problems to state and national populations? Is it safer or worse? What injury problems does that target population think are important to change? On what injury problems does an agency's or employer's funding source focus? Do injury data identify problems that have been selected as priorities in Healthy People 2010 (a set of health goals and objectives for the United States) or a comparable state document?

Several types of epidemiologic data can be collected in order to assess injury status. These data assist in the priority selection process by providing information about the existence of actual and potential injury problems. These data identify where injury problems are; who is at risk; and which problems are, or have the potential to be, increasing or decreasing. These include morbidity, mortality, disability, incidence, prevalence, distribution, and trends across recent time frames. These data should be collected for the target population and at least one comparison population. Comparison populations can be groups similar to the target population, the state population that is home to the target population, or the population of the entire country. It also is important to collect the injury data by subgroup (e.g., gender, racial or ethnic group, geographic group) when available because this may help to pinpoint specific targets of intervention. Incidence rates highlight new cases of an injury problem in a population. They are the most common means to measure and compare the frequency of an injury problem in a population; the higher the incidence rate, the greater the problem. Prevalence rates look at all the cases of an injury problem in a population, new and old. Years of potential life lost (YPLL) rates look at premature death in a given population from specific injury problems.

Epidemiologic data for all reportable cases may not be communicated to local health departments. The CDC, through publications such as the *Morbidity and Mortality Weekly Report* (*MMWR*), the National Center for Health Statistics, and state and local health departments have a vast array of health status data available for use. The challenge is to locate the data that are most specific to the target population.

f. Identify the ethical and legal issues involved in the collection and use of data.

An *ethical issue* refers to situations where competing values are at play and a judgment needs to be made about what is the most appropriate course of action.

No study that uses human subjects can begin unless the potential participants (or their legal representative for those not competent and/or of legal age) have been properly informed about the study and agree to participate. One of the most basic concerns when collecting and using data with humans is privacy. The privacy of participants must be protected. Another concern is anonymity, which means that information cannot be linked to the participant who provided it. No identifying information (e.g., the participant's name, social security number, home address) can be attached to the data collected.

Some studies require that participants be known and therefore the information is not anonymous. Although such studies may not be anonymous, they can be confidential. This exists when the researcher knows the participants' identities and promises not to reveal those identities to others. The advantage of a confidential study is the ability to be able to collect data from the same group of people more than once and the ability to follow up. However, the greatest advantage of conducting a confidential study is that often many people are more likely to tell the truth or share personal information if such information cannot be linked back to them, as only the researcher knows their true identities.

Data analysis can create ethical issues. These ethical concerns can arise from lack of knowledge about appropriate analyses, carelessness in conducting the analyses, or deliberate misuse of analyses. The impact can have lasting effects. Inappropriate data analyses can lead to harm of a person or property, implementation of inappropriate polices or interventions, and the waste of time, effort, and resources.

If the researcher lacks the knowledge and skills needed to complete a data analyses, they should seek assistance from statistical experts, and they should always double-check their data entry and the results of the data analyses. It is important to understand the nature of the data prior to beginning the analysis. Researchers should always report all their findings, not just the ones that turned out the way they wanted them to turn out.

g. Identify how a variety of factors (including age, gender, race, ethnicity, access to economic resources, community norms) may influence the collection, interpretation, and use of injury data.

Most data collection efforts select a particular type of injury and a particular group of people to focus. Choosing the group of people from whom data will be collected can influence their interpretation and use.

Some injuries appear more often for some groups than others. They can vary according to age, gender, race, ethnicity, access to economic resources, and community norms. When determining who is affected by a particular type of injury, it is important to consider all of these characteristics. They shape a person's beliefs, values, preferences, and life experiences. Those factors also strongly affect how a person responds to prevention efforts.

By focusing on a small segment of the population—the segment affected most by a particular type of injury—a researcher can do two things: (1) design a prevention program tailored to the needs, preferences, and life circumstances of that group and (2) maximize the use of resources by targeting efforts where they will have the greatest impact.

h. Define quantitative and qualitative forms of data and give examples of their use in constructing and evaluating injury prevention programs. Describe the benefits and limitations of each kind of data.

Quantitative data are numbers. Data collection methods that result in quantitative data can be analyzed through the appropriate use of descriptive and inferential statistics.

1. Descriptive statistics provide methods of organizing, summarizing, and communicating data. Most injury statistics are descriptive in nature. Total sums, ratios, averages, and percentages are examples of descriptive statistics.
2. Inferential statistics provide methods for making inferences from the descriptive data. Research reports usually use inferential statistics. Examples of such statistics include statistics indicating differences between groups and statistics showing relationships. A college or university course in statistics is needed to properly understand and interpret the use of inferential statistics. Chi-square, t-test, and analysis of variance are examples of specific types of inferential statistics used in research.

Qualitative data are words or pictures. Qualitative data are read or observed in order to determine general patterns. They then are reanalyzed to determine specific categories. One way to use qualitative methods is to develop and delineate program elements before initiating a program; in other words, for program planning. The choice of a qualitative method is based on whether it is the best method given the question being asked.

The types of qualitative methods include:

- ▶ A *case study* addresses questions of how or why something occurred.
- ▶ *Observation* refers to using one's own eyes to collect data. Data collection can be done in several different ways: use of cameras, coding events as they occur, and making detailed notes and logs of occurrences and observations.
- ▶ *In-depth individual interviews* are the most widely used. This is an in-depth, open-ended questioning of an individual. It uses questions requiring more than a yes-or-no response and encourages an explanation.
- ▶ The *focus group* method involves conducting an interview with a group of individuals where open-ended questions are posed. It often is used in program planning and evaluation.
- ▶ *Surveys with open-ended questions* appear at the end of a questionnaire, such as, "Anything else? What suggestions do you have?"
- ▶ *Narrative* methods are rarely used in injury program planning and evaluation. The narration or text comes from diaries, memos, reports, videos, and newspapers.

The benefits and limitations for each of the qualitative methods are summarized in Table 2-1.

i. Explain the importance of data for use in priority setting, program planning, quality improvement, evaluation, and advocacy in injury prevention.

Gathered data can provide evidence that an injury problem exists, and that it is important to know of its existence and to set priorities. Actually, severe injuries are rare events in the life of most individuals, and few persons can get any clear understanding of their importance as a social and economic problem solely from their own experience. Injury data can be used to evaluate the quality and effectiveness of interventions that have been implemented. Experts serving as advocates about a specific injury problem can testify (e.g., before city or county officials) using data to plead the case for resolving the injury problem.

j. Describe how qualitative and quantitative data can be used in conducting an assets-and-needs assessment of a community of interest.

An asset assessment collects data that focuses on the strengths, assets, abilities, and resources that exist and are available. An asset assessment attempts to answer the questions: What resources exist within the community experiencing the injury

Table 2-1 Summary of Benefits and Limitations to Using Qualitative Methods

Method	Key benefits for use in planning and evaluation	Key limitations for use in planning and evaluation
Case study	Allows for an understanding of context as an influence on the program or participant	Complex, overwhelming amount of data; definition of case
Observations	Can identify sequence of causes and effects; may identify new behaviors or events	Difficult to obtain reliable data unless one uses recording devices; sampling frame difficult to establish
Individual in-depth interviews	Provides rich insights into personal thoughts, values, meanings, and attributions	Identifying individuals who are willing to be open
Focus groups	Inexpensive given the amount and type of data; get collective views rather than individual views	Need training in managing the group process; need a good data recording method
Survey with open-ended questions	Very inexpensive method of data collection	Poor handwriting and unclear statements make data useless
Narrative designs	Very inexpensive data collection; provides insights into social and cultural influences on thoughts and actions	Requires special training in data analysis; may not have credibility with stakeholders; difficult to select the most relevant texts to the injury problem or program

Source: Issel, 2004.

problem? What do community members view as strengths and resources within their community? And to what extent are the resources available to address an injury problem?

A needs assessment collects and analyzes data to determine if the target population's needs are being met regarding a defined, specific injury problem. Data from a needs assessment helps identify goals, problems, or conditions that the injury program should address. In this way, it is a starting point for planning, implementing, and evaluating a program.

k. Demonstrate the ability to present data in a clear and understandable manner for different audiences.

Graphs are the best way to present data. These visual methods can make the point much stronger than simply describing the data. While they can be powerful methods, they also have the potential to ruin a presentation if they convey the wrong message or they confuse the audience.

Five basic types of graphic presentations are commonly used in making a pictorial presentation of the data. There are more complex types that are used for specific purposes, but rarely are used. Most presentation software packages have a built-in graph creation tool and will meet the needs of most presenters. The five types of graphic presentations are: area, column, bar, line, and pie chart. Examples of these are shown in Figure 2-1.

Area graphs (Figure 2-1a) show the relationship of different parts to a whole over time. *Column* graphs (Figure 2-1b) show the differences in individual values vertically. It can be used to show the differences between values in different time periods or other data groups. *Bar* graphs (Figure 2-1c) show the differences in individual values horizontally. It is not a good choice for showing values in different time periods. *Line* graphs (Figure 2-1d) show values at different points in time. It is usually best to have equal time intervals along the horizontal axis of the graph. *Pie* graphs (Figure 2-1e) show the proportions of each segment of a whole.

Tables

The basic structure of a table is a set of columns and rows that contain the data and usually contain either a row or column (or both) of headings that organize the data. A table is generally less effective than a graph because it only shows the data, whereas the graph shows an interpretation of the data, which is easier for the audience to understand.

Descriptive Statistics

At the minimum, basic findings should be presented in basic descriptive statistics form. Tables for descriptive statistics also should be used. The main descriptive statistics should include central tendency: mean, median, and mode. *Mean* is the arithmetic average; *median* is the middle number, which divides the distribution of numbers exactly in half; and *mode* is the most-often-occurring number.

Percentages are useful in descriptive statistics to present if done correctly. Percentages can provide a clear picture of data or can mislead if presented incorrectly. Percentages always should be compared to the total number from which they come. For example, to show how many motor vehicle passengers wear a seat belt, a researcher could say *x* percent of the occupants wore them. This percentage is meaningless. Is the data *x* percent of 1,000 or *x* percent of 200,000 occupants? Therefore, when showing percents, always present the total number of the participants or the "N." "N" stands for number of subjects. It is used in statistics to show the total number in the study population or any subgroup that is being compared statistically. The best way to show percentages is to state the "N" along with the percent; for example, "650 out of 750,

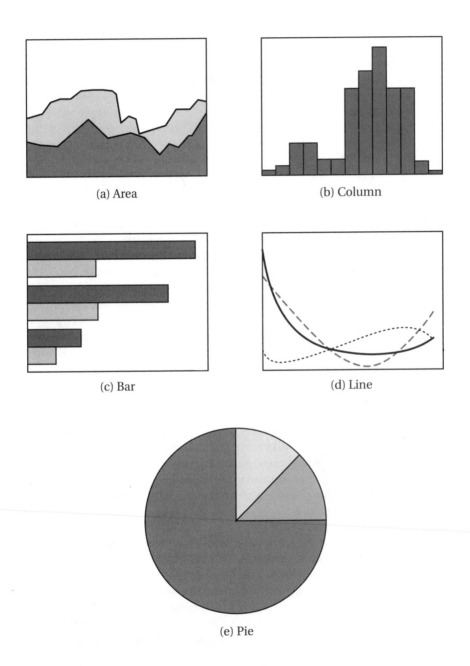

(a) Area

(b) Column

(c) Bar

(d) Line

(e) Pie

Figure 2-1 Graphs. (a) Area (b) Column (c) Bar (d) Line (e) Pie

or 89.3 percent, of the participants in a school district requested access to inexpensive bike helmets."

Rates (e.g., unintentional injury death rate in 2005 was 38.1 per 100,000 population) compare occurrences in groups of 100 or 1,000 or 10,000 and are commonly used in descriptive statistics and epidemiology data. Ratios (e.g., about 1 out of 9 people sought medical attention for any injury) also are a common form of descriptive statistics and may be of value to the planner under the appropriate circumstances. Percentages (e.g., unintentional injury deaths were up 1 percent this year compared to last year) and rates commonly are used in program planning.

Problems of Statistical Analysis*

Statistics play an important role in injury prevention and control. The reasons statistics are not used more are probably because of what some call a "statistical neurosis." An early statistician coined a phrase that has since been repeated to generations: "It's not that the figures lie—it's that the liars figure." Although deceptive figures can appear in injury data, it is probable that the largest number of statistical studies are compiled by those desiring to inform rather than misinform. Nevertheless, a statistic that misleads through honest error can be just as confusing as one that is deliberately constructed to misrepresent. The following section discusses several sources of error found in injury data; these may be divided into the following groups: sources of error in collection, presentation, and interpretation.

Sources of Error in the Collection of Injury Data

Deliberate suppression. There are several forms of suppression. One can be attributed to administrative self-protection rather than to darker motives. Keeping the injury rate down is a perennial concern of administrators. Frequently, a slightly injured worker is immediately returned to the job to keep the factory safety record spotless, even if the injured worker should be home after the injury resting and caring for his or her injury.

Failure to complain. Because an injury is not known until someone reports it, any statistic that purports to represent the total number of any type of injury that has taken place is necessarily an informed guess based on the addition of an estimated number of unreported injuries of the same type. Certain types of injuries tend to be reported with much greater accuracy than others. For example, motor vehicle deaths usually are reported quite accurately because there are legal requirements to make such reports and great value is placed on human life.

---

*The following content relates to the core competency but not to any single objective. It appears because of the problems prevalent in dealing with statistics and data (Thygerson, 1992).

However, motor vehicle collisions causing less than a hundred dollars' worth of damage may go unnoticed, and even unreported, as a result of legal stipulations and a $100-deductible insurance coverage that may not require their reporting. Even reports of damage costs may be totally in error because most estimated costs are quite subjective in nature.

Variations in the definition of certain injuries. There is one obstacle hindering a uniform system of injury reporting that will not be overcome until all jurisdictions employ similar definitions for classifying injuries: Different definitions yield different data. A review of drowning literature demonstrates a lack of a standard definition of drowning. One review found a total of 33 different definitions to describe drowning incidents—20 for drowning and 13 for near-drowning (Papal et al., 2005). This variability in definitions makes it very difficult to assess and analyze the problem of drowning.

A prime example of this is the National Safety Council's tracking of motor vehicle deaths in relation to that of the National Highway Traffic Safety Administration (NHTSA). Virtually every year, the two groups report on the same topic and produce two different numbers. How does it happen? Is one of them wrong? Not necessarily. The answer a researcher gets varies depending on which questions they ask and what they are learning. The National Safety Council, when tracking motor vehicle deaths, defines such deaths as traffic or nontraffic fatalities that occur within 1 year of the crash. A nontraffic fatality is a death that occurred off a public roadway, such as in a parking lot or driveway.

NHTSA's estimates do not include nontraffic deaths and include only those deaths that occur within 30 days of the incident. For example, if someone were in a car crash and in a coma for 9 months before dying, that person would not be included in NHTSA's estimate. Neither organization is "wrong," but they are asking different questions and considering different types of information (Parker, 2006).

Differences in the reporting of injuries within the same area. Everyone has his or her own biases. If a relative or someone with high status has an injury, a person may never report it in order to keep a record clear of any blemish that might hinder future promotions and advancements for that person. An example was given by William Tarrants:

> A mid-western manufacturing plant with a fairly stable injury frequency rate decided to hire a full-time safety manager to see if this rate could be cut down. Within a short time after the safety manager was hired, the injury frequency rate nearly doubled. Should we conclude that the safety manager caused these injuries and quickly fire him? A closer look revealed that the safety manager instituted a new injury investigation and reporting system that produced more reports of disabling injuries, thus increasing the frequency rate.

Lack of uniformity in collecting and recording techniques. Tallying the number of known injuries is a considerably more complicated process than it would seem to be. A motor vehicle crash is usually witnessed and reported, whereas an injury in a home involving minor cuts or burns is rarely reported.

Sources of Error in the Presentation of Injury Data

When a researcher considers injury data, there is probably no assertion more misleading than the frequently heard statement: "the figures speak for themselves." Because long columns of figures convey an impression of actuality, it is essential to discuss the more common misunderstandings that arise from faulty presentation of data.

Misleading use of simple sums rather than rates. The fact that Town A records 50 motor vehicle deaths as compared with 100 reported by Town B does not necessarily mean that Town B is twice as death ridden as Town A. If Town B has four times the population of Town A, the reverse is true. Total injury and death figures do not become meaningful until they are transformed into rates (ratios or percentages) based on the total population under consideration. Similarly, this principle applies to changes in the incidence of injuries. Town C, in 2010, may report twice as many injuries as it did in 2000—yet its population may have doubled during this period. If this is true, then the injury rate remains the same.

Misleading use of averages and percentages. The precaution of translating simple sums into averages and percentages does not assure the proper presentation of data; these measures can be misleading as raw totals. Consider the following statement: "The average number of injuries per family in the Lakeview residential area is three per year." This statement gives the impression that each family living in the Lakeview residential area has about the same number of injuries each year. This assumption may not be correct at all. A count reveals that five families live in the area. Three households report one injury, whereas the fourth family reports two injuries that year. The fifth family has a total of 10 among its members. Thus the "average" figure obtained by adding the total number of injuries and dividing by five is mathematically accurate but misleading. As this illustration demonstrates, an *average* is meaningless without information about the variation of the measures that compose it.

Pitfalls of graphic presentations. For some, long columns of figures and numbers are not only impressive but also downright intimidating. For this reason, statisticians, epidemiologists, and publicists often present their findings graphically or pictorially. Although this method presents material in quick, easy-to-comprehend form, it also can mislead the one assessing the information.

Sources of Error in the Interpretation of Injury Data

The "self-evident" conclusion. Mark Twain observed that there are three kinds of lies: plain lies, damned lies, and statistics. This humorous statement implies that statistics can be manipulated to support any point of view. The use of statistics, however, should not be completely dismissed, because statistics mislead and confuse only when one does not know how to interpret them. There are elaborate formulas for determining the significance and reliability of a statistic.

The problem with many of the sources of injury data are (1) the information is incomplete, (2) reporting is done only on severe types, (3) information is not easily available or not made public, (4) inaccuracies are included, and (5) the variations in definition of injury can lead to misinformation.

For instance, the statement that "four times more fatalities occur on the highways at 7 PM than at 7 AM" can be misleading. People may fail to realize that more people are killed in the evening than in the morning simply because more people are on the highways at that hour to be killed.

A person often hears that "off-the-job activities are more dangerous than workplaces because more injuries occur off-the-job" or that "the bathroom is the most hazardous room in the home because more deaths occur in the bathroom than any other room." The originators of these statements fail to consider the differences in the quantity of exposure to hazards, the types of exposure, and other influencing factors.

The confusion of correlation with cause. A favorite method of searching for "causes" is to hunt for statistical associations. It often is claimed, without real justification, that there are associations and correlations between contributing factors and injuries. Individuals sometimes have difficulty contrasting the association of these factors with the total situation; illustrations are given in Table 2-2. The central point is that a genuine association exists only when two things appear together *either more frequently or less frequently than would normally be expected.*

Whenever two factors are associated, there are at least four possibilities as to why:

1. A causes B (epileptic seizure causes motor vehicle crash).
2. B causes A (motor vehicle crash causes seizure due to head injury).
3. Both A and B are caused by C (both seizure and motor vehicle crash are caused by flickering roadside lights).
4. A and B are independent and the "association" is by chance.

The previous list shows how a statistical association never identifies the cause; it merely states that two factors move together, without indicating why. To explain what causes what, inferential statistics must be used, and this requires specialized training.

Table 2-2 When Does a Percentage Indicate a Statistical Association?

If:	We need to know:	Before trying to decide:
40 percent of fatal accidents involve drivers who drink alcohol	What percent of all driving is done by drivers who drink?	Whether drivers who drink contribute more or less than their share of fatal crashes
50 percent of injuries to boys in the first three grades of school are due to lack of safety knowledge	What percent of all boys of similar age lack safety knowledge?	Whether lack of safety knowledge is associated with school injuries to boys
30 percent of fatalities involve vehicles being driven too fast	What percent of all driving is done beyond the speed limit?	Whether driving too fast is correlated with fatal crashes
300 percent as many deaths occur off the job as on the job	What percent of time is spent both on the job and off the job?	Whether a worker is safer at work than elsewhere

Sometimes an association or correlation is highly significant, even though the question of causes remains unanswered. For example, several insurance companies found that boys making good grades had fewer motor vehicle crashes than students making low grades. The company did not need to know the cause of this association—this fact alone was enough to permit them to cut premiums for boys who could show an average grade of "B" or better.

The Centers for Disease Control and Prevention (CDC) established the National Center for Injury Prevention and Control in 1992.

Conclusion

Injury prevention efforts rely heavily on data, and this data comes from a number of sources. Many national and state government agencies and other organizations collect, analyze, and disseminate injury data. They vary in scope and in the extent to which they provide information. Significant advances have been made for injury surveillance and evaluation of programs, but more could be done. This chapter focuses on accessing, interpreting, using, and presenting injury data.

Data collection and analysis can reveal an important injury problem because the injury incidences may be some distance in time and location from one another. Data can provide the answers to the 5W and H questions—who, what, where, why, when, and how—all necessary in selecting and later evaluating an intervention program.

References

Doll, L.S, S.E. Bonzo, J.A. Mercy, and D.A. Sleet. (2007). Handbook of injury and violence prevention. New York: Springer.

Issel, L.M. (2004). Health program planning and evaluation. Sudbury, MA: Jones and Bartlett Publishers.

National Center for Injury Prevention and Control. (2001). Injury fact book 2001–2002. Atlanta: Centers for Disease Control and Prevention.

National Safety Council. (2007). Injury facts. Itasca, IL: National Safety Council.

Papal, Hoelle R. and A. Edris. (2005). Systematic review of definitions for drowning incidents. *Resuscitation* 65(3):255–264.

Parker, James G. (2006). Safety by numbers: Where does data come from? *Safety and Health* 174:5:68–69.

Thygerson, A.L. (1992). Safety, 2nd edition. Sudbury, MA: Jones and Bartlett Publishers.

CHAPTER 3 ▶

Program Planning

CORE COMPETENCY 3: Ability to design and implement injury prevention activities.

---

a. Identify and explain the roles of national, state, and local level agencies and organizations that can serve as resources for prevention efforts.

Many agencies and organizations work toward reducing America's injury problem. Tables 3-1, 3-2, 3-3, and 3-4 provide a brief overview of national, state, and local level agencies and organizations involved in addressing different unintentional injury prevention efforts. These agencies and organizations have made important contributions to injury prevention. However, fragmentation exists, and the government at all levels could play a larger role.

b. Explain the role and benefits of collaboration in prevention efforts.

The injury prevention field is large and has a diversity of groups and approaches. Most efforts by government agencies use the public health approach with its methods and strategies unique to the public health field. Those outside of the public health arena also focusing upon injury prevention include fire services, law enforcement agencies, school systems, workplaces, and recreational groups. See Table 3-5 for examples of people and groups who often work together on public

Table 3-1 Federal Government Agencies

Agency	Role
National Center for Injury Prevention and Control	Works to reduce mortality, morbidity, disability, and costs related to injuries—intentional and unintentional
Consumer Product Safety Commission (CPSC)	Charged with protecting the public from unreasonable risks of serious injury or death from consumer products
Maternal and Child Health Bureau	Promotes the health of mothers and children
Indian Health Service	Focuses upon the health of Native Americans
National Highway Traffic Safety Administration (NHTSA)	Attempts to reduce injuries resulting from motor-vehicle crashes; sets and enforces safety standards for motor vehicles
Occupational Safety and Health Administration (OSHA)	Establishes occupational safety and health standards; conducts inspections to ensure compliance with the standards
National Institute of Occupational Safety and Health	Focuses on research and training related to occupational safety and health; makes recommendations to OSHA

Table 3-2 Examples of National Nonprofit Organizations

Organization	Role
AAA Foundation for Traffic Safety	Education and research on motor vehicle crashes
American Association of Poison Control Centers	Gathers poison incident data and provides education
Brain Injury Association	Increase awareness and promote prevention of brain injury
Children's Safety Network	Resource center for child and adolescence injury prevention
Insurance Institute for Highway Safety	Sponsored by automobile insurance companies; focuses on the main factors involved in motor vehicle collisions
Mothers Against Drunk Driving (MADD)	Increase awareness about drunk driving and solutions to drunk driving and underage drinking drivers
National Fire Protection Association (NFPA)	Educate the public and develop fire codes and standards
National Safe Kids Worldwide	Promotes childhood safety through community-based strategies
National Safety Council	Provides training and consulting with the goal of improving safety in various injury problems (e.g., agriculture, construction, utilities)
Safe USA	Alliance of organizations focusing upon research, service, training, communication, and policy development related to injury prevention

Table 3-3 National Professional Organizations

American Academy of Orthopaedic Surgeons
American Academy of Pediatrics, Section on Injury and Poison Prevention
American Alliance for Health, Physical Education, Recreation and Dance
American College of Emergency Physicians, Trauma Care and Injury Control Committee
American College of Surgeons, Committee on Trauma
American Public Health Association, Injury Control and Emergency Health Services Section
American Society of Safety Engineers
American Trauma Society
Emergency Nurses Association
International Association of Chiefs of Police
International Association of Fire Chiefs
International Association of Firefighters
State and Territorial Injury Prevention Directors' Association
Wilderness Medical Society

Table 3-4 Examples of State and Local Government Agencies and Organizations

Agency or organization	Role
Child Death Review Teams	Gather and analyze data surrounding child deaths
Emergency Medical Services (EMS)	Care of injured victims and transportation to hospital emergency departments
Fire Services Agencies	Firefighting and rescue operations Fire prevention safety education programs
Labor and Occupational Agencies	Investigate worksite injuries Develop and implement prevention programs
Law Enforcement Agencies	Enforce injury-related laws (e.g., traffic) Provide programs (e.g., bike safety)
Public Health Departments	Identifies injury problems Plans, implements, and evaluates injury prevention programs
State Highway Offices	Develops a state highway safety plan Administers federal funding
State Department of Education	Develops school curriculum involving safety (e.g., school bus, pedestrian, driver education)
State Transportation Department	Licensing of drivers Construction and maintenance of roads and highways
State Occupational Safety and Health Administration	Develops and implements prevention programs Investigates workplace injuries Provide input on regulations

Table 3-5 Examples of People and Groups Commonly Found in a Public Health
Injury Prevention Coalition (*if applicable to the injury problem)

Local government representatives
Health care providers
Local college/university faculty (e.g., departments of health, sociology, education)
Health care administrators
Cooperative extension employees
School district faculty and/or administrators*
Target population representatives
Law enforcement representatives*
Fire service*
Emergency medical services*
Local health department employees
Local recreation department employees*
Agency on Aging*
Business owners and managers
Service organizations (e.g., Rotary, Lions Club, Kiwanis)
Chamber of Commerce

health coalitions. They may differ in their approaches from those in governmental public health agencies. Finding effective ways to coordinate and collaborate these various groups possessing different backgrounds in terms of training and strategies can be challenging.

Coordinating and collaborating ideally involves the formation of coalitions and partnerships. A *coalition* is formed when groups come together to work toward common goals and objectives. *Advisory boards* are groups of individuals that represent stakeholders and members of the target population. Advisory boards are common at worksites, school systems, and health care facilities.

A coalition of groups brought together to address a common injury problem in a target population can be powerful. Important benefits for organizing a coalition for program planning include pooling resources, decreasing unnecessary duplication of efforts, increasing efficiency in program delivery—including and integrating diverse perspectives in the planning process—increasing political clout, improving the ability to gain access to hard-to-reach populations, and creating greater credibility than an individual institution can have (Hodges, 2005).

c. Identify types/examples of current and potential stakeholders/partners and their current prevention activities.

The lead agency or institution must have the resources necessary to organize and maintain the coalition; if not, the coalition may not work. The lead agency or institution will be largely responsible for a number of important tasks. Someone from the lead group will need to perform clerical work (e.g., making phone calls, photocopying). The lead group facilitates the logistics of coalition meetings by making reminder phone calls, securing meeting locations, providing refreshments, and so forth. It is usually the lead group that coordinates coalition activities and fund-raising.

Who is needed on a coalition? It is imperative to have stakeholders. These are the people who will be most affected by the work of the coalition. Examples of stakeholders include members of the target population, those responsible for implementing interventions in the target population, and the staffs of organizations that may be affected by the programs developed by the coalition. Community opinion leaders also should be on your coalition.

d. Describe how to identify and prioritize injury problems and interventions.

Many health problems exist—communicable and chronic diseases, violence, substance abuse, and unintentional injuries, the focus of this book. Prioritizing the allocation of resources to prevent these problems can be difficult. The same goes for specific injury types within the realm of unintentional injuries—which deserves top priority? Which problems will benefit the most from an intervention?

This objective's content contains two sections: (1) identifying injury problems and (2) prioritizing injury problems and interventions.

Identifying Injury Problems

LEADING CAUSES OF DEATH

The National Center for Injury Prevention and Control's Web site (www.cdc.gov/ncipc) provides three listings of leading causes of death: (1) all deaths, (2) all injuries, and (3) unintentional injuries only. In recent years, unintentional injury deaths rank as the fifth leading cause of all deaths. They are the leading cause of death in those between age 1 and 44 years.

YEARS OF POTENTIAL LIFE LOST

Another approach toward identifying health problems is the years of potential life lost (YPLL). The YPLL is calculated by subtracting a person's age at death from their life expectancy. Such calculations are difficult because each person may have a different life expectancy at any given time. The age of 75 years increasingly is being used to calculate YPLL because life expectancy for a child born today is about 75 years. YPLL weights deaths of very young person as more than the death of a very old person. See the National Center for Injury Prevention and Control

Web site for the data. Unintentional injuries account for more YPLL than any other leading cause of death.

ECONOMIC COST

The costs of unintentional injuries are immense—in the billions of dollars. Economic cost data are hard to locate, and even the experts disagree on the estimates obtained. The National Safety Council (2007) estimates the annual costs from all unintentional injuries to exceed $625 billion. This large monetary loss includes such things as wages and productivity losses, medical expenses, administrative expenses, property damage, and so forth.

NEWSPAPER AND MASS MEDIA ACCOUNTS

The quotable Will Rogers said, "All I know is just what I read in the papers, and that's an alibi for my ignorance." Newspapers and other types of mass media can bring attention to an injury problem that few other ways can. However, the reporting may portray only the bizarre and catastrophic types of events. Moreover, for surveillance purposes, they greatly underreport the occurrence of injuries.

SURVEILLANCE SYSTEMS

Governments at all levels maintain surveillance systems intent on gathering injury data. Some types of injuries receive much greater attention than others. A later chapter provides information about these surveillance systems.

Prioritizing Injury Problems and Interventions

The objective for this section includes "prioritizing injury problems" and "prioritizing injury interventions." Within this section is information and procedures useful for doing both: prioritizing injury problems and injury interventions.

The following poem, a classic in public health, shows the difficulty of decision making as to which injury intervention should be selected:

The Parable of the Dangerous Cliff
Twas a dangerous cliff, as thy freely confessed,
    Though the walk near its crest was so pleasant;
But over its terrible edge there had slipped
    A duke, and a full many peasant.
The people said something would have to be done,
    But their projects did not at all tally.
Some said, "Put a fence 'round the edge of the cliff,
    Some, "An ambulance down the valley."

The lament of the crowd was profound and was loud,
  As their hearts overflowed with their pity;
But the cry for the ambulance carried the day
  As it spread through the neighboring city.
A collection was made, to accumulate aid,
  And dwellers in highway and alley
Gave dollars or cents—not to furnish a fence—
  But an ambulance down in the valley.

"For the cliff is all right if you're careful," they said;
  And if folks ever slip and are dropping,
It isn't the slipping that hurts them so much
  As the shock down below—when they're stopping."

So for years (we have heard), as these mishaps occurred
  Quick forth would the rescuers sally,
To pick up the victims who fell from the cliff
  With the ambulance down in the valley.

Said one, to his plea, "It's a marvel to me
  That you'd give so much greater attention
To repairing results than to curing the cause;
  You had much better aim at prevention.
For the mischief, of course, should be stopped at its source,
  Come, neighbors and friends, let us rally.
It is far better sense to rely on a fence
  Than an ambulance down in the valley."

"He is wrong in his head," the majority said;
  "He would end all our earnest endeavor.
He's a man who would shirk this responsible work,
  But we will support it forever.
Aren't we picking up all, just as fast as they fall,
  And giving them care liberally?
A superfluous fence is of no consequence,
  If the ambulance works in the valley."

The story looks queer as we've written it here,
  But things oft occur that are stranger.
More humane, we assert, than to succor the hurt,
  Is the plan of removing the danger.
The best possible course is to safeguard the source;

Attend to things rationally.
Yes, build up the fence and let us disperse
With the ambulance down in the valley.

Written in 1895 by Joseph Malins, English poet

National Health Goals: Healthy People Objectives

Healthy People is a set of health objectives for the United States to achieve over 10 years. It can be used by many different people, states, communities, professional organizations, and others to help develop programs to improve health. These can serve to prioritize injury prevention efforts by stressing and therefore prioritizing these objectives over other injury problems that went unlisted.

Nearly all states, the District of Columbia, and Guam have developed their own Healthy People plans. The *Healthy People Toolkit*, which can be useful in setting and using objectives, is available on the Web at www.health.gov/healthypeople/state/toolkit. Individuals, groups, and organizations are encouraged to integrate Healthy People into current programs, special events, publications, and meetings.

The overall health goals in Healthy People are to (1) increase quality and years of healthy life and (2) eliminate health disparities (differences in disease and death rates between racial and ethnic subgroups). See Table 3-6 for the objectives relating to unintentional injuries.

Hanlon Method or Basic Priority Rating System*

Establishing priorities from a multitude of health problems, many of which are injury problems, is a necessary and increasingly difficult task. Administrators and managers often are faced with decreasing resources. A method to establish priorities that is reasonable and easy to calculate is a necessary tool.

The Hanlon method is a rating system, using various data to quantify problems and their interventions when prioritizing is necessary (Hanlon and Pickett, 1984). Hanlon's approach has been codified into a simple formula known as the Basic Priority Rating System (BPRS). This method prioritizes health problems based on the size of the problem, the severity or importance of the problem, and the potential effectiveness of interventions.

---

*This section is adapted from the National Association of County and City Health Officials (1991). APEXPH Workbook: Assessment protocol for excellence in public health. Washington, DC: National Association of County and City Health Officials. Note: For this objective, the term *interventions* was added by the authors.

Table 3-6 Healthy People 2010 Objectives Relating to Unintentional Injuries

The following objectives are a distillation of the injury prevention objectives. This list includes the objectives contained in the "official" list of Related Injury Objectives from Other Focus Areas and additional objectives believed to be important to the field.

15-1. Reduce hospitalization for nonfatal head injuries to 54 hospitalizations per 100,000 population.

15-2. Reduce hospitalization for nonfatal spinal cord injuries to 2.6 hospitalizations per 100,000 population.

15-3. Reduce firearm-related deaths to 4.9 per 100,000 population.

15-4. Reduce the proportion of persons living in homes with firearms that are loaded and unlocked to 16 percent.

15-5. Reduce nonfatal firearm-related injuries to 10.9 injuries per 100,000 population.

15-6. (Developmental) Extend state-level child fatality review of deaths due to external causes for children aged 14 years and under.

15-7. Reduce nonfatal poisonings to 292 nonfatal poisonings per 100,000 population.

15-8. Reduce deaths caused by poisonings to 1.8 deaths per 100,000 population.

15-9. Reduce deaths caused by suffocation to 2.9 deaths per 100,000 population.

15-10. Increase the number of states and the District of Columbia with statewide emergency department surveillance systems that collect data on external causes of injury to all states and D.C.

15-11. Increase the number of states and the District of Columbia that collect data on external causes of injury through hospital discharge data systems.

15-12. Reduce hospital emergency department visits caused by injuries to 112 hospital emergency department visits per 1,000 population.

15-13. Reduce deaths caused by unintentional injuries to 20.8 deaths per 100,000 population.

15-14. (Developmental) Reduce nonfatal unintentional injuries.

15-15. Reduce deaths caused by motor vehicle crashes to 9.0 deaths per 100,000 population and 1 death per 100 million vehicle miles traveled (VMT).

15-16. Reduce pedestrian deaths on public roads to 1 pedestrian death per 100,000 population.

15-17. Reduce nonfatal injuries caused by motor vehicle crashes to 1,000 nonfatal injuries per 100,000 population.

15-18. Reduce nonfatal pedestrian injuries on public roads to 21 nonfatal injuries per 100,000 population.

15-19. Increase use of safety belts to 92 percent of the total population.

15-20. Increase use of child restraints to 100 percent of motor vehicle occupants aged 4 years and under.

15-21. Increase the proportion of motorcyclists using helmets to 79 percent of motorcycle operators and passengers.

15-22. Increase the number of states and the District of Columbia that have adopted a graduated driver licensing model law to all states and D.C.

15-23. (Developmental) Increase use of helmets by bicyclists.

Table 3-6 Healthy People 2010 Objectives Relating to Unintentional Injuries (continued)

15-24. Increase the number of states and the District of Columbia with laws requiring bicycle helmets for bicycle riders to all states and D.C.

15-25. Reduce residential fire deaths to 0.6 deaths per 100,000 population.

15-26. Increase functioning residential smoke alarms to 100 percent of residences with a functioning smoke alarm on every floor.

15-27. Reduce deaths from falls to 2.3 deaths per 100,000 population.

15-28. Reduce hip fractures among older adults to 491.0 fractures per 100,000 females aged 65 years and older and to 450.5 fractures per 100,000 males aged 65 years and older.

15-29. Reduce drownings to 0.9 drownings per 100,000 population.

15-30. Reduce hospital emergency department visits for nonfatal dog bite injuries to 114 hospital ER visits per 100,000 population.

15-31. (Developmental) Increase the proportion of public and private schools that require use of appropriate head, face, eye, and mouth protection for students participating in school-sponsored physical activities.

Source: www.safetypolicy.org.

Components of this method include:

▶ Component A: Size of the problem
▶ Component B: Seriousness of the problem
▶ Component C: Estimated effectiveness of an intervention
▶ Component D: PEARL factors (propriety, economic feasibility, acceptability, resource availability, legality)

The scores assigned to the components can be biased by the personal preferences of those involved in the planning process. Group consensus and consistency can occur when precise definitions and good data are used. The members of the group have to work together throughout the process.

Component A: Rate the size of the problem. The first factor to determine is the size of the problem (A). The decision of how to define size is usually a group consensus. Most often this involves the number of persons affected by the problem. The score corresponding to the size of the problem (see Table 3-7) is used as the value of that factor and is placed in the formula. Another method for determining the size of the problem is the use of mortality data to rate the size of the problem (see Table 3-8). They are given as per 100,000 people in a population. The injury problem with the highest frequency receives a rating of 10, and the injury problem with the lowest frequency receives a rating of 0 or 1. The other injury problems are placed in between. Nationally, for example, 7.1 poisoning deaths per 100,000 could indicate that poisoning should have a priority over fall-related deaths, which has 6.0 deaths per 100,000. These data can be obtained from state health department offices of vital records or by accessing the CDC Web site.

Table 3-7 Scores for Percentage of Population Affected

Percentage of population affected	Score
25% or more	9 or 10
10% through 24.9%	7 or 8
1% through 9.9%	5 or 6
.1% through .9%	3 or 4
.01% through .09%	1 or 2
Less than .01% (1/10,000)	0

Table 3-8 Scores Based on Mortality Data

Death rate per 100,000 population	Score
Motor vehicle crashes	15.5
Poisoning	7.1
Falls	6.0
Choking	1.6
Drowning	1.2
Fires	1.0

Disability, pain, and quality of life should be considered, although difficult to quantify. Thus, the size of the problem ought to be viewed from various angles and incorporate a diversity of measures or indicators. The scoring scale can be in any fashion meeting the group's approval. Once the estimated size is determined, a score ranging from 0 to 10 is inserted into the formula.

Component B: Rate the seriousness of the problem. Not all injury problems are equal in seriousness (B). Factors indicating seriousness include the degree of:

1. Urgency for addressing the problem
2. Severity of the problem
3. Economic losses possible from the problem

Each of these three elements of seriousness can be rated on a scale of 0 at the lowest end to 10 on the highest end. An average score is derived from the three elements that represent the score for B in the formula. Note that in the formula, seriousness (B) is considered twice as important as size (A). See Table 3-9 for more information.

Seriousness is best determined through contact with experts, as well as through input from key stakeholders on the long-term consequences of the problem. Fatality rate and premature mortality represented by YPLL for persons dying before age 65 both can help determine severity. The degree of economic loss is focused on individual loss due to disability and death, but it also might include the societal costs of providing care and the loss of revenue from disabled individuals.

Table 3-9 Scores for Seriousness of an Injury Problem

How serious an injury problem is considered	"Seriousness" rating
Very Serious (e.g., very high death rate, great impact on others)	9, 10
Serious	6, 7, 8
Moderately Serious	3, 4, 5
Not Serious	0, 1, 2

The group should be careful not to bring the issues of size or preventability into their discussion because they fit elsewhere into the formula.

Component C: Rate the effectiveness of available interventions. Scoring the effectiveness of the interventions uses a scale of 0 to 10. This may be may be the most subjective component of the formula. Interventions for which there is considerable favorable evidence would be rated highest, where "favorable" means having a significant effect on the problem. The choice of intervention deserves considerable attention, in terms of whether and how it has the potential to affect the factors leading to a potential injury.

There is data available from studies that document how successful interventions have been. See Table 3-10 for more information about the effectiveness of available interventions.

Locating information about the effectiveness of interventions requires an extensive literature search. An excellent source is SafetyLit, an online source for recent research about injury prevention. It can be accessed at http://safetylit.org. Later chapters of this book also highlight the best practices and evidence-based interventions for injury prevention. The CDC's Guide to Community Preventive Services available online at www.thecommunityguide.org provides information about the effectiveness of some community-based injury interventions. Also, the Harborview Injury Prevention and Research Center, found online

Table 3-10 Scores for Effectiveness of Available Interventions

Effectiveness of available interventions in preventing the injury problem (in percent)	"Effectiveness" rating
Very effective: 80 to 100 effective	9, 10
Relatively effective: 60 to 80 effective	7, 8
Effective: 40 to 60	5, 6
Moderately ineffective: 20 to 40 effective	3, 4
Relatively ineffective: 5 to 20 effective	1, 2
Almost entirely ineffective: less than 5 effective	0

at http://depts.washington,edu/hiprc/index.html, offers best practices information about unintentional injury interventions.

Component D: *Apply the "PEARL" test.* PEARL consists of a group of factors with a high degree of influence in determining whether a particular intervention can actually be carried out. PEARL is a mnemonic for:

- ▶ Propriety: Is a program for the injury problem suitable?
- ▶ Economics: Does it make economic sense to address the problem? Are there economic consequences if a program is not carried out?
- ▶ Acceptability: Will the community accept a program? Is it wanted?
- ▶ Resources: Is funding available or potentially available for a program?
- ▶ Legality: Do current laws allow program activities to be implemented?

Any health problem receiving a "no" on any question should either be dropped from consideration because it is impossible or impractical at the moment or the reason for the "no" answer to be considered and, if it can be corrected, consideration of the injury problem might continue. It may not be possible to apply the PEARL scoring until a substantial amount of information has been collected about the problem.

CALCULATE PRIORITY SCORES FOR THE INJURY PROBLEMS

Scores for each injury problem are calculated from the ratings recorded in columns A, B, and C of Table 3-11. Priority scores are entered in column E on the table. Use the following formula for these calculations with the letters representing the scores in columns A, B, and C from the table:

$$D = [A + (2 \times B)] \times C$$

Using dog bites, an example of the calculation for these values appear in columns A, B, and C:

Column A = 2 (size)
Column B = 6 (seriousness)
Column C = 2 (intervention)

The following calculation would be carried out for the priority rating to be recorded in column D:

$$D = [2 + (2 \times 6)] \times 2 = 28$$

ASSIGN RANKS TO THE INJURY PROBLEMS

Once priority scores have been recorded for all injury problems, assign a priority rank for each injury problem, based on the size of the of the priority scores, and

Table 3-11 Injury Problem Priority Setting

Injury problem	A Size 0 to 10	B Seriousness 0 to 10	C Effectiveness of intervention 0 to 10	D Priority score (A+2B)C	E Rank
Dog bites	2	6	2	28	7

record it in column E. For example, the health problem with the highest priority score should be given a rank of 1, the problem with the next highest score, a rank of 2, and so on. Injury problems with the same priority score should be given the same priority rank.

Bracketology: Choosing a Single Injury Problem or Intervention

Bracketology is a tool for judging and determining which single injury problem should be focused on or which single intervention is preferred to be used. It is a strategy of binary pairings that finally determine what is thought to be the best. The bracket is laid out like a graph for a sport tournament (e.g., basketball, tennis); see Table 3-12.

After generating a list of injury problems or a list of potential interventions, place them in the bracket on the left side of the bracket. Evaluate each binary pairing and select the best in the pair. For interventions use either the criteria listed on page 74, known as the Runyan criteria (1998), to make judgments or use those known as PEARL, which were discussed with the Hanlon method previously. Continue through the bracket until one injury problem is focused on or a single intervention is determined to be the best. When dealing with interventions, a weakness of this approach is that it generates a single best intervention. However, this criticism could be overcome by selecting the final two or four interventions. A mixture of interventions is best because a single intervention rarely solves the problem.

Table 3-12 Bracket: Selecting the Best Dog Bite Intervention Example

Enforce unrestrained/
free-roaming animal law

Neuter/spay dogs

Ban high-risk breeds

Dog training (socialization)

Euthanize vicious dogs

Media campaign (prevention)

"User pays" liability insurance

Educate dog owners (dog
selection & training, being alert)

For injury interventions, use these criteria (Runyan, 1998) for judging the merits of the binary pairings until you reach what is considered the best choice:

► **Effective**: Does it work? This is the most important criteria and ideally relies on prior intervention evaluations which may not be available.
► **Preferences**: Is the intervention option compatible with the preferences, wishes, and cultural beliefs of the affected population?
► **Costs**: What are the costs of doing the intervention (e.g., implementation costs) versus the costs of not doing it (e.g., medical costs, lost wages)?
► **Restriction of personal freedom**: How much and what type of restriction on freedom is associated with the intervention?
► **Stigmatizes**: Does it stigmatize individuals who have some distinguishing characteristic (e.g., poverty, disability)?
► **Feasible**: Can the intervention be implemented? Is it technologically feasible?
► **Other criteria**: What other criteria might be appropriate to the situation?

Physician advice can enhance an individual's knowledge about preventing injuries.

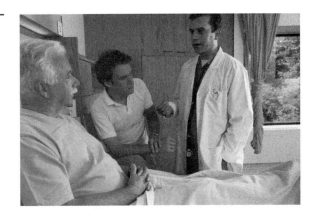

Paired-Comparison Analysis: Determining Priorities

A practical technique for comparing options is the paired-comparison analysis. It is useful where priorities are not clear or are competing in importance. It provides a framework for comparing each option against all others and helps to show the difference in importance between them. After generating a list of either injury problems to be ranked or interventions to be selected (e.g., using brainstorming, Haddon matrix, 3Es), the next step involves deciding which option—among multiple options—to select.

Paired-comparison analysis is useful especially where objective data is absent as may be the case for some injury problems. This analysis makes it easy to choose the most important problem to solve or select the solution or intervention that will provide the greatest benefit. *When evaluating injury interventions*, use either the PEARL criteria or the Runyan criteria (1998). *When prioritizing injury problems*, use the criteria from the Hanlon method to determine the seriousness: urgency for addressing the problem, severity of the problem, and economic losses of the problem.

The directions for using paired-comparison analysis are:

1. Beginning at the top of each column on Section #1, compare each pair listed on Section #2, while asking yourself, "If I could choose only one, which would it be?" Circle the number corresponding to your choice.
2. Continuing down each column, compare and choose one of the two options.
3. Count the number of times each number was circled on Worksheet #1, and fill in the blanks next to the corresponding number on Worksheet #2.

The result of these paired choices is a set of options, rank-ordered in terms of what options were chosen more often. It is useful where options are not clear or are competing against each other for resources and implementation.

Paired-comparison analysis is an objective and simple technique for comparing many options—too many to rank easily just by inspection, but not so many that the table size becomes unmanageable.

Table 3-13 Section #1

1-2						
1-3	2-3					
1-4	2-4	3-4				
1-5	2-5	3-5	4-5			
1-6	2-6	3-6	4-6	5-6		
1-7	2-7	3-7	4-7	5-7	6-7	
1-8	2-8	3-8	4-8	5-8	6-8	7-8

Table 3-14 Section #2

Option	Number of times selected	Rank
1)		
2)		
3)		
4)		
5)		
6)		
7)		
8)		

e. Describe how to locate and evaluate the best sources of information (or "evidence") available on which to base intervention decisions.

Finding intervention strategies need not be difficult. Nevertheless, finding the right strategies that are appropriate for the target population takes time. In fact, a major weakness within the injury prevention field is the scarcity of evaluations of interventions. Interventions and programs that have proved to be successful exist in the literature under such titles as best practices and evidence based.

A first step is to review the literature conducted with a focus on professional journals and from government agencies that conduct research. Going to the Web site of the Society for Advancement of Violence and Injury Research (SAVIR) can be very helpful. This organization is devoted to scholarly activity injury prevention, research, consultation, and evaluation. Attending professional meetings and conferences is another way to find out what is happening in the injury prevention field regarding effective programs and innovative strategies. Looking at Web sites on programs that work or best-practices programs will help in this process as well. Good sources for locating "what works" are in Table 3-15.

Table 3-15 Web Sites for Best-Practices for Unintentional Injuries*

Harborview Injury Prevention and Research Center
http://depts.washington.edu/hiprc/practices/index.html

Safety Lit: Injury Prevention Update
www.safetylit.org

Guide to Community Preventative Services
www.thecommunityguide.org

Cochrane Collaboration
www.thecochranelibrary.com

National Library of Medicine—PubMed
www.ncbi.nlm.nih.gov/entrez/query.fcqi

Safe Communities—U.S. Department of Transportation
www.nhtsa.dot.gov/safecommunities/ServiceCenter/showcase/showcase.htm

Colorado Prevention Leadership Council
www.nhtsa.dot.gov/safecommunities/ServiceCenter/showcase/showcase.htm

Minnesota Department of Health
www.health.state.mn.us/injury/best/index.cfm

Ontario Injury Prevention Resource Centre
www.opha.on.ca/resources/injurybp.pdf

National Resource Center for Safe Aging
www.safeaging.org/model/default.asp

*All accessed during April 2007.

f. Describe various levels where prevention activities can be focused (e.g., individual, institutional, community, public policy).

The Spectrum of Prevention, developed by Larry Cohen, is a tool for developing a multifaceted, comprehensive approach to injury prevention across six inter-related levels. Activities at each of these levels have the potential to support each other and promote injury prevention (Cohen, 1999). The spectrum emphasizes the importance of influencing policy and legislation, an area that the Haddon matrix does not specifically address. See Table 3-16 below.

Table 3-16 Spectrum of Prevention

Level of spectrum	Definition of level	Examples
1. Strengthening individual knowledge and skills	Enhancing an individual's capability of avoiding injury	Physician advising patient during check-ups about unsafe practices; bicycle sales people demonstrating proper helmet use; training expectant mothers on the correct use of car seats
2. Promoting community education	Reaching groups of people with information and resources to promote injury prevention	Mass media campaigns (e.g., communitywide learn-to-swim program at local swimming pool)
3. Educating providers	Informing providers who will transmit skills and knowledge to others	Teach pediatricians the value of advising their patients about unsafe practices
4. Fostering coalitions and networks	Bringing together groups who can conserve resources, foster cooperation, increase credibility, and impacts of their efforts	Safe Kids Worldwide
5. Changing organizational practices	Adopting regulations and shaping norms to improve safety	Hiring crossing guards for school crossings; sobriety checkpoints
6. Influencing policy legislation	Developing strategies to change laws and policies to influence outcomes	Mandatory helmet laws for bikes and motorcycles

Source: Adapted from Cohen, L. and S. Swift. (1999). The spectrum of prevention: Developing a comprehensive approach to injury prevention. *Injury Prevention* 5:203–207.

Because injury problems often are complex, the best solutions are usually comprehensive and address all levels of the spectrum. There is a need to look at all the different locations where an intervention can be the most effective. The spectrum helps determine at what levels the intervention should be implemented. To say "have your car safety inspected" is one thing, but how can vehicle owners be convinced to have a safety inspection performed? Perhaps a coalition is needed for an educational outreach to vehicle owners. Perhaps training service station attendants and car dealerships can help to promote inexpensive safety inspections with their customers. Passing a law requiring all vehicles to be periodically safety inspected by a licensed mechanic could be accomplished and fits into the sixth level.

g. Demonstrate the use of a conceptual model (e.g., Haddon matrix, social ecological model, etc.) for identifying intervention opportunities.

Haddon Matrix

The Haddon matrix was introduced in Chapter 1. Here is an example of using the steps of the Haddon matrix to identify interventions involving motor vehicle crashes (Haddon, 1980). The same procedures can be used for any injury problem.

Step 1: Place each known risk or causal factors in the appropriate phase. Causal factors include the *causes of the event* and the *causes of the injury*. Note that the phases are horizontal to represent a time sequence from pre-through postevents. The example provided involves motor vehicle crashes.

The sequence of an injury incident is shown as a continuum—going from left to right, a logic time sequence.

Preevent (injury-causing event)	Event (injury/damage during actual injury-causing event)	Postevent
1. Inexperience/deficient driving skills	5. Ejected from vehicle	9. Improper or no immediate first aid
2. Sideswipes another vehicle	6. Drove off of road and hit sign pole	10. Delay calling EMS
3. Brake failure	7. Head rest too low for occupant when vehicle hit from rear	11. Construct vehicle with less expensive fenders
4. Cultural norms permitting speeding and red light running	8. Poor road maintenance after snow storms	12. Not enough personnel for EMS ambulances

Step 2: For each of the risk or causal factors in Step 1, determine an *intervention* and place it in the appropriate phase. Numbers in both Step 1 and 2 match. A main concept is despite fastening a safety belt or having a cell phone in the preevent phase, it is when they "come into play" or being used in the case of an "event" (e.g., crash, drowning, poisoning, fall) that determines what phase they are in.

Preevent (reduce number of injury-causing event—education, legislation, enforcement)	Event (reduce damage or harm during actual injury-causing event—technology, engineering)	Postevent (response to and treatment and rehabilitation of injury)
1. Driver education, graduated licensing 2. Adequate lane markings 3. Vehicle safety inspection of brakes, tires 4. Media campaign showing that speeding and red light running does not save time	5. Occupant "packaging" (seat belts, child restraint seats, air bags) 6. Breakaway posts and sign poles 7. Head rest raised to proper level 8. Letters to the editor complaining about poor road maintenance after snow storms	9. Proper first aid and emergency provided quickly at the scene 10. Cell phones and adequate EMS 11. Accessible and low cost of vehicle-damage repair 12. Conduct EMT recruitment and classes

Step 3: Place each *intervention* (from Step 2) in the appropriate phase and epidemiological category. The numbers match those in Steps 1 and 2. This is the Haddon matrix.

	Preevent (reduce number of injury causing events)	Event (reduce damage or harm during actual injury-causing event)	Postevent (response to and treatment and rehabilitation of injury)
Human (host)	1. Driver education, graduated licensing	5. Occupant "packaging" (seat belts, child restraint seats, air bags)	9. Proper first aid and emergency care provided at the scene
Carrier of agent (mechanical form of energy)	3. Vehicle safety inspection of brakes, tires	7. Head rest raised to proper level	11. Accessible and low cost of vehicle-damage repair

	Preevent (reduce number of injury causing events)	Event (reduce damage or harm during actual injury-causing event)	Postevent (response to and treatment and rehabilitation of injury)
Physical environment	2. Adequate lane markings	6. Breakaway posts and sign poles	10. Cell phones and adequate EMS
Social environment	4. Media campaign showing that speeding and red light running does not save time	8. Letters to the editor complaining about poor road maintenance after snow storms	12. Conduct EMT recruitment and classes

Some things to consider are:

▶ All the cells may not be filled.
▶ It is usually impossible to implement all of the interventions.
▶ An individual may complete the matrix, but a group completing the matrix may be faster and more creative.

Other considerations include:

▶ Priority and emphasis of an intervention should be placed on the most effective strategy—which one works, is based on evidence, and is cost effective.
▶ A "mixed strategy" should be used to address each of the three phases or time periods of the injury incident (e.g., preevent, event, postevent).
▶ "Passive" or automatic measures rather than "active" ones requiring a person's action are often more effective.

Another version of the Haddon matrix has the epidemiological factors going horizontally across the matrix and the time phrases going vertically. However, it seems logical to show the injury sequence going left to right horizontally. Note that many experts divide the environmental factors into two types: (1) physical and (2) social. See the following example.

	Human (host)	Agent	Physical environment	Social environment
Preevent				
Event				
Postevent				

Once the interventions have been identified, you can prioritize them using one of the several methods (e.g., paired-comparison analysis, Hanlon method) found in this chapter's objective d: "describe how to identify and prioritize injury problems." Though the objective d refers to injury problems, the same methods for prioritizing can be applied to interventions.

h. Provide examples of interventions that use education/ behavior change, legislation/enforcement, and technology/ engineering to prevent injuries. Describe how they can work together to create a comprehensive program.

The three types of interventions in this objective are known as the 3Es of Prevention—education, enforcement, and engineering. See Table 3-17 for examples of 3Es interventions.

Table 3-17   Examples of 3E Interventions

Education/behavior change	Legislation/enforcement	Technology/engineering
High school driver education	Speed limit laws	Motor-vehicle occupant restraints: seat belts, air bags, child carriers
	Drunk driving laws	
Hunter safety courses		
	Wearing occupant restraints	Padded dashboards
Swimming classes		
		Break-away sign posts
Boating safety courses	Wearing of motorcycle helmets	
		Helmets
Safety posters at worksite		
	Requiring wearing of personal flotation devices while boating	Personal flotation devices
Brochures and pamphlets featuring safety		Detectors: smoke, carbon monoxide
DVDs/videos on safety	Wearing "hunter" orange while hunting	Child-resistant packaging
	Building codes & inspections	
	Prohibiting fireworks	
	Requiring smoke detectors in residences	

Engineering attempts to provide automatic protection.

Education attempts to persuade people to adopt safer behaviors.

Enforcement attempts to reduce dangerous behaviors.

Educational interventions are probably most familiar because they are generally the easiest things to do. Still, educational interventions may not be the most effective thing to do to reduce the incidence of an injury problem. They can be more effective when they accompany one of the other Es.

Education attempts to initiate behavioral changes by informing a target group about potential hazards, explaining risks, and persuading people to adopt safer behavior. Education will not always cause individuals to change their behavior, but it can make them more receptive to additional interventions.

Enforcement tries to reduce dangerous behaviors through legislation and enforcement of that legislation. Legislation can target behaviors by individuals, manufacturers, and local governments.

Examples of state and community injury-related laws:

▶ Restricting the sale or giving of alcohol to minors
▶ Requiring building codes and standards
▶ Regulating the speed of motor vehicles

It has long been believed that to effectively combat a specific injury problem, a law must be passed with severe penalties and strict enforcement. For most laws to be effective, they should focus on:

- ▶ Having a likelihood of apprehension to be perceived as being high
- ▶ Delivering swift penalties
- ▶ Having a penalty that does not have to be extreme or severe

Engineering interventions make changes to the environment or product design to automatically protect everyone. This is called a *passive* or *automatic intervention*, because it requires no work on the part of the individual. Interventions that do not require direct action by an individual usually are more effective. Examples of engineering interventions include padded dashboards, child-proof medicine caps, and break-away highway sign posts.

An effective intervention combines strategies from each of the 3Es; for example:

- ▶ Enforcement—enact law
- ▶ Education—inform people about the new law and why it is necessary and the consequences if it is broken
- ▶ Engineering—use an ignition interlock system to detect a drinking driver

These three approaches can work together by focusing on the same injury problem. Using school children as pedestrians can illustrate how all three strategies can focus upon the same problem—a shotgun approach rather than a single intervention. See Table 3-18.

i. For a given injury problem, choose and justify an intervention based on (1) relevant data, (2) characteristics of the intended audience, (3) a conceptual model or theory (e.g., social ecological model, stages of change), and (4) evidence related to "best practice."

Injury Problem: Falls Among the Elderly

(1) RELEVANT DATA*

The elderly are susceptible to falls largely due to the weakening of bones and the loss of mobility that come with aging. Advanced age, multiple medications, and multiple pathologies are factors that increase the risk for falls. Falls are the leading cause of injury-related deaths for males 80 and older and for females 75 and older. One-fourth of those who sustain a hip fracture die within 1 year and another 50 percent never return to their prior level of mobility or independence.

---

*Data in this section comes primarily from the National Center for Injury Prevention and Control. Falls Among Older Adults: Summary of Research Findings. Available at: www.cdc.gov/ncipc/pub-res/toolkit/SummaryOfFalls.htm. Accessed: July 5, 2007.

Table 3-18 3Es for the Same Injury Problem

Education/behavior change	Legislation/enforcement	Technology/engineering
School teachers devoting time in class instructing students on how to properly cross a street and obeying the crosswalk guards	School crossing guards on duty before and after school; presence of a police car in the proximity of the school	Pedestrian warning signs; school crossing signs; road marked with a crosswalk; flashing yellow lights to caution drivers

More than 50 percent of falls occur in the home, and those that happen on stairs and steps are the most deadly. Many falls are caused by tripping on loose rugs or exposed electrical cords inside the home. Outside the home, injuries are sustained in falls from ladders and when stepping into holes and depressions on the property.

Facts About Falls

▶ In the United States, one of every three adults 65 years or older will fall each year. More than 10,000 people over age 65 die from fall-related injuries annually.
▶ By the year 2020, the cost of fall injuries is expected to reach $32.4 billion.
▶ Falls account for 87 percent of all fractures for people 65 years and older. They are also the second leading cause of spinal cord and brain injury among older adults.

(2) CHARACTERISTICS OF THE INTENDED AUDIENCE

▶ **Age:** The risk of falling and being injured increases with age. Of all fall deaths, more than 60 percent involve people ages 75 years or older. People who are 85 or older are 10 to 15 times more likely to suffer hip fractures than those between the ages of 60 and 65.
▶ **Gender:** Women experience more fall-related injuries than men and sustain 75–80 percent of all hip fractures. This may be related to the higher prevalence of osteoporosis among women. However, the rate of deaths from fall-related injury is higher among men.
▶ **Health conditions:** The risk of fall-related injury is greater for people with osteoporosis, arthritis, neurological and musculoskeletal disabilities, visual impairment, Alzheimer's disease, dementia, and clinical depression.
▶ **Medication:** Some medicines can cause drowsiness or dizziness, and some drugs can interact with other medicines or alcohol and cause problems that may lead to falling.
▶ **Lifestyle:** Lack of regular exercise or physical activity, poor nutrition, low calcium and vitamin D intake, smoking, excessive alcohol use, substance

abuse, and misuse of medication are all associated with a higher risk of fall injury.

(3) DESCRIPTION OF INTERVENTION PROGRAM*

Objectives and methods of the Fear of Falling intervention. The primary objective of the intervention *A Matter of Balance* was to reduce fear of falling. The secondary aim was to increase physical, social, and functional activity. Three hypotheses were tested:

1. Fear of falling will decrease in intervention subjects as compared to control subjects.
2. Self-efficacy and a sense of control regarding risk of falling will increase in intervention subjects as compared to control subjects.
3. Physical and social activity will increase in interventions subjects as compared to control subjects.

The intervention was designed with the aim of implementing and experimentally evaluating the efficacy of this eight-session group intervention in 20 senior housing projects randomly assigned to either receive the group intervention or to serve as controls and dissemination of the program to a broader community of users.

The intervention was a group program consisting of eight 2-hour sessions scheduled twice a week for 4 weeks. The techniques used in these group sessions were videotape, lecture, group discussion, mutual problem solving, role playing, exercise training, assertiveness training, home assignments, and behavioral contracting. The early session focused on attempting to change attitudes and self-efficacy prior to attempting changes in actual behavior. This "cognitive restructuring" involved instilling beliefs such as greater perceived control, greater confidence, and a realistic assessment of failures through use of a documentary-style video presenting older adults expressing fears about falling contrasted to others expressing positive attitudes.

Subsequent program content involved varying activities included training exercises on how to shift to more positive cognitions. The cognitive restructuring component was reinforced by instructional material regarding incidence of falls, risks of falling, skill training in falls prevention, and what to do if one falls. The benefits of exercise to improve strength and balance were emphasized. Strength training exercises were included in six of the eight sessions. Assertiveness techniques also were taught in the context of encouraging discussion with health care providers and family about concerns about falling.

The final stage of the intervention was to focus on individual behavior change by correcting home hazards, enforcing the importance of regular physical exercise, and trying to get participants to resume a formerly restricted activity.

---

*Adapted from: National Center for Safe Aging, Fear of falling: A matter of balance.

Enrollment into the *Fear of Falling* study consisted of 434 randomized subjects who expressed concerns about falling and resulting limitation of daily activities. Subjects were recruited from senior housing complexes in the greater Boston area and started on an eight session, biweekly group intervention.

(4) EVIDENCE RELATED TO "BEST PRACTICE"*

Major findings. The results were categorized as being immediate effects or long-term effects.

Immediate Effects

▶ Reduced fear of falling
▶ Increased confidence in managing falls
▶ Increased level of intended activity
▶ Increase mobility control

Long-Term Effects

▶ Reduced fear of falling
▶ Increased confidence to manage falls
▶ Increased mobility range
▶ Enhanced social behavior

It also was found that maintenance of program effects would likely be enhanced with one or more booster sessions about 3 months after the program. There was no increase in falls for participants.

j. Design an implementation plan to include a description of the intended audience, goals and objectives, proposed activities, evaluation component, timeline, and resources.

The process of developing a injury prevention program involves a series of steps. Several successful models have been developed to assist those who wish to develop a injury prevention program. Those include the PRECEDE/PROCEED model, the Multilevel Approach to Community Health (MATCH), and the consumer-based planning models that are based on health communication and social marketing such as CDCynergy and Social Marketing Assessment and Response Tool (SMART). Each of these planning models has its strengths and weaknesses; each has its components that makes it unique.

---

*Adapted from: National Center for Safe Aging, Fear of falling: A matter of balance.

The suggested steps for program planning appear here. The planner(s) may conduct the planning activities in another order than the one presented.

Step 1: Assess the Needs of the Target Population.

This step is referred to as a needs assessment. A *needs assessment* is the process of collecting and analyzing information and developing an understanding of the issues, resources, and constraints of the target population. The assessment's purpose is to determine whether the needs of the people are being met.

Step 2: Convene an Advisory or Planning Committee.

Community members should be involved in the entire planning process. Target population and stakeholder involvement is necessary during the planning and implementation stage. This involvement of target population members helps develop program ownership, which is critical for the program's acceptance. They can provide critical insight that could make or break the program's efforts.

Step 3: Write a Mission Statement.

The mission statement is a narrative statement describing the focus of the program, which often includes the program intent and philosophy.

MISSION STATEMENT

Each organization, public or private, should have a mission statement. Every project or service can benefit from its own mission statement. The program goals evolve from the mission statement, and the objectives evolve from the goal or goals. Once the mission statement is in place, the task of developing the outcome or goal of the project, along with the specific objectives, needs to occur. Objectives outline in measurable terms the desired changes that should occur in the target population as a result of the intervention and provide the basis of evaluation for the program.

A useful mission statement's key elements include:

▶ Statement of the key elements of the philosophy, values, and program beliefs
▶ Statement of the commitment the organization has to growth, stability, and survival
▶ Description of the target populations and markets to be served
▶ Statement of the desired public image of the services or programs to be offered

Table 3-19 displays examples of mission statements.

Table 3-19 Examples of Mission Statements

Alaska Injury Prevention Center

The Mission of the Alaska Injury Prevention Center [AIPC] is to prevent unintentional and intentional injuries, thereby reducing the pain and suffering resulting from these tragedies to the people of Alaska.

To accomplish this mission, AIPC sponsors projects and works with communities to promote bicycle helmets, car seats, pedestrian reflectorization, drowning prevention, suicide prevention, firearm safety, seat belts, booster seats, ice grippers for seniors, work place safety, etc.

American Trauma Society

To save lives through improved trauma care and injury prevention.

Southeastern Regional Injury Control Network

The Southeastern Regional Injury Control Network is dedicated to developing a coordinated, effective approach to unintentional and intentional injury control in the southeastern states.

Michigan Department of Community Health

The mission of the Injury Prevention Section is to promote public health prevention approaches to reduce morbidity, mortality and risk behaviors related to unintentional and intentional injuries.

The Section provides leadership, training, public education, funding support and technical assistance for the development, implementation and evaluation of community-based primary prevention programs, and surveillance related to the leading causes of injuries. Section staff also serve on various state, regional, and national committees to provide consultation and facilitate cooperation among agencies to foster focused support for policies and programs designed to reduce the impact of injuries in the state.

In addition, Section staff are responsible for developing research grant proposals, conducting data analysis, and writing scientific articles and reports based upon the research findings resulting from surveillance and community projects.

Senior Injury Prevention Project of Alameda County [California]

To reduce the number of preventable injuries to older adults in Alameda County and to raise awareness regarding the need for county-wide older adult injury prevention programs.

Injury Prevention Coalition of the South Plains [Texas]

To reduce injuries and injury-related costs throughout the South Plains by working cooperatively with all Coalition partners and by utilizing expanded data sources, expanded partnerships, citizen involvement and input, and integrated and comprehensive injury control systems.

Step 4: Write Program Goals and Objectives.

PROGRAM GOALS

After finalizing the mission statement, planners then develop a program goal (or goals). This is a statement that provides specific long-term direction for the program. Often considered a broad statement of direction, the goal is used to present the overall intent or desired outcome of a program or project.

Program goals often are written in general terms, lacking program or project specifics or details. Often, this translates into meaning that the goal is not measurable, because it lacks specific assessment criteria. This understanding of a goal differs from the understanding of program objectives because objectives generally contain measurable specifics. Measurable specifics include such information as deadlines (e.g., by the year 2010) and rates of increase or decrease for an injury problem.

The goal generally takes time to accomplish (e.g., weeks, months, even years). Some examples of program goals include:

▶ To decrease bicycle-related head injuries by encouraging the use of bicycle helmets through offering discount coupons to parents
▶ To decrease child pedestrian morbidity and mortality by altering the manner in which the community thinks about and approaches pedestrian safety

OBJECTIVES

Once the program goals are in place, the program objectives can be written. An *objective* is defined as a specific statement of short-term application, usually written in terms that are measurable. Objectives often include activities that have a specific time limit or timeline for completion and expected results of each activity. Each objective should be in line with a program goal and directly related to reaching that goal.

Types of objectives. Most objectives will be directed toward the individuals or institutions that will be the targets of the intervention. Other objectives should be written for the program planning and implementation staff. While different terminology may be used, the important thing to remember is that a direct relationship exists between the objectives and the goals that are written.

Program objectives are measured as part of the outcome evaluation. They are directly connected to accomplishing the project or program goal and focus on how the program will create a change in morbidity, mortality, and quality of life.

Behavioral or action objectives are behaviors or actions that are considered to be the cause of the injury problem that the program is attempting to change. Measurement of the attainment of this type of objective is part of impact evaluation.

Process objectives relate to those factors examined in the process evaluation. There are two types: (1) learning objectives that reflect a desire for a change in knowledge, attitudes, or specific skills or practices and (2) administrative objectives relating to the activities of the project and the tasks that are completed along the way.

Developing an objective. Four elements should be included:

1. Who: Identify the target population affected or expected to engage in the desired behavior.
2. What: Identify the outcome to be achieved—what change is desired.
3. How much: Identify the specific criteria for deciding when the outcome has been successfully achieved.
4. By when: Identify the time period within which the outcome is expected to occur.

Objectives should be written in clear but simple language, should be action oriented, and should be measurable.

Step 5: Review Best-Practice or Evidence-Based Interventions.

Basing a new program on other successful programs is important. A review of the professional literature and other documents will help generate a list of potential interventions. Best practices can be found in the professional literature in professional journals, government organizations, and on Web sites. Refer to this chapter's objective d and Table 3-15 for sources of best practices. Locating what works may not always be possible because many interventions have not been adequately evaluated.

Step 6: Select an Intervention.

The number of activities in an intervention may be many or only a few. It has been shown that multiple activities often are more effective than a single activity. Few people change their behavior based on a single exposure. Interventions can be developed to focus upon an injury problem of a target at any or all levels (e.g., individual, interpersonal, organization, public policy).

Step 7: Plan Evaluation.

Evaluation should be designed as a continuous process. Select evaluation methods and questions that will facilitate process, impact, and outcome evaluation. Record-keeping methods must be developed so that the necessary data are available for the evaluators. If an outside evaluator is needed for the project, that evaluator should be brought in during the planning phase to develop the evaluation plan as early as possible.

Step 8: Pilot Test the Intervention.

A pilot test, with a small group that represents the target population, helps identify potential flaws or problems with the intervention. Information from this step can help make corrections that could save resources and time later.

Step 9: Implement the Program.

Carry out the intervention's activities. Phasing in the intervention gradually is suggested (small groups instead of the entire population).

Step 10: Evaluate the Results.

Evaluation is when planners determine the worth or value of the intervention effort. Two forms of evaluation are: (1) *formative*, which is done during the planning and implementing stages to improve or refine the program, and (2) *summative*, which begins with the development of goals and objectives and is conducted after implementation of the intervention to determine the program's impact on the target population.

k. Describe and understand how cultural, socioeconomical, political, and physical environment factors may influence a prevention effort.

Many factors affect prevention efforts. Examples of such factors include cultural, social, economic, political, and physical factors. As a result, the efforts of each community varies.

> *Cultural factors.* A community's beliefs, traditions, and prejudices can affect injury prevention efforts. For example, the beliefs of a community about specific injury prevention efforts can influence policymakers on whether they will spend money for prevention programs (e.g., free or loaned child car restraint seats for those who cannot afford them). Cultural factors often tie closely to social factors (next).

> *Social factors.* The influence of social norms can be positive or negative and can change over time. Alcohol consumption represents a continuing negative social norm in the United States. The normal expectation among

the two-thirds of Americans who drink seems to be that drinking is fun. People in their pursuit of having fun will drink and drive despite the fact that almost half of all fatal motor vehicle crashes involve alcohol (National Safety Council, 2007).

Economic factors. National and local economies can affect prevention efforts. An economic downturn means that fewer tax dollars will be available for injury prevention programs. This occurs because revenue shortfalls cause agencies to experience budget cuts. When money is short, efforts such as poison control centers become targets for cutbacks.

Political factors. Decisions made by those in political offices, either nationally or locally, can improve or jeopardize prevention efforts by the decision they make. The concern is over greater or lesser governmental participation in injury prevention issues. For instance, a long-term debate has involved mandatory motorcycle helmets.

Physical factors. Location, climate, and community size can influence the type of injuries that are likely to occur. For example, higher rates of motor vehicle deaths occur in rural areas compared with urban locations (largely due to higher speeds); and Alaska commercial fishermen have high drowning rates (largely due to the cold water in which they may be immersed). Community size means that larger communities may have more injury problems, but they also have the potential for more injury prevention resources.

Conclusion

Measures to prevent and reduce injuries have been in existence since ancient times (e.g., shoes to protect against sharp stones). Many worked so well (e.g., evacuation in times of floods and volcanic eruptions) that they are still in use.

Traditional, often ineffective, approaches to injury prevention have been based largely on piecemeal, unsystematic perceptions of injury causes and intervention options. Utilization of the criteria listed here will aid in determining interventions:

- ▶ Priority should be given to interventions that will be the most effective in reducing injury losses and need not be based on causes that contributed to the incident. Some examples of this would be using a net for an acrobat rather than urging him or her to "perform safely" and not to fall; placing thermal insulation on the handles of cooking pots and pans rather than telling users never to touch them with their bare hands; or putting shoes on children rather than cautioning them not to stub their toes.
- ▶ A mixture of interventions is best because a single intervention rarely solves the problem.

▶ In many cases, the less that the people to be protected must do, the more successful the intervention. Automatic ("passive") measures do not require the person to do something, and manual ("active") measures require that they do.
▶ Consideration of the cultural, social, and political forces sometimes will determine an injury prevention program's success or failure.

References

Centers for Disease Control and Prevention. Fatalities and injuries from falls among older adults—United States, 1993-2003 and 2001-2005. *MMWR*, 2006;55:45;1221-1224.

Cohen, L. and S. Swift. (1999). The spectrum of prevention: Developing a comprehensive approach to injury prevention. *Injury Prevention* 5:203-207.

Haddon, W. (1980). Advances in the epidemiology of injuries as a basis for public policy. *Public Health Reports* 95: 411–421.

Hanlon, J.J. and G.E. Pickett (1984). Public health: Administration and practice. St. Louis, MO: Times Mirror/Mosby.

Hodges, B.C. and D.M. Videto. (2005). Assessment and planning in health programs. Sudbury, MA: Jones and Bartlett Publishers.

National Association of County and City Health Officials. (1991). APEXPH Workbook: Assessment protocol for excellence in public health. Washington, DC: National Association of County and City Health Officials.

National Center for Safe Aging. Fear of Falling: A Matter of Balance. Available at: www.safeaging.org/model/programs/fearoffalling/fearoffalling_eval.asp#eval. Accessed: July 5, 2007.

National Safety Council. (2007). Injury facts. Itasca, IL: Author.

Runyan, C.W. (1998). Using the Haddon matrix: introducing the third dimension. *Injury Prevention* 4:302-307.

CHAPTER 4 ▶

Program Evaluation*

CORE COMPETENCY 4: Ability to evaluate injury prevention activities.

Evaluations can be easy or difficult. Some people dread doing them while others enjoy the activity. Some evaluation data seldom gets used while other data prove useful. Nevertheless, the principles of evaluation must be understood and followed. Funding agencies want to know if their funds contributed to preventing injuries, and injury prevention professionals should want to know if their time and efforts made a difference.

Evaluation is the process of determining whether programs—or certain aspects of programs—are appropriate, adequate, effective, and efficient and, if not, how to make them so. In addition, evaluation shows if programs have unexpected benefits or create unexpected problems. All programs to prevent unintentional injury need to be evaluated whether their purpose is to prevent a problem from occurring, to limit the severity of a problem, or to provide a service.

Evaluation is much easier than most people believe. A well-designed and well-run injury prevention program produces most of the information needed to appraise its effects. As with most tasks, the key to success is in the preparation. A program's accomplishments—and the ease with which a researcher can evaluate those accomplishments—depend directly on the effort put into the program's design and operation.

However, that is the problem: whether it is wiser to spend a lot of resources running the injury prevention program or to spend some resources determining

---

*This chapter is largely adapted from Thompson and McClintock (2000).

if the program is even worth running. Many experts recommend the second option: Programs that can demonstrate, through evaluation, a high probability of success also have a high probability of legislative, community, technical, and financial support.

a. Understand the importance of evaluation and why and when evaluation should be done.

There is a growing need for well-designed evaluations of interventions and programs in injury prevention. In addition, there is an increased focus on the use of best-practice and evidence-based interventions to improve such programs and interventions. Data gathered during evaluation enable managers to create the best possible programs, to learn from mistakes, to make modifications as needed, to monitor progress toward the program's goal, and to judge the program's ultimate outcome. See Table 4-1 for more on why to evaluate these programs.

Indeed, not evaluating an injury prevention program is irresponsible because, without evaluation, one cannot tell if the program benefits or harms the people the program is trying to help. Just as doctors would not use a vaccine that was untested, researchers should not use injury interventions that are untested. Ineffective or insensitive programs can build public resentment and cause people to resist future, more effective, interventions.

Evaluation also will show whether interventions other than those planned by the program would be more effective. For example, program staff might ask

Table 4-1 Why Evaluate Injury Prevention Programs?

• To learn whether proposed program materials are suitable for the people who are to receive them
• To learn whether program plans are feasible before they are put into effect
• To have an early warning system for problems that could become serious if unattended
• To monitor whether programs are producing the desired results
• To learn whether programs have any unexpected benefits or problems
• To enable managers to improve service
• To monitor progress toward the program's goals
• To produce data on which to base future programs
• To demonstrate the effectiveness of the program to the target population, to the public, to others who want to conduct similar programs, and to those who fund the program

Source: Thompson and McClintock, 2000.

police officers to talk to students about the hazards of drinking and driving. The hope might be that the stories the police tell about the permanently injured and dead teenagers they see in car crashes would scare the students into behaving responsibly.

Evaluation might show, however, that many teenagers do not respect or trust police officers and therefore do not heed what they say. Evaluation also would show what type of people the students would listen to—perhaps sports stars or other young people (their peers) who are permanently injured because of drinking and driving. The right message delivered by the wrong person can be nonproductive and even counterproductive.

A side benefit of formal evaluation is that the people who are served by the program get an opportunity to say what they think and to share their experiences. Evaluation is one way of listening to the people a program is trying to help. It lets them know that their input is valuable and that the program is not being imposed on them.

Another side benefit is that evaluation can boost employee morale—program personnel have the pleasure of seeing that their efforts are not wasted. Evaluation produces evidence to show that their work is paying off or that management is taking steps to see that needed improvements are made.

A third side benefit is that, with good evaluation before, during, and after a program, the results may prove so valuable that the news media or scientific journals will be interested in publishing them. In addition, other agencies or groups may see how well the program has worked and want to copy it.

b. Understand how evaluation should be integrated into intervention design and implementation.

Evaluation is a complex process that has to be actively implemented and effectively put into action at all levels and phases of a project. Ongoing and regular evaluation of a program should be conducted. The most useful approach to evaluation is through the development of goals, general objectives, and specific objectives. Goals and objectives are looked at to determine if they have been met, if outcomes are realized, to what extent they have been met, and what still needs to be done. Comparing what the objectives state with what was supposed to be done and with what actually happened is fundamental.

The information needed to evaluate the effects of a program will develop naturally and almost effortlessly if the researcher puts the necessary time and resources into designing a good program, pilot testing the proposed procedures and materials, and keeping meticulous records while the program is in operation.

To be most effective, evaluation procedures and activities must be woven into the program's procedures and activities. When planning a program, also plan how to judge its success.

Include the following components in the design of a program:

▶ A plan for pilot testing all the program's plans, procedures, activities, and materials (formative evaluation)
▶ A method for determining whether the program is working as it should and whether it is reaching all the people it was planned to serve (process evaluation)
▶ A system for gathering the data needed to evaluate the final results of the program (impact and outcome evaluation)

c. Describe formative, process, impact, and outcome evaluation and describe when and how to use each of these.

Ideally, evaluation is an ongoing process that begins as soon as the idea for an injury prevention program is conceived, interweaving with program activities throughout the life of the program and ending after the program is finished. Sometimes evaluation continues for years after the program ends to see if program effects are sustained over time. By evaluating each step, a program can catch and solve problems early, which not only saves time and money but makes success more likely.

Evaluation has four stages that are begun in this order: formative, process, impact, and outcome. Planning for each stage begins while an injury prevention program is being developed, and no stage is truly complete until the program is over.

Formative Evaluation

Description. Formative evaluation is the process of testing program plans, messages, materials, strategies, or modifications for weaknesses and strengths *before* they are put into effect. Formative evaluation also is used when an unanticipated problem occurs *after* the program is in effect.

Purpose. Formative evaluation ensures that program materials, strategies, and activities are of the highest possible quality (quality assurance). During the developmental stage of a program, the purpose is to ensure that the program aspect being evaluated (e.g., a home visit to check smoke detectors) is feasible, appropriate, meaningful, and acceptable for the injury prevention program and the target population. In the case of an unanticipated problem after the program is in effect, the purpose is to find the reason for the problem and then the solution.

When to conduct. Conduct formative evaluation when a new program is being developed and when an existing program is (1) being modified, (2) having problems with no obvious solutions, or (3) being adapted for a new setting, population, problem, or behavior.

Target population. Who is asked to participate in formative evaluation depends on the evaluation's purpose. For example, if a researcher is pilot testing materials for a new program, select people or households at random from the target population. If he wants to know the level of consumer satisfaction with his program, he selects evaluation participants from people or households who have already been served by the program. If he wants to know why fewer people than expected are taking advantage of the program, he should select evaluation participants from among people or households in the target population who did *not* respond to his messages.

Type of information produced by formative evaluation while a program is being developed. Whether the program being developed is surveillance or intervention, new or adapted, the formative evaluator's first concern is to answer questions similar to these:

- ▶ **Introduction:** When is the best time to introduce the program or modification to the target population?
- ▶ **Plans and Strategies:** Are the proposed plans and strategies likely to succeed?
- ▶ **Methods for Implementing Program:** Are the proposed methods for implementing program plans, strategies, and evaluation feasible, appropriate, and likely to be effective or are they unrealistic, poorly timed, or culturally insensitive?
- ▶ **Program Activities:** Are the proposed activities suitable for the target population? In other words, are they meaningful, barrier-free, culturally sensitive, and related to the desired outcome? For example, is the literacy level appropriate? Would a bicycle rodeo appeal to teenagers or would they see it as childish? Is a lottery for child safety seats acceptable or will some members of the population see it as gambling?
- ▶ **Logistics:** How much publicity and staff training are needed? Are sufficient resources (human and fiscal) available? Are scheduling and location acceptable? For example, would scheduling the program during the normal workday make it difficult for some people in the target population to use the program?
- ▶ **Acceptance by Program Personnel:** Is the program consistent with the staff's values? Are all staff members comfortable with the roles they have been assigned? For example, are they willing to distribute smoke detectors door-to-door or to participate in weekend activities in order to reach working people?

► **Barriers to Success:** Are there beliefs among the target population that work against the program? For example, do some people believe that children are safer if they are held by an adult than if they are restrained in a car seat?

Finding solutions to unanticipated problems after a program is in operation. If a program is already in operation but having unanticipated problems, evaluators can conduct formative evaluation to find the cause. They look at the same aspects of the program as they do during the developmental stage of the program to see (1) what is the source of the problem and (2) how to overcome the problem.

Methods. Because formative evaluators are looking for problems and obstacles, they need a format that allows evaluation participants free rein to mention whatever they believe is important. In such a case, qualitative methods (personal interviews with open-ended questions, focus groups, and participant observation) are best. A closed-ended quantitative method would gather information only about the topics identified in advance by program staff or the evaluator.

Occasionally, however, quantitative surveys may be appropriate. They are useful when the purpose of evaluation is to find the level of consumer or staff satisfaction with particular aspects of the program.

How to use results. Well-designed formative evaluation shows which aspects of a program are likely to succeed and which need improvement. It also should show how problem areas can be improved. Modify the program's plans, materials, strategies, and activities to reflect the information gathered during formative evaluation.

Ongoing process. Formative evaluation is a dynamic process. Even after the injury prevention program has begun, formative evaluation should continue. The evaluator must create mechanisms (e.g., customer satisfaction forms to be completed by program participants) that continually provide feedback to program management from participants, staff, supervisors, and anyone else involved in the program.

Telephone interviews are more rapid and less expensive than personal interviews.

Process Evaluation

Description. Process evaluation is the mechanism for testing whether the program's procedures for reaching the target population are working as planned.

Purpose. Process evaluation counts the number of people or households the program is serving, determines whether the program is reaching the people or households it planned to serve, and determines how many people or households in the target population the program is *not* reaching.

When to conduct. Process evaluation should begin as soon as the program is put into action and continue throughout the life of the program. Therefore, a researcher needs to design forms for process evaluation while the program is under development.

Important factor to consider before beginning the process evaluation. The evaluator and program staff must decide whether the program should be evaluated on the basis of the number of people contacted or the number of contacts with people. The distinction is important.

For the *number of people contacted*, count only *once* each person in the target population who had contact with the program regardless of how many times that person had contact.

For the *number of contacts with people*, count *once* each time the program had contact with a member of the target population regardless of how many times some people had contact.

Obviously the number of *contacts with people* should be the same as, or higher than, the number of *people contacted*.

This distinction is especially meaningful when a person may receive independent value or additional benefit from each contact with the program.

Target population. For process evaluation, the target population is the people or houses actually reached, whereas the program's target population is the people or households desired to reach.

Methods. Keep track of all contacts with the people or households who are served by the program. If appropriate, keep track of all program-related items distributed to, or received from, the target population.

> ▶ **Direct Contacts:** One method of keeping track of direct contacts is to use simple encounter forms, which can be designed to collect basic information (1) about each person or household that has direct contact with the program and (2) about the nature of the contact. Using these forms, a researcher can easily count the number of people or households served by

the program, the number of items distributed during a product distribution program, or the number of items returned to a product-loan program. The forms must be designed while the program is being developed and ready for use as soon as the program begins.

▶ **Indirect Contacts:** Not all contact with a program is direct. A program's target population may be reached directly, indirectly, or both. For example, many school-based programs provide information to schoolchildren (direct) who, in turn, take the information home to parents (indirect). Other programs train members of the target population as counselors (direct) to work with their peers in the school community (indirect). Such methods have been used by programs to promote the use of bicycle helmets. Often, a program's stated purpose is to reach community members through indirect methods. However, programs often have an indirect effect that was not planned.

To estimate the number of people the program reaches indirectly, ask the people with whom the program has direct contact to keep track of their contacts (the people to whom they give the program's information or service). For this purpose, they could use a system similar to the program's system of keeping track of its direct contacts.

Sometimes, however, asking people with whom the program has direct contact to keep track of their contacts is impractical, unreliable, or both. In such a case, devise a reliable method for estimating the number of indirect contacts. For example, estimate that half the third graders who attended a safety training program would speak to their parents about the information given to them.

▶ **Items Distribute or Collected:** Track items collected from the target population or given away during a safety product distribution campaign.

How to use results. Use the results of process evaluation to show funding agencies the program's level of activity (i.e., the number of people of households who have received the program's service). If the process evaluation shows some unexpected problems, especially if it shows the program is not reaching as many people in the target population as expected, do some more formative evaluation. That could include, for example, personal interviews with a random selection of people in the target population who had *not* participated in the program. In addition, much of the information gathered during the process evaluation can be used for impact and outcome evaluation when calculating the effect the program has had on the target population.

Impact Evaluation

Description. Impact evaluation is the process of assessing the program's progress toward its goals (i.e., measuring the immediate changes brought about by the program in the target population).

Purpose. To learn about the target population's changes in knowledge, attitudes, and beliefs may lead to changes in injury prevention behavior. For example, evaluators might want to know whether people are more likely to buy a bicycle helmet or smoke detector than they were before the program began. They also might want to know whether people understand better the risks associated with not wearing seatbelts while driving.

At this stage, evaluators are not necessarily measuring changes in behavior (e.g., increases in the number of people using a bicycle helmet or smoke detector). Although information about behavior could be used to measure impact, it is a better measure of program outcome, which is the final stage of evaluation. To qualify for funding, programs need to incorporate evaluation—at least as far as the impact stage—into their program design.

When to conduct. Take baseline measurements of the target population's knowledge, attitudes, and beliefs immediately before the first encounter with the target population (e.g., before the first training class or before any products are distributed). Begin measuring changes in knowledge, attitudes, and beliefs immediately after the first encounter. (Also see the explanation on Methods.)

Target population. For impact evaluation, the target population consists of people or households that received the program service.

Design. Well-designed impact evaluation has two aspects:

1. It measures the baseline knowledge, attitudes, and beliefs of the target population *and* demonstrates how these change as a result of the program.
2. It eliminates the possibility that any demonstrated change could be attributed to some factor outside the program by controlling for the effect of outside influences on the program's results.

Outside influences to be eliminated as explanations for change. The two influences that must be eliminated as explanations for change in the participants' knowledge, attitudes, beliefs, or behaviors are *history* and *maturation*.

Methods. Measure the target population's knowledge, attitudes, beliefs, and behaviors *before* any individual or group receives the program service (baseline measurement) and again *after* the first person or group receives the service. Compare the two measurements to learn what changes occurred as a result of the program. Be careful not to conclude that a program brought about *all* change shown by these comparisons.

Knowledge, attitudes, and beliefs almost always are measured by a survey instrument, such as a questionnaire containing closed-ended items (e.g., multiple-choice questions). For example, ask each person attending a training class to complete a questionnaire before and after the class to discover how much his or her knowledge, attitudes, and beliefs changed as a result of the training program.

Occasionally, however, knowledge, attitudes, and beliefs are assessed by direct observation. For example, an observer might check to see that seatbelts are positioned correctly or smoke detectors installed correctly. Evaluators also might observe group discussions to watch and listen for signs of participants' attitudes or beliefs. Observation is often more costly, less efficient, and less feasible than administering a survey instrument.

How to use the results. If the results are positive, use the results of impact evaluation to justify continuing a program. If the results are negative, justify revising or discontinuing the program. Obviously, if impact evaluation shows that the program is ineffective, outcome evaluation is not necessary. Programs with positive results are likely to receive further funding; programs with negative results obviously will have a more difficult time getting funds. However, if an evaluator can show why the program was ineffective and how it could be modified to make it effective, the program may be able to justify receiving further funds.

Outcome Evaluation

Description. Outcome evaluation is the process of measuring whether a program met its ultimate goal of reducing morbidity and mortality due to injury. Decisions about whether to continue funding a program often depend on the results shown by outcome evaluation; good-quality outcome evaluation depends on a good design for the injury prevention program itself.

Purpose. The only difference in purpose between impact evaluation and outcome evaluation is the program effect that is measured. Impact evaluation measures changes in knowledge, attitudes, beliefs, and (possibly) preventive behaviors. Outcome evaluation measures changes in preventive behaviors and in related morbidity and death.

When to conduct. For ongoing programs (e.g., a series of fire-safety classes given each year in elementary schools), conduct outcome evaluation as soon as enough people or households have participated in the program to make outcome evaluation results meaningful. Depending on the number of children in the fire-safety classes, conduct outcome evaluation; for example, every year, every 3 years, or every 5 years.

For one-time programs (e.g., a 6-month program to distribute free smoke detectors to low-income households), begin outcome evaluation as soon as the program is complete. Consider also conducting outcome evaluations, for example, a year or 3 years after the program is complete to learn how well the program's effects were sustained over time.

Preparation for outcome evaluation, however, begins when the program is being designed. The design of the program affects the quality of the data for an outcome evaluation. Furthermore, baseline data must be collected immediately before participants have their first encounters with the program.

Target population. For outcome evaluation, the target population is all the people or households that received the program service.

Methods. The methods used for measuring changes in behavior are essentially the same relatively easy methods as those used to measure changes in knowledge, attitudes, and beliefs during impact evaluation. In general, however, measuring changes in morbidity and mortality is not so easy. For example, a researcher can measure the change in helmet-wearing behavior of children who participated in a safety training class soon after the class is over (see Methods in the section on impact evaluation). Measuring the reduction in morbidity and mortality as a result of those same children's change in behavior is much more difficult.

A major cause of this difficulty is that the number of people who will die or suffer serious morbidity as a result of most unintentional injuries is small. In contrast, everyone has a certain attitude and behaves in a certain way with regard to the injury-preventive devices (e.g., bicycle helmets, smoke detectors) that the program is encouraging people to use. Therefore, documenting changes in morbidity and mortality that are directly the result of a program to reduce most unintentional injuries requires a vastly larger study population than does documenting changes in attitudes, beliefs, and behaviors.

In addition to a large study population, documenting changes in morbidity and mortality requires a long-term study, which is both expensive and time consuming. So what to do? Convert data on behavior change into estimates of changes in morbidity and mortality.

When a long-term study is not feasible, convert the more readily accessible information on changes in behavior into estimates of changes in morbidity or mortality. The procedure on how to accomplish this is beyond the scope of this book. Therefore, an epidemiologist, a university epidemiology class, or an epidemiology book (Merrill and Timmreck, 2006; Rivara et al., 2001) are sources of information recommended.

How to use results. Use positive results of outcome evaluation as even stronger evidence than the results of impact evaluation to justify continued funding for a program. If the results (positive or negative) are likely to be of value to researchers or other programs to prevent unintentional injury, it may be possible to publish them in scientific journals.

Possible future study. For a behavior for which data are not available on the relationship between that behavior and risk for death or injury, consider doing a study to produce this information. Justify the cost by stressing the importance of quantifying relationships between a certain behavior and risk for morbidity and mortality. The data produced by the study then could be published and used in outcome evaluation by other injury prevention programs.

Table 4-2 Which State of Evaluation Are You Ready For?

To learn which state of evaluation a program is ready for, answer the following questions; then follow the directions provided after the answer.

Q. Does the program meet any of the following criteria?

- It is just being planned and you want to determine how best to operate it.
- It has some problems you do not know how to solve.
- It has just been modified and you want to know whether the modifications work.
- It has just been adapted for a new setting, population, problem, or behavior.

Yes to any of the four criteria. Begin formative evaluation.

No to all criteria. Read the next question.

Q. The program is now in operation. Do you have information on who is being served, who is not being served, and how much service you are providing?

Yes. Read next question.

No. Begin process evaluation. You also may be ready for impact evaluation. Read next question.

Q. Your program has completed at least one encounter with one member or one group in the target population (e.g., completed one training class). Have you measured the results of that encounter?

Yes. Read next question.

No. You are ready for impact evaluation. If you believe you have had enough encounters to allow you to measure your success in meeting your overall program goals, read the next question.

Q. For Ongoing Programs:

- Has sufficient time passed and have you had contact with a sufficient number of people to allow you to measure how well the program has done in meeting its ultimate goal of reducing morbidity and mortality? See when to conduct in Outcome Evaluation section.

Q. For One-Time Programs:

Is the program complete?

Yes. You are ready for outcome evaluation.

No. Reread the previous questions, and, if you are still unclear, reread this section's content. If you remain uncertain, you may need to contact a professional consultant.

Source: Thompson and McClintock, 2000.

d. Describe the use of qualitative and quantitative methods in evaluation, and explain the benefits and limitations of each method.

Qualitative Research

Because qualitative methods are open ended, they are especially valuable at the formative stage of evaluation when programs are pilot testing proposed procedures, activities, and materials. They allow the evaluator unlimited scope to probe the feelings, beliefs, and impressions of the people participating in the evaluation and to do so without prejudicing participants with the evaluator's own opinions. They also allow the evaluator to judge the intensity of people's preference for one item or another.

Qualitative methods are useful for testing plans, procedures, and materials if a problem arises *after* they are in use. Using these methods, evaluators can usually determine the cause of any problem. See Table 4-3 for further information on different qualitative methods. Armed with knowledge about the cause, program staff can usually correct problems before major damage is done.

For example, a researcher put an advertisement in the local newspaper offering smoke detectors to low-income people. Not as many people responded as expected, and she wasn't able to determine why. Conducting formative evaluation using qualitative methods will usually reveal the reason. Perhaps the advertisement cannot be understood because the language is too complex, perhaps the target population seldom reads newspapers, perhaps most people in the target population cannot go to the distribution location because it is not on a public transportation line, or perhaps the problem is due to some other factor. Whatever the cause, once the researcher learns what the problem is, she is in a position to remedy it.

Quantitative Research

Quantitative methods are ways of gathering objective data that can be expressed in numbers (e.g., a count of the people with whom a program had contact, the percentage of change in a particular behavior by the target population). Quantitative methods are used during process, impact, and outcome evaluation. Occasionally, they are used during formative evaluation to measure, for example, the level of participant satisfaction with the injury prevention program.

Unlike the results produced by qualitative methods, results produced by quantitative methods can be used to draw conclusions about the target population. See Table 4-4 for advantages and disadvantages of survey instruments. For example, suppose everyone in a focus group (randomly selected from bicyclists in the target

Table 4-3 Qualitative Methods of Evaluation

Method	Purpose	Number of people to interview or events to observe	Resources required
Personal interviews	To have individual, open-ended discussion on a range of issues; to obtain in-depth information on an individual basis about perceptions and concerns	The larger and more diverse the target population, the more people who must be interviewed	Trained interviewers; written guidelines for interviewer; recording equipment; a transcriber; a private room
Focus groups	To have an open-ended group discussion on a range of issues; to obtain in-depth information about perceptions and concerns from a group	4 to 8 interviewees per group	Trained moderator(s); appropriate meeting room; audio and visual recording equipment
Participant-observation	To see firsthand how an activity operates	The number of events to observe depends on the purpose; to evaluate people's behaviors during a meeting may require observation of only one event (meeting), but to see if products are installed correctly may require observation of many events (installations)	Trained observers

Table 4-3 Qualitative Methods of Evaluation (continued)

Method	Advantages	Disadvantages
Personal interviews	Can be used to discuss sensitive subjects that the interviewee may be reluctant to discuss in a group; can probe individual experience in depth; can be done by telephone	Time consuming to conduct interviews and analyze data; transcription can be time consuming and expensive; participants are one-on-one with interviewer, which can lead to bias toward "socially acceptable" or "politically correct" responses
Focus groups	Can interview many people at once; response from one group member can stimulate ideas of another	Individual responses influenced by group; transcription can be expensive; participants choose to attend and may not be representative of target population; because of group pressure, participants may give "politically correct" responses; harder to coordinate than individual interviews
Participant-observation	Provides firsthand knowledge of a situation; can discover problems the parties involved are unaware of (e.g., that their own actions in particular situations cause others to react negatively); can determine whether products are being used properly (e.g., whether an infant car seat is installed correctly); can produce information from people who have difficulty verbalizing their points of view	Can affect the activity being observed; can be time consuming; can be labor intensive

Source: Thompson and McClintock, 2000.

population) wears a helmet while riding. Researchers then cannot conclude that all bicyclists in the target population wear helmets. However, let's say that, instead of a focus group, researchers conducted a valid survey (a quantitative method) and found that 90 percent of respondents wear helmets while bicycling. They then could estimate that the percentage of bicyclists who wear helmets in the target population is in the 85 percent to 95 percent range.

Table 4-4 Advantages and Disadvantages of Methods of Administrating Survey Instruments

Method	Advantages	Disadvantages
Personal interviews	Least selection bias: can interview people without telephones, even homeless people; greatest response rate: people are most likely to agree to be surveyed when asked face-to-face; visual materials may be used	Most costly: requires trained interviewers and travel time and costs; least anonymity: therefore, most likely that respondents will shade their responses toward what they believe is socially acceptable
Telephone interviews	Most rapid method; most potential to control the quality of the interview: interviewers remain in one place, so supervisors can oversee their work; easy to select telephone numbers at random; less expensive than personal interviews; better response rate than for mailed surveys	Most selection bias: omits homeless people and people without telephones; less anonymity for respondents than for those completing instruments in private; as with personal interviews, requires a trained interviewer
Instruments to be completed by respondent	Most anonymity: therefore, least bias toward socially acceptable responses; cost per respondent varies with response rate: the higher the response rate, the lower the cost per respondent; less selection bias than with telephone interviews	Least control over quality of data. Dependent on respondentís reading level; mailed instruments have lowest response rate; surveys using mailed instruments take the most time to complete because such instruments require time in the mail and time for respondent to complete

Source: Thompson and McClintock, 2000.

e. Understand effective means of communicating evaluation results as well as the role of evaluation in identifying the key components of an intervention that are effective, for whom they are effective, and under what conditions they are effective.

Several kinds of reports are suggested.

1. An executive summary briefly outlines the evaluation, its major findings, and recommendations for the program.
2. A research report provides a detailed description of the evaluation activities, findings, conclusions, recommendations, and insights.
3. Reports to the public include press releases given to local media, press conference, presentations to select groups, Web site containing the data, results, and recommendations.

The information should be presented graphically by using colorful and easy-to-read charts, graphs, and pictures.

Outline of an evaluation report:

1. Summary

   - What were your goals?
   - What were your objectives?
   - How did you evaluate the program?
   - What were the major results of the evaluation?

2. Background of the program

   - Why was this program done?
   - Who were you trying to reach?
   - How long did the program run?

3. Description of the evaluation

   - What was the evaluation design?
   - How was the data collected?
   - How were the participants selected?

4. Program results

   - What were the results (for each objective)?
   - Are there any interesting quotes or stories about people who participated in the program?

5. Discussion of results

   - How do you explain the findings?

6. Conclusions and recommendations

- What do you recommend regarding changes in the program?

f. Identify potential stakeholders/partners and resources to assist in conducting an evaluation.*

An evaluation begins by engaging stakeholders (i.e., the persons or organizations having an investment in what will be learned from an evaluation and what will be done with the knowledge). Stakeholders must be engaged in the inquiry to ensure that their perspectives are understood. When stakeholders are not engaged, an evaluation might not address important elements of a program's objectives, operations, and outcomes. Therefore, evaluation findings might be ignored, criticized, or resisted because the evaluation did not address the stakeholders' concerns or values. After becoming involved, stakeholders help to execute the other steps. Identifying and engaging the following three principal groups of stakeholders are critical:

1. **Those involved in program operations** (e.g., sponsors, collaborators, coalition partners, funding officials, administrators, managers, staff). Persons or organizations involved in program operations have a stake in how evaluation activities are conducted because the program might be altered as a result of what is learned. Although staff, funding officials, and partners work together on a program, they are not necessarily a single interest group. Subgroups might hold different perspectives and follow alternative agendas; furthermore, because these stakeholders have a professional role in the program, they might perceive program evaluation as an effort to judge them personally. Program evaluation is related to but must be distinguished from personnel evaluation, which operates under different standards.

2. **Those served or affected by the program** (e.g., clients, family members, neighborhood organizations, academic institutions, elected officials, advocacy groups, professional associations, skeptics, opponents, staff of related or competing organizations). Although engaging supporters of a program is natural, individuals who are openly skeptical or antagonistic toward the program also might be important stakeholders to engage. Opposition to a program might stem from differing values regarding what change is needed or how to achieve it. Opening an evaluation to opposing perspectives and enlisting the help of program opponents in the inquiry might be prudent because these efforts can strengthen the evaluation's credibility.

3. **Primary users of the evaluation.** These are specific persons who are in a position to do or decide something regarding the program. In practice,

---

*Source for this objective: Centers for Disease Control and Prevention, 1999.

primary users will be a subset of all stakeholders identified. A successful evaluation will designate primary users early in its development and maintain frequent interaction with them so that the evaluation addresses their values and satisfies their unique information needs.

The scope and level of stakeholder involvement will vary for each program evaluation. For example, stakeholders can be directly involved in designing and conducting the evaluation. Also, they can be kept informed regarding progress of the evaluation through periodic meetings, reports, and other means of communication. Sharing power and resolving conflicts helps avoid overemphasis of values held by any specific stakeholder. Occasionally, stakeholders might be included to use their involvement in an evaluation to sabotage, distort, or discredit the program. Trust among stakeholders is essential; therefore, caution is required for preventing misuse of the evaluation process.

g. Identify potential barriers to specific types of evaluation and approaches to overcome these.

Potential barriers for evaluation a program include:

- ▶ Limited funds
- ▶ Limited staff time and capabilities
- ▶ Length of time allotted to the program
- ▶ Restriction in hiring consultants (if needed)
- ▶ Policies limiting the ability to gather information from the public
- ▶ Lack of management support for evaluation
- ▶ Difficulty in choosing a comparison (control) group
- ▶ Failing to be specific as to what is to be measured (most measure behavior rather than the injury)

Limited resources (the most commonly used excuse for having weak evaluations) may force a choice between process evaluation and outcome evaluation. If the researcher must choose, some experts recommend using the outcome evaluation. This certifies that the objectives were accomplished. Other experts may advise using the process evaluation to help manage the program well.

Despite barriers, it is beneficial to determine if the program is on track and how well it worked. Some form of evaluation for almost any size of budget is possible.

h. Develop an evaluation plan for an intervention.

Every evaluation must contain certain basic components. (See also Table 4-5 for a breakdown of the steps in an evaluation.) By creating a plan to evaluate an intervention, an evaluation will be easier to complete.

Table 4-5 Steps Involved in Any Evaluation

1. Write a statement defining the objective(s) of the evaluation.
2. Define the target population.
3. Write down the type of information to be collected.
4. Choose suitable methods for collecting the information.
5. Design and test instruments appropriate to the chosen methods for collecting the information.
6. Collect raw information.
7. Process the raw information.
8. Analyze the processed information.
9. Write an evaluation report describing the evaluation's results.

A clear and definite objective. *Write a statement defining clearly and specifically the objective for the evaluation.* Without such a statement, evaluators are unfocused and do not know what to measure. The statement will vary depending on the aspect of the program that is being evaluated. For example, before the program begins, test any materials to distribute to program participants. In such a case, the evaluation objective might read something like this:

> *To learn whether the people in our target population can understand our new brochure about the benefits of smoke detectors.*

The evaluation objective for a completed program might read like this:

> *To measure how many deaths were prevented as a result of our program to increase helmet use among teenage bicyclists in XYZ County.*

A description of the target population. *Define the target population and, if possible, the comparison (control) group.* Be as specific as possible. The target population will vary depending on the reason for the evaluation. A later section discusses how to select an appropriate target population at each stage of evaluation. An example definition of a target population might read like this:

> *All children from 8 through 10 years old who own bicycles and who attend public schools in XYZ County.*

A description of what is to be evaluated. Write down the type of information to be collected and how that information relates to the program's objectives. For example, if the goal of the program is to increase the use of smoke detectors among people with low incomes, the description of the information needed during the first state of evaluation might read like this:

> *For baseline information on our target population, we need to know the number and percentage of people with incomes below $_____ in the city of XYZ who now have smoke detectors in their homes.*

Specific methods. *Choose methods that are suitable for the objective of the evaluation and that will produce the type of information desired.* The previous objective C. discusses the four stages of evaluation and mentions the methods most suitable for each stage.

Instruments to collect data. *Design and test the instruments to be used to collect information.*

Raw information. *Collect raw information from the members of the target population.* Raw information is simply the information collected as the program is run (e.g., the number of people who came to a location, the number of items distributed). Raw information is information that has not been processed or analyzed.

Processed information. *Put raw information into a form that makes it possible to analyze.* Usually this means entering the information into a computer data base that permits the evaluator to do various statistical calculations.

Analyses. *Analyzing either quantitative or qualitative information requires the services of an expert in the particular evaluation method used to gather the information.*

Evaluation report. *Write a report giving results of the analyses and the significance (if any) of the results.* This report could be as simple as a memo explaining the results to the program manager. However, it could also be an article suitable for publication in a scientific journal or a report to a congressional committee. The type of report depends on the purpose of the evaluation and the significance of the results.

References

Centers for Disease Control and Prevention. (1999). Framework for program evaluation in public health. *Morbidity and Mortality Weekly Report* 48(RR11):1–40.

Merrill, R.M. and T.C. Timmreck. (2006). Introduction to epidemiology. Sudbury, MA: Jones and Bartlett Publishers.

Rivara, F.P., P. Cummings, T.D. Koepsell, D.C. Grossman, and R.V. Maier. (2001). Injury control: A guide to research and program evaluation. New York: Cambridge University Press.

Thompson, N.J. and H.O. McClintock. (2000). Demonstrating your program's worth: A primer on evaluation for programs to prevent unintentional injury. Atlanta: Centers for Disease Control and Prevention, National Center for Injury Prevention and Control.

CHAPTER 5 ▶

Program Management

CORE COMPETENCY 5: Ability to build and manage an injury prevention program.

This chapter focuses on the public health approach to injury prevention. Individual safety practices, though important, are excluded.

Effective program management is one of the most crucial—and most often overlooked—factors. Program management usually requires time and practice to develop. New program managers can learn from their more experienced colleagues.

a. Describe how to establish and maintain an advisory group to assist with the development and monitoring of goals for injury prevention within a population (e.g., a community, a state, among children, among Latinos).

An advisory group or committee offers suggestions and technical assistance and should represent the community. Some may confuse the advisory committee with a coalition. The term *coalition* represents a broad variety of collaborative organizations such as advisory committee, alliances, networks, task forces, and the like. In other words, the word coalition might be applied to any of the preceding groups.

Recruiting the right committee members is important. Start by identifying organizations that already work on the identified injury problem and for other groups that should be involved. Once these organizations are known, consider

An advisory group should represent the community.

who will best represent each organization on the advisory committee. Although a top management person can make decisions for his or her organization and bring credibility to the committee, staff members may be more in touch with the issues and be more committed, enthused, and available than a top leader.

Many advisory groups welcome individuals onto the committee. These may include community leaders, community members, or people who have directly experienced the problem.

Consider the number of organizations and the diversity of membership when forming the advisory group. If a committee has more than 12 to 18 people, more resources are needed and developing a group identity may take longer. The number of committee members also is determined by the task being undertaken.

At the first advisory group meeting, the lead agency should clearly define the purpose of the committee. Each member should introduce him- or herself, identify his or her role on the committee, and what his or her organization's interest and expectations are in participating on the committee. Estimate how much to realistically expect of members. Anticipate that members will not always fulfill their commitments.

The lead agency should expect to provide clerical work (mailings, typing of agendas and minutes, making reminder calls); meetings (planning agendas, providing refreshments, coordinating with the committee chairperson); public information (developing materials, press releases); coordinating activities (media campaigns, special events); and possible fund-raising.

Maintain an advisory group's morale by:

▶ Sharing the power and leadership
▶ Recruiting and involving new members
▶ Preventing frustration
▶ Sharing successes

The advisory group will maintain its vitality as long as it addresses issues brought up by its members and honest dialogue is found, in which members can be frank without feeling threatened because of what they express. Using humor and finding a bright side to issues and discussions transcends all cultures.

Advisory groups do not last forever. The group should be dissolved if it does not achieve its goals or if it is no longer effective.

b. Develop a long-range plan for injury prevention and identify issues that may impact program goals, implementation, and sustainability

Injury prevention programs can extend over 1 year, 5 years, or even 10 years. If a program involves a long-range program, every effort should be made to ensure that potentially new activities fall within the scope of the long-range plans. There should only be one overall master plan, and it should be the only one used. If a program is developed without coordinating it with the master plan, efforts will be going in several directions. This defeats the program's mission and long-range plans. A policy should be established that requires only one long-range plan: that all activities stay within the plan and within the mission statement and goals.

Plans should be comprehensive, meaning that an awareness of most, if not all, of the needs within a community or institution are known. A list of such needs should be kept and revised periodically. It should include the need to improve or expand existing programs as well as to add new programs. Prioritization of such a list can be converted into either goals for the year or longer-range goals. This avoids letting others distract from the program's mission and goals.

Each injury prevention program has its own set of limitations, impediments, and barriers to implementation. It would be almost impossible to list them all; however, refer to Table 5-1 for examples.

Table 5-1 Examples of Some Possible Problems

• Lack of financial support
• Placing personnel in positions for which they are not trained or qualified
• Legal and regulatory matters not correctly attended to
• Cultural, ethnic, and racial issues not considered or accounted for
• Improper or inadequate manpower, equipment, facilities, and the like
• Lack of administration support
• Personnel leaving or being reassigned
• Lack of vitality in the personnel and group due to the excessive length of the program

If the administration likes a program, sees value in it, and will support it, implementation and success are more likely to occur. Make sure that everyone knows about the program. This can be done by displaying the mission statement wherever and whenever possible. The mission statement can serve as a rallying cry and motivator for staff when things get bogged down.

c. Identify key funding sources for injury prevention activities.

Major funding sources include public and private sources.

Grants: Funding awarded for experimental, demonstration, or research projects in which success is uncertain. Most grants are awarded to non-profit organizations.

Contracts: Money allocated to supply specified services to a funding agency. Contracts are usually awarded for programs that originate with the funding source.

Public funds: Money raised through taxes and administered by federal, state, and local government.

Private funds: Money raised and administered by private organizations, such as corporations, foundations, and charities. Often available as grants, private funds are awarded for new and/or experimental projects.

Where to locate sources of funding for injury prevention:

Foundation sources. A foundation is a private nonprofit organization. They are usually established by wealthy individuals or corporations as an efficient way of dispersing grants to aid a variety of social causes. With few exceptions, they make grants only to other tax-exempt, nonprofit organizations. Foundations sometimes are difficult to discover. The following publications can help:

- The Foundation Directory (http://fdncenter.org)
- National Directory of Corporate Giving

Corporate grants. These are more difficult to obtain than foundation funding. Contacting the company's corporate contributions or similar office is advised.

Government grants. These are issued through a request for proposal (RFP) or a request for application (RFA). An RFP solicits bids from contracts while an RFA solicits proposals for grants. Most grants go to nonprofit organizations. Federal RFPs and RFAs are published in the *Federal Register* (call 202-523-5240) or a local library may have a copy. State and local RFPs and RFAs appear in a state register. The *Catalog of Federal Domestic Assistance* also is helpful for locating grant money.

In addition, RFPs are available over the Internet. On the Internet, go to www.grants.gov. This Web site is a central storehouse for information on over 1,000 grant programs and access to approximately $400 billion in annual awards. By registering once on this site, an organization can apply for grants from 26 different federal agencies.

The National Center for Injury Prevention and Control's Web site, www. cdc.gov/ncipc, announces funds for various types of injury prevention programs.

d. Prepare a proposal for funding from an external source.

At a minimum, the cover letter should contain the name and address of the organization submitting the proposal and a concise summary of the problem and the proposed program. To establish credibility, it may include personal and organizational credentials and a statement of the organization's capability and experience in the area. Also include the total funding requirement. It must contain the contact person's name, mailing and e-mail addresses, a telephone number, and an authorized signature from a chief administrator along with an offer to provide additional information as needed.

Grant proposals have several common elements. These elements may have different names, be grouped differently, or be in a different sequence. An agency may set a page limitation (e.g., 10 or 15 pages of double-spaced typing). Most grant proposals contain these elements:

- ▶ **Abstract**: Prepare a summary of the proposal in a page or less.
- ▶ **Background**: Include what the organization has done in the past with data to support.
- ▶ **Target population**: Offer a description of who will benefit from the program. The target group should be described in detail, and their location in the geographical area covered by the program should be indicated. A description of the group's involvement in the planning process also is important.
- ▶ **Goals/objectives**: Goals are the outcomes of the program; objectives are the specific accomplishments to be achieved. The specific objectives should be included in measurable form. Although behavioral objectives are not necessarily required, they lend themselves well to the grant application specifications. A timetable for accomplishing the objectives should also be included.
- ▶ **Evaluation plan**: Include both the process and outcome measures to be used in evaluating the program's success. A plan for evaluation is often a key part of the proposal. The methodology to be used should be described in detail.
- ▶ **Management plan**: Describe who the key personnel are and their roles in the program.

▶ **Budget**: Itemize all expenses and give a detailed justification for each, if possible. A budget sheet is usually included in the application. Because budget forms vary from agency to agency, the funding agency form should be used when possible. Grant proposal budgets have some commonality. Usually they list salaries by position. Fringe benefit costs are ordinarily figured as a percentage of salary. The total varies but is usually about 25 percent of the total salary cost. Itemize supplies and materials by major types (e.g., office supplies, mail, telephone, printing). Equipment is usually a separate category. Categorize travel as in country/out of country or in state/out of state. Identify indirect costs (e.g., utilities, space). Although negotiable, it may approach 50 percent of salaries and wages.

e. Demonstrate the ability to create, justify, and manage a budget.

Each organization will have its own particular format for developing budgets. Most organizations have a financial officer (e.g., chief financial officer, accountant) to set the rules and accounting procedures. In outlining a budget, itemize in detail the costs of the anticipated expenditures. The list in Table 5-2 will help in creating a budget.

All the expenditures should be appropriately justified in the proposal narrative. The amount requested from the funding agency should not exceed its maximum allowable limits unless the organization is willing to pay the difference.

Table 5-2 Typical Budget Items

Personnel
• Salaries and wages
• Fringe benefits
• Consultants and contracts
Nonpersonnel
• Space—office, storage
• Equipment lease, rent, purchase, maintenance
• Supplies, materials, copying, printing
• Travel and per diem
• Telephone, computer lines, utilities
• Miscellaneous expenses (e.g., postage and delivery)

Justify why each type of expense is needed. Attach a narrative statement justifying the request for each category in the budget (e.g., supplies, materials, copying, printing). The justification should describe the:

1. Injury problem to be addressed.
2. Scope or level of the problem in the community.
3. Mission of the project.
4. Specific objectives of the program.
5. Intervention to be used.
6. Capacities of the organization that will conduct the program.
7. Overall significance of the program—one paragraph why the program should be done in the community, at this time, and by this organization.

Managers of an organization must understand the budget and must ask questions until they understand where the money is and why. The control of the budget should not be left to an accountant. A weekly meeting or a thorough reading of budget status and cash flow reports is essential for good management. Budget monitoring is needed to ensure that accounts are not overspent and money is not wasted.

f. Demonstrate the ability to prioritize the allocation of resources (e.g., personnel, financial, space, time, equipment) to align with program goals.

Because resources are valuable, they need to be used wisely. Time should be spent putting the resources where they can have the greatest opportunity to make an impact. There are more financial demands than fiscal resources. Often there are a dozen or more places to spend every dollar. The prioritizing methods, paired-comparison method, and bracketology (described in Chapter 3) may be useful for ranking resources.

g. Develop a plan for hiring, supervising, and promoting the professional development of staff.

For a program to be successful, it has to have good people. Thus, the selection and/or hiring of well-qualified personnel are important. Hiring and promoting mistakes are costly. The consequences include poor performance and rapid turnover.

Unless there is internal promotion for a position, it is necessary to attract a large, diverse applicant pool so that several highly qualified applicants can be chosen for an interview (Johnson and Breckon, 2007). The size of the applicant pool depends on several factors (e.g., title of the position, responsibilities, salary, perks). A regional or national search using national journals or placement services and contacting colleges may be necessary. Personal networking with people likely to know potential candidates can be rewarding. Many of the best positions are filled this way.

Use an application form to collect the information about the applicant. It may reveal more than a resume. Check references before scheduling interviews—this verifies the information provided on the application form (Wurzbach, 2004). The references also may reveal the applicant's strengths and weaknesses, sometimes missing in a resume or application form. Be aware that personality conflicts and unfair judgments may occur. Contact former employers only when the hiring process has narrowed the selection down to two or three finalists and permission has been given by the applicants.

Personal interviews allow for the opportunity to discover information about the individual that cannot be noted on the application form or from reference checks. An interview can help determine if there is a match between the applicant and the interviewer for both parties. Consider hiring personnel from the target population. This helps to increase program acceptance and provides valuable insight into the community and its members.

It is easier to choose a person familiar to the administration to head up a program instead of hiring another more qualified person. Current staff should considered who might be qualified for and interested in an open position. Promoting from within an organization usually helps morale, and the person is a known entity—no surprises about his or her work habits and personal attributes. Internal candidates know the organization and its staff. The advantage of recruiting externally is that a new person brings new insights and perspectives. They also may bring experience and training not found among the current staff.

h. Demonstrate knowledge of ethical issues that may arise in injury prevention practice.

Ethical issues involve opinions about what is good or bad. Laws assume there is a single correct behavior, whereas ethics deal with beliefs, values, and preferences of individuals or groups. Ethics is concerned with debatable and controversial issues. Ethical decisions are intensely personal. When dealing with the public, ethical and legal concerns vary from overall commitments to do public good to concerns with fairness and equality for each individual.

Many injury prevention programs are designed for and delivered to children. This can pose special ethical problems. Children who are old enough to understand that they are being asked to participate in a program must provide assent to be in the program. The refusal of either the child or the parent must be honored.

The most basic responsibility is to do no harm. There is the need to ensure that participants are making the decisions voluntarily and are well informed about those decisions when involved in an injury prevention program. Educators should not make decisions for participants or to pressure them for the preferred behavior. In most noneducational interventions, signed consent forms should be used. When in doubt, legal advice should be obtained, especially when developing new programs.

Examples of some injury prevention controversies include:

- ▶ Mandatory use of safety devices (e.g., motorcycle helmet)
- ▶ Various efforts to control drunk drivers
- ▶ Banning specific breeds of dogs from a community
- ▶ Effectiveness of some safety education programs

i. Describe ways that injury prevention can be integrated into other programs and identify common barriers to integration.

Many times it is advantageous to combine efforts and resources with other programs. This can include sharing of data, using other personnel and experts, and reducing duplicating efforts. During such integration, a program can be enhanced and strengthened, and the program's image increased, therefore impressing funders (e.g., legislature, foundation, government agency).

Barriers to integrating into other programs include:

- ▶ Turf problems: who gets the credit and recognition
- ▶ Limited resources: competing for the same funds or believing that there are resources available for only one program
- ▶ Rationale of having no time: no time for committee meetings, no time for training
- ▶ Philosophical differences: believing that one program should have priority over another; that one program is better than another; or that planners of one program are inferior (e.g., in experience, training)

j. Demonstrate the ability to leverage program success to further program growth.

Success provides evidence that the program and its intervention works plus its personnel are capable. Moreover, if a program has effectively achieved its goals and objectives in one part of a community's population, it is easier to convince an administration and funding agencies that spreading the program to other part of a community is wise and can be effective. In other words, when an injury prevention program shows that it saves money and prevents suffering, this can be used as leverage to continue or even increase an injury prevention program's resources.

Money plays a major factor in starting a program but also enhancing it. When only one program is involved, a cost description can be conducted. Cost description is a presentation of expenses related to the program. A cost analysis can provide about information about the efficiency of a program. For example, a cost analysis reveals the dollars spent per program participant. These findings can be compared to other programs in order to determine if the program is more or less efficient than similar programs.

If two programs are involved, a cost-effectiveness analysis answers the question of whether program A or program B has more effect for the dollars expended. Another way of stating this is to ask which treatment or intervention is the best for the money. A cost-effectiveness analysis always compares the costs of two programs against one type of impact that is measured the same way in both programs. Economic analyses can be very complex and involved and can require a high degree of economics knowledge.

k. Demonstrate the ability to develop and use performance standards to monitor program success.

The format for reporting on the progress and evaluation of injury prevention programs may be predetermined by the funding agency. In particular, state programs that receive federal funding are required to report on a standard set of performance measures. A *performance measure* is a "quantitative" indicator that can be used to track progress toward an objective. Again, each funding agency will have a set of performance measures and definitions. The language of performance measurements is different from that used by evaluators and can cause confusion. Table 5-3 shows some comparisons of performance measurement and evaluation terms.

Table 5-3 Comparing Performance Measurement and Evaluation Terms

Performance measurement terms	Evaluation terms
Measure type	Goal
Numerator	Sample
Denominator	Sample population
Data resources	Data collection methods

Although the funding agency may need standard reports from all programs, the data reported may not be in a format that the program managers find helpful in their program management. In such cases, evaluations may have a dual focus of providing the performance measure data that is more immediately useful for program management and improvement.

Conclusion

Building and managing an injury prevention program involves "business-like" activities. Some professionals entered the injury prevention field not realizing that good, effective programs run very similar to good, profitable businesses. This chapter included funding, budgeting, allocating resources, and development of a staff—recruiting, hiring, supervising, and promoting.

References

Johnson, J.A. and D.J. Breckon. (2007). Managing health education and promotion program: Leadership skills for the 21st century, 2nd edition. Sudbury, MA: Jones and Bartlett Publishers.

Wurzbach, M.E. (editor). (2004). Community health education and promotion: A guide to program design and evaluation, 2nd edition. Sudbury, MA: Jones and Bartlett Publishers.

CHAPTER 6 ▶

Information Distribution

CORE COMPETENCY 6: Ability to disseminate information related to injury prevention to the community, other professionals, and key policymakers and leaders through diverse communication networks.

Communication skills are not just the ability to communicate verbally with others but also the ability to guide discussions, to answer questions, and to listen and appreciate various points of view. In addition, written communication skills are essential for grant writing, generating reports, and mail/e-mail communication.

a. Identify and differentiate the components and methods of designing and delivering effective messages for different audiences.

Massive amounts and types of materials exist. First attempts may not try to "reinvent the wheel" and will use existing materials. However, along the way nothing may be found that will quite do. It then must be decided to adapt an existing piece of material versus starting from scratch.

The message must:

▶ Meet the program's objectives
▶ Fit the audience's learning style (e.g., visual, auditory)
▶ Present concepts in an simple, organized way

Visuals should be clear and easy to understand.

▸ Fit the culture, values, and beliefs of the audience
▸ Show photographs and visuals relevant to the culture
▸ Written or narrated at an appropriate reading/comprehension level

The following guidelines may help in developing and adapting materials appropriate for an injury prevention program and its audience.

Text, narrative. Include only a few concepts and only information that enable the user to follow the message. Use short sentences and words. Use active language. Use words and phrases familiar to the audience. In narratives, be sure the pace and intonation are appropriate. Use visuals that reinforce text and/or narrative. Visuals should make sense to the audience. Quote credible spokespeople in written text. Make messages believable and practical.

Visuals. Choose photographs, images, or drawings that are clear and easy to understand. Use visuals that show specific examples of the behavior described. Cartoons and drawings should be life-like. Avoid diagrams, graphs, and other complicated visuals. Illustrate only the desired behaviors, not those to be avoided. Limit the number of visuals to emphasize the most important points, and place them in an order that can be understood. Illustrations should reflect the ethnic and cultural background of the intended audience. Place the people in everyday settings, using familiar belongings and wearing familiar clothes.

Format. Use only a few concepts and pages. Leave enough space between text and visuals to allow the eye to move easily from one to the other. Place related messages and illustrations together. Typeface with serifs, such as Times Roman and Century Schoolbook, is generally considered easier to read. Use colors appropriate and acceptable to the audience. Use everyday people or situations that represent the audience. Use a paper that is thick enough to withstand repeated use (e.g., 20 to 60 pound bonded paper).

Pretesting. Use focus groups, interviews, and other reviews to help determine whether the material is acceptable to the intended audience and the individuals who will be distributing the material.

b. Demonstrate the ability to prepare different types of written documents (e.g., written testimony, public health brief, fact sheet, press release, letter to the editor, policy statement, Web site content) to effectively communicate information about injury.

Writing skills can be the ticket to greater career achievement. In a labor force full of mediocre writers, someone who writes well is bound to stand out—and succeed.

Written testimony. Providing a professional testimony is an easy and effective medium for promoting an injury prevention program at all levels—institutional, local, state, national, or international. Professional written testimonies often occur in the form of a letter. Points to remember when writing a testimony include:

- ▶ Make sure the letter is addressed correctly.
- ▶ Keep the letter to less than one page in length.
- ▶ Always write in letterhead stationery or plain white paper. Do not use scented paper or decorative designs.
- ▶ Type or word process the letter.
- ▶ Check and double-check spelling and grammar.
- ▶ Include a return address and phone number.

Public health brief. These manuscripts are short reports of a study or an evaluation. Their content includes an introduction, methods, results, discussion, references, and tables/figures. The outline is similar to a journal article's abstract.

Be prepared to write different types of documents to communicate information about injuries.

Fact sheet. While the format for fact sheets varies, good ones have several things in common. They are well-organized and cover the specific topic with enough depth for the reader to have an understanding of the topic. Fact sheets are one to two pages. If statistical information is given, use charts or graphs to make them easier to comprehend. If several subjects need to be covered, it is best to write separate fact sheets. Using the five Ws and H (who, what, when, where, why, and sometimes how) can be helpful.

Press release. Submit press releases when there is something important to say, such as the start of a new program, a change in an existing program affecting many people, or the results of a program. Include local statistics and quotes from specialists. It should be sent to the news director of the local radio, television, or newspaper. Suggested guidelines for a press release include:

- Identify the organization, use letterhead or printed press release forms, and state the name and telephone number of a contact person for additional information.
- Cite a release date with a caption, such as "for release on (date)."
- Create a headline that may not be used, but tells the editor about the contents.
- Length—do not use more than one page.
- Use a consistent style—critical information appears in the first paragraph using the five Ws (who, what, when, where, why, and sometimes how)—and keep it simple, short, and focused.
- Check and double-check names, titles, dates, spelling, numbers, and grammar.
- Submit photos (e.g., 5x7 or 8x10 black-and-white glossies), but do not submit color photos; a digital photograph could be sent either through the Internet or on a CD, but check what medium the organization prefers.

Letter to the editor. This is an excellent way to respond to a newspaper when it has run a story or an editorial on an issue of concern in which the injury prevention is involved. They will lose their impact if sent too often and may not be printed. The letter should be short; no more than 400 words. Being short makes it more likely to be read. The most important point should appear in the first paragraph. If the letter is a response to a specific article, editorial, or another letter, refer to the title, date, and author in the opening sentence.

Policy statement. A policy statement contains several parts: (1) a general statement of intent or goals of the policy, a description of the organization (i.e., people and their duties), (2) identifying the procedure or mechanism for developing and carrying out of the policy, and (3) identifying the expected as well as possible unintended consequences that will occur as a result of the policy.

Web site content. Writing for a Web site is different than writing for printed material. Guidelines include:

- ▶ *Use clear and simple language.* Reading from computer screens is tiring for the eyes and about 25 percent slower than reading from a printed page. Some techniques are to avoid slang or jargon, use short words (e.g., use "begin" rather than "commence"), avoid complex sentence structure, and use active instead of passive verbs (active = measured, recorded; passive = is, are).
- ▶ *Limit* each paragraph to one idea.
- ▶ *Front-load content,* which means putting the conclusion first followed by the who, what, where, when, why, and how. Use newspaper articles as a reference.
- ▶ *Bold* important words and two to three words that describe the main point of the paragraph.
- ▶ *Use lists* because they are easier to scan and less intimidating.

c. Be able to serve as a resource to the public, media, and policy makers when appropriate and be able to provide referrals to other resources.

The term "expert" carries credibility and prestige that can serve a researcher well and can enhance an injury prevention program. Reading a couple of books, skimming a dozen journal articles, and researching on the Internet seldom is enough to qualify someone as an expert. Perhaps the best preparation for becoming known as an expert is to have a book published. However, until that happens there are other things that can qualify someone as an expert (these would be in a specialized field):

- ▶ Gain work experience
- ▶ Attend conferences and workshops
- ▶ Join and become involved in the professional organization associated with the field
- ▶ Converse with the best in the field
- ▶ Read broadly on the topic
- ▶ Determine a particular niche—keep a narrow focus; avoid becoming a "jack of all trades and a master of none"

Once someone has done all this, write articles for a local newspaper or professional journals covering that area of expertise. Editors are constantly looking for unique and information-packed articles. The more articles, the more of an expert a person will become.

In addition, seek opportunities to speak as often as possible. When articles begin to get published, request to speak with and be interviewed by the media.

Be prepared to be inter-
viewed by both broadcast
and print media.

It has been said many times that there are no new ideas under the sun; however, the mission of an expert is to take those ideas, add to them, reshape them, and create information that is uniquely his or hers. Content credibility leads to personal credibility.

d. Demonstrate the ability to be effectively interviewed by both broadcast and print media on an injury topic.

Before the interview, ask the reporter about the questions or areas that will be covered during the interview. Prepare the answers and practice answering. Also, give a reporter a list of questions to be asked. These may or may not be used. Most radio or television interviews allow about 15 to 20 seconds to respond to a reporter's question. Therefore, using short sentences in an interesting way is necessary. Use simple, easily understood words, and avoid jargon and technical terms whenever possible. If the answer is not known, say so—do not try to bluff. Respond by saying that the matter will be looked into and an answer will be given at a later date.

Many interviews are conducted over the telephone. In the case of radio or television, it may or may not be live. Studio interviews are used for live talk shows, which sometimes have listener call-ins.

Be poised, speak clearly, and keep eye contact with the reporter. For television, dress in soft, medium, or pastel colors. Avoid very dark or light clothing and con-trasting patterns and stripes. Avoid noisy bracelets or bright, sparkling jewelry.

Conclusion

Communication skills, both in verbal and written materials, can greatly enhance the cause of injury prevention. Although the inexperienced professional may lack in ability, skills can be enhanced and honed through practice.

CHAPTER 7 ▶

Stimulate Change

CORE COMPETENCY 7: Ability to stimulate change related to injury prevention through policy, enforcement, advocacy, and education.

Injury prevention efforts advocate a positive change. Such change can be slow and gradual or fast. Change can be wide in scope, affecting a large number of people, or limited, affecting only a small number of people. Injury prevention–related policies, enforcement, advocacy, and education all aim to implement change.

a. Develop and implement a culturally appropriate marketing plan to promote an injury prevention activity (e.g., within an organization or a given community).

Social marketing aims to influence voluntary behavior of a target population. It also focuses on the beneficial aspects and on understanding the perspective of the recipient on how those benefits are valued and perceived. Social marketing adapts the four "Ps" of marketing:

- ▶ *Promotion*: encompasses the more visible publicity type of activities (e.g., advertising, incentives, face-to-face selling, public relations).
- ▶ *Place*: refers to where the product is available (e.g., clinic, billboard, within a store). Places should be convenient, comfortable, and credible.

- ▶ *Price*: focus not only on the charge for the service, but also on the secondary costs (e.g., transportation, loss of peer group status).
- ▶ *Product*: refers to the physical good, service, or idea that is delivered with the intent of being beneficial to the target population.

b. Describe the differences between policy, education, lobbying, and advocacy as tools to stimulate change in the community.

Education, lobbying, and advocacy play an integral role in shaping policy at all levels of government.

- ▶ **Policy:** course of action to guide present and future decisions. It is a plan of what to do in a particular situation that has been agreed to by a group of people or a government. Although laws are policies, not all policies are laws.
- ▶ **Education:** process of changing behavior in such a way as to reduce unintentional injuries.
- ▶ **Lobbying:** process of trying to influence policymakers (e.g., legislators) in favor of a specific cause. Grassroots lobbying occurs when an appeal to the general public is made asking them to try to influence specific legislation.
- ▶ **Advocacy:** organizations or groups collectively conduct activities ranging from building a statewide coalition to testifying before a legislative committee to persuading a professional organization to include injury prevention on an annual conference agenda. Advocacy steers public attention from a particular type of injury as a personal problem to a public health issue.

Education, lobbying, and advocacy play an integral role in shaping policy at all levels of government.

c. Identify key prevention policies, laws, or regulations that address injury.

Injury prevention usually begins with education or advice giving and continues through other interventions if the preceding one is not effective. For example, if education about a policy fails to reduce the injury rate, then an inducement may be attempted; if that fails, coercion may be tried; if that fails, laws or regulations may be enacted. Laws and regulations, then, are one way to deal with an injury problem, and they indicate that other injury prevention efforts have been ineffective. See Table 7-1 for examples of this process. The whole process may take years or decades before an effective intervention is found or developed. Therefore, an existing policy, law, or a regulation usually indicates that other interventions have failed to reduce a particular type of injury.

d. Identify gaps in policies, laws, regulations, and enforcement that, if addressed, could reduce injury in the community.

An objective assessment of traffic laws is conducted by the Insurance Institute for Highway Safety (IIHS), which not only evaluates traffic laws but also rates them. Their ratings can be found at www.iihs.org/laws/state_laws/measure-up.html.

Table 7-1 Examples of Policies, Laws, and Regulations

Policy, Law, or Regulation	Example
Policy: an established course of action that must be followed	Businesses shall establish rules that prohibit the use of cellular telephones while driving company vehicles.
Law: a rule of conduct established and enforced by the authority, legislation, or custom of a given community, state, or nation	Require motor vehicle occupants to be appropriately restrained with safety belts or safety seats. Building codes shall require four-sided isolation fencing around residential swimming pools. The fencing shall be of appropriate height and with self-closing and self-latching gates.
Regulation: an authoritative rule dealing with a procedure	Communities shall ensure that playground equipment and surfaces meet the most recent CPSC and ASTM safety standards. Implement and enforce building codes that require the installation of hard-wired smoke alarms with battery back-up in all new home construction.

Hold a press conference for a significant announcement or a timely event.

The IIHS definition of what was "good" appears here. States and communities not within the "good" category would be deemed to have a gap in their laws, which could reduce injury if they were legislated and enforced.

Good alcohol laws: An administrative license revocation law that mandates at least a 30-day revocation for a violation with few or no exceptions for hardship; a law under which it is illegal to drive with a blood alcohol concentration (BAC) at or above 0.08 percent; a readily enforceable law under which it is illegal for anyone younger than 21 to drive with any measurable BAC (enforcement is impeded in some state because police must suspect that a young driver has a high BAC before administering an alcohol test to check for any measurable BAC); and sobriety checkpoints must be permitted.

Good safety belt use laws: Law allows primary enforcement (police may stop and ticket motorists for belt law violations alone); fines and/or license points are imposed for violations; and law applies to occupants in rear as well as front seats.

Good child restraint use laws: All children younger than 13 in all vehicle seats are required to ride in infant restraints, child seats, or safety belts; and enforcement is primary, which means that the vehicle can be stopped for no other reason than a child is not being protected by an infant restraint, child seat, or safety belt.

Good motorcycle helmet use laws: All motorcycle riders must wear helmets. Helmets are highly effective in protecting motorcycle riders' heads in a crash. Law enforcement officers in universal helmet law states can easily observe and

Gaps are found in state motorcycle helmet use laws that could, if enacted, reduce injury if they were legislated and enforced.

cite motorcycle riders who are not wearing a helmet; this likely explains why helmet use rates are well above 90 percent in universal helmet law states.

Good red light camera enforcement: Law grants specific statewide authority for camera enforcement. A red light camera is a system that automatically detects whether a vehicle has run a red light, and if so, photographs the car's license plate. The vehicle's owner is sent a ticket or warning.

e. Identify potential partners and opponents in influencing policies, laws, regulations, and enforcement and distinguish their roles.

An important principle for an advocacy is that many partners should be included. Forming a group to advocate for or against an issue can be more effective than an individual voice because a group can share responsibilities and complete more tasks. Policymakers and decision makers listen because they know that the group is large and politically powerful. Understanding the values, needs, and concerns of opponents to an issue and identifying areas of common ground can result in more realistic options that will create additional advocates.

Considerations for the type of partners to seek include partners who can:

▶ **Lead someone directly to the target population.** This saves a lot of time and effort instead of having them come to the researcher. For example, for a bicycle helmet program, form a partnership with the school district and the Parent-Teacher Association (PTA) to access elementary school children.

▶ **Provide greater impact.** Credible and well-respected groups can provide a positive impact. An example is associating with a medical association because, as a whole, physicians are well respected.

▶ **Provide resources.** Finances, materials, and personnel are needed. A Fortune 500 company or foundation often have the needed resources.

f. Describe the role the media and other communication channels play in public education and how to utilize these channels to shape public opinion about injury prevention.

Media refers to news programs, talk shows, editorials, and public service announcements (PSAs). Involving the media can greatly increase the likelihood of an advocacy's success. The media can increase the public's and decision makers' awareness of an injury problem. Attempts should be made to put the advocacy's message in as many places and in as many formats as possible. The idea is to influence policymakers, community decision makers, and to change the target population's perception about an injury problem.

Involve the media by:

▶ **Issuing press releases.** Obviously, press releases should announce something new. Think of ways to make the story attractive by building it around "hooks." A "hook" attempts to attract people to the story. Hooks might involve injuries occurring around a holiday or seasonal event, an anniversary of an injury prevention program, or a human interest story.

▶ **Holding a press conference.** These should be held only if there is something significant to announce; a timely event and/or controversial news. Notify editors and producers several days in advance. Hold the conference in a quiet location and in the morning for better media coverage. Provide a press kit containing a fact sheet and a press release. Limit the spokesperson's statements to no longer than 3 to 5 minutes. Provide time for a question-and-answer segment if possible.

▶ **Contacting individual reporters.** Attempt to be a good source of information for reporters. They are always looking for a good story. Suggest in-depth reports or feature stories.

g. Identify information on the cost of injury and be able to describe its application in policy making.

Injuries are costly, and these amounts can be collected and computed. The losses are staggering. Publicizing these costs raises public and official awareness, yet opposition to some injury prevention programs exists because of their economic impact on some segment of the population. Consequently, this often inspires opposition for various economic reasons (e.g., requires a tax increase, adds to the price of a product). For example, automobile manufacturers resisted implementing designs to improve safety and landlords resisted building codes. Therefore, policymakers should be very much aware of the opposition they may face when a program is proposed.

h. Demonstrate the ability to work effectively with advocacy groups (e.g., MADD) to advance injury prevention policies, laws, or regulations.

Other groups or agencies may already be trying to reach the same target population with the same objectives. Collaboration can prove to be helpful, especially when in agreement with the other groups on all aspects of the injury problem. Cooperative arrangements offer an excellent way to expand limited resources and present a more powerful image.

Many reasons can be given for individuals being in an advocacy organization or becoming involved in advocacy activities. In some cases, they have had a personal experience, especially one that is negative or traumatic. Many advocacy organizations were developed because an individual or a small group of people decided to take action. Such an example is Mothers Against Drunk Driving (MADD), which was founded by Candy Lightner after her own daughter was killed by a drunk driver. See Table 7-2 for more examples or search the Internet for additional information.

i. Demonstrate the ability to use research and evaluation to develop culturally appropriate policy, advocacy, and education initiatives.

Research and evaluation are essential in determining whether policy, advocacy, or educational attempts are worth the effort. Research and evaluation provides a strong factual base upon which to base a successful program. Any proposed initiative should be based on data collected from research or an evaluation. Useful data includes showing that the:

▶ **Injury problem is important.** Comparing injuries with other causes of morbidity and mortality can impress people about the magnitude of the injury problem.

Table 7-2 Examples of Injury Prevention Advocacy and Trade Organizations

AAA Foundation for Highway Safety	National Commission Against Drunk Driving
American Academy of Pediatrics	National Council of Fireworks Safety
American Association of Poison Control Centers	National Fire Protection Association
American Fire Sprinkler Association	National Fire Sprinkler Association
Automotive Coalition for Traffic Safety	National Organization for Youth Safety
Brain Injury Association	National Program for Playground Safety
Center for Auto Safety	National Safety Council
Citizens for Reliable and Safe Highways	National Youth Sports Safety Foundation
Common Sense About Kids and Guns	No Dog Bites
Every 15 Seconds	Operation Lifesaver
Farm Safety 4 Just Kids	Parents Against Tired Truckers
Foundation for Aquatic Injury Prevention	Perils for Pedestrians
Home Safety Council	Remove Intoxicated Drivers
Kids In Danger	Safe Kids Worldwide
Kids 'N Cars	Safety Forum
Mothers Against Drunk Driving	Think First Foundation
National Bicycle Safety Network	Trauma Foundation
National Coalition for School Bus Safety	

Also comparing different injuries occurring among a community or region can be useful in setting priorities as to what injuries should be focused on.

▶ **Target population is the correct one.** Expending efforts and finances targeting the wrong group is a waste of resources and affects credibility if future programs are instigated.

▶ **Intervention has the potential to be effective.** Research identifying the best practices for many injury problems have been completed and are available.

▶ **Public opinion data.** Whether it is from existing data or commissioned surveys, public opinion data can provide evidence of public concerns about the injury problem. Giving the findings to elected officials and other community decision makers helps keep the issue on their agenda. This data also provides content for press releases.

▶ **Opponent information.** Knowing opponents' strategy and tactics can help evaluate the appropriateness of an advocacy's strategy and tactics.

▶ **Financial impact documentation.** This can persuade critics to reevaluate their position and can increase trust in an advocacy.

j. Demonstrate the ability to translate policy into organizational plans and programs.

The development of written policies is an important step in building a solid base for an organization desiring a successful injury prevention program. However, if the policies are never implemented, the organization will be no better off than before their development.

Implementation begins with the distribution of the policies to those who will be affected by them. Some ideas for carrying out this process include (1) distributing the policies with a letter of explanation, (2) presenting them at a gathering of the organization, and (3) holding a special meeting for the specific purpose of explaining the policies.

k. Understand how policy change can have positive or negative effects on injury outcomes.

National, state, local, and organizational political forces can affect the ability to implement an injury prevention program and to receive the necessary resources. Decision makers may or may not approve the program initiative based on politics. Knowing ahead of time what is and is not politically supported will help decide how to proceed.

CHAPTER 8 ▶

Professional Career Management

CORE COMPETENCY 8: Ability to maintain and further develop competency as an injury prevention professional.

Professionals generally want to maximize their achievement, status, and/or income. Thus, they most often will aspire to obtain the most responsible, highest paid position they qualify for and feel comfortable in. Having a career path in mind provides a realistic plan and timetable for acquiring the necessary knowledge and skills.

a. Demonstrate the ability to access and use key journal and electronic resources to obtain updated information regarding injury prevention.

The professional should keep well informed and up-to-date on developments and changes in the injury prevention field. Some of the professional journals accompany a membership to a particular professional organization while others require an individual or department subscription to access them. Making periodic visits to a university library helps. Some organizations have access to electronic versions of the journals. See Table 8-1 for some journals related to injury prevention.

Electronic access to journals accommodates the busy professional. In addition, the Web sites of various organizations related to injury prevention also can be accessed on the Internet. These Web sites can serve as valuable resources (see Table 8-2).

Table 8-1 Journals Related to Injury Prevention

Academic Emergency Medicine	Injury Control and Safety Promotion
Accident Analysis & Prevention	Injury Prevention
American Journal of Emergency Medicine	International Journal of Epidemiology
American Journal of Epidemiology	International Journal of Injury Control and Safety Promotion
American Journal of Health Behavior	Journal of the American Medical Association
American Journal of Health Education	Journal of Community Health
American Journal of Public Health	Journal of Emergency Medicine
American Journal of Preventive Medicine	Journal of Public Health Policy
Annals of Emergency Medicine	Journal of Safety Research
Annals of Epidemiology	Journal of Trauma
Annual Review of Public Health	Morbidity and Mortality Weekly Report
Canadian Journal of Public Health	New England Journal of Medicine
Cochrine Database of Systematic Reviews	Pediatrics
Disaster Management and Response	Prehospital Emergency Care
Disaster Medicine and Public Health Preparedness	Preventive Medicine
Disaster Prevention and Management	Public Health Reports
Disasters	Safety and Health
Emergency Medicine Journal	Safety Science
Evaluation	Sports Medicine
Fire Safety Journal	Traffic Injury Prevention
Health Education and Behavior	Traffic Safety
Health Education Research	Trauma
Injury	Wilderness and Environmental Medicine

Note: Use a search engine such as Google or Yahoo to locate Web pages for more information.

Table 8-2 Electronic Resources Related to Injury Prevention

National Center for Injury Prevention and Control
www.cdc.gov/ncipc/ncipchm.htm
This site provides injury data for every U.S. state, suggested references and resources for your library, and links to government and nonprofit injury prevention sites worldwide. Funding opportunities are given, and fact sheets are available.

(continued)

Table 8-2 Electronic Resources Related to Injury Prevention (continued)

Children's Safety Network
www.childrenssafetynetwork.org
Geared primarily toward health professionals, this site includes information about various resources and publications on injury prevention for children and adolescents.

Injury Control Resource Information Network
www.injurycontrol.com/icrin/frameicrin.htm
This site provides injury data for every U.S. state, suggested references and resources for your library, and links to government and nonprofit injury prevention sites worldwide, as well as current job listings for injury professionals.

Injury Prevention Web
www.injuryprevention.org
This site provides injury data for every U.S. state, suggested references and resources for your library, and links to government and nonprofit injury prevention sites worldwide.

National Highway Traffic Safety Administration
www.nhtsa.dot.gov
This comprehensive site on motor vehicle safety provides information on vehicle safety, crash test results, recall lists, technical bulletins, public information, and educational materials.

National SAFE KIDS Worldwide
www.safekids.org
This site has information on injury topics relevant to children including bicycle safety, water safety, playground safety, child passenger safety, and more.

National Safety Council
www.nsc.org
This site addresses all aspects of safety in the environment, at the workplace, in the community, and at home. Resources include fact sheets and helpful tips, campaign materials, and upcoming conferences.

SafeUSA
www.safeusa.org
Developed through a partnership between the CDC and a collection of major public and private organizations, this site addresses safety in the home, at school, at work, on the move, and in the community. Visitors will find easy-to-read facts and information along with useful tips for prevention.

State and Territorial Injury Prevention Directors Association (STIPDA)
www.stipda.org
Resources on this site include educational materials and links to state injury programs.

U.S. Consumer Product Safety Commission
www.cpsc.gov
The U.S. Consumer Product Safety Commission (CPSC) is charged with protecting the public from unreasonable risks of serious injury or death from more than 15,000 types of consumer products under the agency's jurisdiction. The CPSC works to ensure the safety of consumer products, such as toys, cribs, power tools, cigarette lighters, and household chemicals.

Table 8-2 Electronic Resources Related to Injury Prevention (continued)

Harborview Injury Prevention and Research Center
http://depts.washington.edu/hiprc/index.html
The University of Washington provides links to Best Practices for: bicycles, child pedestrians, choking and suffocation, drowning, falls, fires and burns, motor vehicles, poisoning, and recreational injuries.

The Community Guide
www.thecommunityguide.org/mvoi/default.htm
Provides evidence-based recommendations showing the effectiveness of selected population-based interventions to reduce motor vehicle occupant injuries. It focuses on three strategic areas:
1. Increasing the proper use of child safety seats
2. Increasing the use of safety belts
3. Reducing alcohol impaired driving

Note: A search engine such as Google or Yahoo is useful for more information or in the Web site address changes.

b. Identify key professional organizations and agencies related to injury prevention and describe how these organizations can assist in maintaining and developing skills.

Professional Organizations Related to Injury Prevention

American Public Health Association (APHA) Injury Control and Emergency Health Services (ICEHS) Section
> The ICEHS is a national forum for all professional committed to the control of violence and unintentional injuries, and to the delivery of emergency health care services. Go to www.icehs.org for more information.

American Society of Safety Engineers (ASSE)
> The American Society of Safety Engineers (ASSE) provides an educational program for members and nonmembers based on the needs of those in occupational safety and health. Go to www.asse.org for additional information. Their Web site provides a list of colleges and universities offering associate, bachelor, masters, and doctoral degrees in the field as well as current job openings in the field.

Association of Schools of Public Health (ASPH) Injury Prevention and Control
> This organization offers advice on improving injury research and training schools in public health and focuses on expanding faculty development and expertise. In addition, they promote professional interest in injury prevention and control among students and faculty. Go to www.asph.org/document.cfm?page=828.

Association of State and Territorial Health Officials (ASTHO)
The ASTHO works to enhance states' capacity to address injury prevention and to raise the visibility of these issues among state health officials and health department staff. Their Web site is www.astho.org.

Association of Schools of Public Health (ASPH) Injury Prevention and Control
The ASPH is the only national organization representing the deans, faculty, and students of the accredited member schools of public health and other programs seeking accreditation as schools of public health. Go to www.asph .org for more information.

Association of Teachers of Preventive Medicine (ATPM)
The ATPM is a national association supporting health promotion and disease prevention educators and researchers. The association focuses on health promotion and disease prevention in the education of physicians and other health professionals. Go to www.atpm.org/about/about.html for more information.

American Trauma Society (ATS)
The society is dedicated to the prevention of trauma and improvement of trauma care with a strong advocate for injury care and prevention. Go to www.amtrauma.org.

Governors Highway Safety Association (GHSA)
This is a nonprofit association representing the highway safety offices of states, territories, the District of Columbia, and Puerto Rico, GHSA provides leadership and representation for the states and territories to improve traffic safety, to influence national policy, and to enhance program management. Its members are appointed by their governors to administer federal and state highway safety funds and implement state highway safety plans. Go to www.nagdhsr.org.

National Association of County and City Health Officials (NACCHO)
The association provides education and training to local health officials and agency staff on engaging the broader local public health system in injury prevention. It also works to create opportunities for the National Center for Injury Prevention and Control (NCIPC) to engage in dialogue with local health officials and market resources to address injury prevention and control issues through organizational publications and the Internet. Go to www .naccho.org/topics/HPDP/injuryprevention.cfm.

Society for Public Health Education (SOPHE)
The SOPHE provides leadership to the health education profession through advocacy, continuing education, and valuable connections and resources. Go to www.sophe.org.

Society for the Advancement of Violence and Injury Research (SAVIR)
The SAVIR promotes scholarly activity dealing with injuries and addresses issues relevant to the prevention, acute care, and rehabilitation of traumatic injury. These aims are achieved through member activities in research, research dissemination, program development and evaluation, consultation, education, and training. Go to www.savir.org.

State and Territorial Injury Prevention Directors Association (STIPDA)
The STIPDA engages in activities to increase awareness of injury as a public health problem; provide injury prevention and control education, training, and professional development; and enhance the capacity of public health agencies to conduct injury prevention programs. Go to www.stipda.org.

Federal agencies related to injury prevention play important roles. They have their own programs and, when involved with legislation, enforce their standards and regulations. They provide some federal resources to the states for training, program development, and research. Federal agencies can have a great impact on state and local public health efforts. See Table 8-3.

Table 8-3 U.S. Federal Agencies

Administration on Aging (AoA)
Bureau of Labor Statistics (BLS)—Census of Fatal Occupational Injuries
Centers for Disease Control and Prevention (CDC)
Fire Administration (USFA)
Health Resources and Services Administration (HRSA)
Healthy People 2010
Indian Health Service (IHS)—Injury Prevention Program
International Collaborative Effort (ICE) on Injury Statistics
National Agricultural Safety Database (NIOSH)
National Center for Health Statistics (NCHS)
National Center for Injury Prevention and Control at CDC (NCIPC)
National Commission Against Drunk Driving (NCADD)
National Highway Traffic Safety Administration (NHTSA)
National Institute for Occupational Safety and Health (NIOSH)
Safe Communities
The National Transportation Safety Board (NTSB)
U.S. Coast Guard (USCG)
U.S. Consumer Product Safety Commission (CPSC)
U.S. Fire Administration (USFA)

Note: Use a search engine such as Google or Yahoo to locate Web sites containing more information.

c. Identify a potential mentor/advisor who has experience in injury prevention and can assist with professional development.

A mentoring relationship between a senior professional and a junior professional has its primary goal to nurture the junior professional's development. A mentor is invaluable in navigating the injury prevention profession. The mentor can guide the mentee in helping build professional networks through personal contacts and participation at professional meetings.

All injury prevention professionals do not necessarily make effective mentors; certain individuals are more effective in the role of developing others. Whether an individual is suited to the role of mentor may depend on his or her own stage of development and experience. For example, a fairly successful individual may have had a specific, or limited, background and may not have enough general experience to offer. Prior to entering into a mentoring relationship, the protégé should assume the responsibility of assessing the mentor's potential effectiveness.

The characteristics that are essential in an effective mentor include:

- ▶ **A desire to help.** Individuals who are interested in and willing to help others. Above all, the mentor should be a supporter of the mentee's efforts and aspirations.
- ▶ **Have had positive experiences.** Individuals who have had positive formal or informal experiences with a mentor tend to be positive mentors themselves.
- ▶ **Good reputation for developing others.** Experienced people who have a good reputation for helping others develop their skills.
- ▶ **Time and energy.** People who have the time and mental energy to devote to the relationship. Availability is one of the most important aspects for the mentor to make a regularly scheduled meeting time. Mentees need to understand that the mentor is likely to have many other responsibilities and should not take advantage of the mentor's willingness to be available.
- ▶ **Up-to-date knowledge.** Individuals who maintain current, up-to-date knowledge and/or skills.
- ▶ **Learning attitude.** Individuals who are still willing and able to learn and who see the potential benefits of a mentoring relationship.
- ▶ **Demonstrated effective mentoring skills.** Individuals who demonstrate effective coaching, counseling, and networking skills.

A mentoring relationship can be very informal. The mentee might discuss career aspirations with the mentor, ask for advice on what to read, and ask about opportunities for gaining the necessary experience.

Reading journals and electronic resources is the best way to obtain updated information.

d. Identify and describe training resources, conferences, and courses that would be appropriate for learning new information on injury prevention strategies, research, and best practices.

Training opportunities can be found at www.InjuryEd.org/training.htm. This Web site lists training programs in five categories: (1) clearinghouses, (2) those lasting less than a day to as long as 5 days, (3) those lasting 5 days to as long as one semester, (4) distance education, and (5) conferences. Upcoming conferences for injury prevention professionals can be found at www.InjuryEd.org/conferences. htm. Checking the Web sites of the professional organizations also can serve as a source for learning about conferences and training opportunities.

SAVIR is an organization devoted to promoting scholarly activity in injury control, addressing issues relevant to the prevention, acute care, and rehabilitation of traumatic injury through multiple activities in research, research dissemination, program development and evaluation, consultation, and education and training. A list of their members is found in Table 8-4.

Table 8-4 Members of the Society for Advancement of Violence and Injury Research (SAVIR)

Alabama
UAB Injury Control Research Center
The University of Alabama at Birmingham
School of Medicine
South Birmingham, AL 35294-2041

(continued)

Table 8-4 Members of the Society for Advancement of Violence and Injury Research
(SAVIR) (continued)

California
San Francisco Injury Center
University of California, San Francisco
San Francisco General Hospital
San Francisco, CA 94110

Southern California Injury Prevention Research Center
UCLA School of Public Health
Los Angeles, CA 90024

Colorado
Colorado Injury Control Research Center
Colorado State University
Fort Collins, CO 80523-6156

District of Columbia
Center for Injury Prevention and Control
The George Washington University Medical Center
Department of Emergency Medicine
Washington, DC 20016

Georgia
Emory Center for Injury Control
Emory University School of Medicine
Department of Emergency Medicine
Atlanta, GA 30303

Iowa
Injury Prevention Research Center
University of Iowa
Iowa City, Iowa 52242

Kentucky
Kentucky Injury Prevention and Research Center
Lexington, KY 40504

Maryland
Center for Injury Research and Policy
Johns Hopkins Bloomberg School of Public Health
Baltimore, MD 21205-1996

Children's Safety Network: Economics and Data Analysis Resource Center
Calverton, MD 20705

Massachusetts
Harvard Injury Control Research Center
Harvard University
School of Public Health
Boston, MA 02115

Table 8-4 Members of the Society for Advancement of Violence and Injury Research (SAVIR) (continued)

Massachusetts (continued)
Motor Vehicle Hazard Archives Project
Public Health Advocacy Institute
Northeastern University School of Law
Boston, MA 02116

Michigan
University of Michigan Injury Research Center
Ann Arbor, MI 48109

North Carolina
Injury Prevention Research Center
University of North Carolina
Chapel Hill, NC 27599-7505

Ohio
Center for Injury Research and Policy
Columbus Children's Research Institute
Columbus, OH 43205

Pennsylvania
Center for Injury Research and Control
University of Pittsburgh Medical Center
Pittsburgh, PA 15261

Firearm and Injury Center at Penn
University of Pennsylvania Health System
Philadelphia, PA 19104-3335

Rhode Island
Injury Prevention Center at RI Hospital
University Emergency Medicine Foundation
Providence, RI 02903

Washington
Harborview Injury Prevention Research Center
Seattle, WA 98104

West Virginia
West Virginia University Injury Control Research Center
Morgantown, WV 26505

Wisconsin
Injury Research Center at the Medical College of Wisconsin
Milwaukee, WI 53226

Note: Use a search engine such as Google or Yahoo to locate Web sites containing more information.

CHAPTER 9 ▶

Motor Vehicle Injuries*

NOTE: The U.S. National Highway Traffic Safety Administration (NHTSA) has replaced the term "accident" with "crash."

Motor vehicle–related crashes are the leading cause of death among children, youth, and young adults in the United States and the leading cause of death from unintentional injury for people of all ages. In 2005, there were 45,800 fatalities in the United States, 2.4 million disabling injuries, and the economic costs were estimated at $247.7 billion (National Safety Council, 2007).

The National Highway Traffic Safety Administration (NHTSA) and the National Safety Council (NSC) count motor vehicle crash deaths using somewhat different criteria. The NSC counts total motor vehicle related fatalities—both traffic and nontraffic—that occur within one year of the crash. The NHTSA counts only traffic fatalities that occur within 30 days of the crash. This means that a difference of about 800 to 1,000 motor vehicle related deaths each year in these two organization's fatality data (National Safety Council, 2007).

Reduction of motor vehicle injuries remains a major public health challenge, despite sharp declines in death rates since 1925 (National Safety Council, 2007). Injury prevention professionals, using a variety of interventions given in this chapter, can impact this major cause of death and disability.

Pathophysiology

There are three types of collisions in a motor vehicle crash (see also Figure 9-1):

---

*This chapter's interventions are adapted from the U.S. Department of Transportation, National Highway Traffic Safety Administration, *Countermeasures That Work* and Centers for Disease Control and Prevention, Guide to Community Preventive Services, *Motor Vehicle Occupant Injury*.

1. Vehicle
2. Human
3. Internal movement within the human body

(a)

(b)

(c)

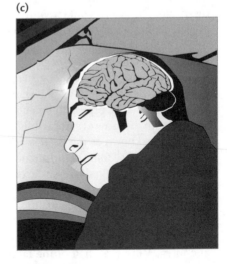

Figure 9-1 There are three types of collisions in a motor vehicle crash: Vehicle, Human, Internal movement within the human body. (a) The first collision in a front impact is that of the car against another object. (b) The second collision in a frontal impact is that of the passenger against the interior of a car. (c) The third collision in a frontal impact is that of the passenger's internal organs against the solid structures of the body.

In the *vehicle collision*, a vehicle strikes another vehicle, a tree, or similar object. The vehicle does not actually stop all at once, but slows down as the front end collapses under the force of the collision, so that at about 30 mph, a vehicle hitting a nonmoving object will crumple about 2 feet. As the vehicle crushes, it absorbs some of the force of the collision. It takes a car about one-tenth of a second to come to a complete stop. Because the crushing of the front end absorbs energy, the longer this impact takes and the more controlled the collapse of the vehicle, the greater the potential is for survival. This first collision only involves the vehicle; the occupants are not injured.

The second type of collision is the *human collision*. At the moment of impact, passengers in the vehicle are still traveling at the vehicle's original speed. When the vehicle comes to a complete stop, the passengers continue to be hurled forward until they come in contact with some part of the vehicle (e.g., the steering wheel, the dashboard, the front window or back of the front seat) or are ejected from the vehicle and strike the road or other outside objects. Humans in a crash can cause serious injuries to other humans when they collide with one another. Front-seat passengers in a vehicle are often hit by rear-seat passengers as they fly forward with incredible force. This "human-body collision" can cause serious injury or death.

The third type of collision occurs in a crash because, even after the human body comes to a complete stop, the internal organs are still moving. During this action, the internal organs slam into one another or the skeletal system. This *internal collision* is what often causes serious injury or death. Imagine what happens when someone's head collides with the windshield of a vehicle. After the person comes in contact with the windshield and is stopped by the solid object, the brain hits the inside of the skull. The result may be a mild concussion or permanent brain damage.

Injuries to children are especially severe. If a child were being held by an adult, then the forward force would be 30 times the child's weight; if the child weighed 20 pounds, then he or she would be moving with a force of 600 pounds—a weight few adults can hold, especially when applied suddenly. The adult's weight, moving forward with the force of several thousand pounds, would press against the child's body. This is known as the *child crusher syndrome*.

It is not just the force of the impact that causes injury, but what the passenger hit inside the vehicle. Hard surfaces create injuries similar to hammer blows, while sharp surfaces function like knives. The windshield can induce especially nasty wounds; it is not unusual to see victims who have been scalped, or have had portions of their faces mangled and lacerated.

The areas of the body most commonly injured are the head, neck, chest, and abdomen. More than half of the fatal and life-threatening injuries come from the victims' bodies hitting the steering wheel, the windshield, and areas of the dashboard.

Risk Factors*

Motor vehicle crashes vary greatly by age and gender. This section discusses these differences as well as other epidemiological factors involved in crashes, such as time and place.

Age of driver. On the basis of number of miles driven, the youngest and oldest drivers have the highest crash rates. For drivers aged 16 to 19, the fatal involvement rate per 100 million vehicle miles traveled is about three times the overall rate for all drivers in passenger vehicles. The rate for drivers aged 75 and over is the highest of all age groups. The same basic "U"-shaped curve is found for crashes involving injury rates, which shows higher rates for younger and older drivers.

Gender. Males have higher involvement rates than females in fatal crashes. For all crashes, females have higher involvement rates than males. In other words, women are involved in more crashes, but more men are killed in crashes. Differences in the rates may be due to differences in the time, place, and circumstances of driving.

Improper driving. Exceeding the posted speed limit or driving at an unsafe speed is the most common error in fatal and nonfatal crashes. Improper driving techniques resulting in crashes are reported in rank order below:

1. Speed too fast or unsafe
2. Right of way
3. Left of center
4. Improper turn
5. Improper overtaking
6. Followed too closely

The highest crash rate is among drivers aged 75 and over.

---

*This section's data comes from the National Safety Council's *Injury Facts* (2007).

Alcohol. The NHTSA reports that about 40 percent of all traffic fatalities each year involve an intoxicated or alcohol-impaired driver. In the United States, alcohol use is the single most frequently noted human factor in fatal crashes.

Time of day. Time of day is an important factor. About 60 percent of all motor vehicle deaths occur during the day. Peak hours for fatalities occur during the afternoon rush hour on weekdays and late night on weekends. However, death rates based on mileage are over two times higher at night than during the day.

Day and month. Motor vehicle death totals vary sharply for different days of the week and different months of the year. Deaths are highest on Fridays, Saturdays, and Sundays. Deaths are at their lowest levels in January and February and increase to their highest levels in July and August.

Location. Motor vehicle deaths occur more frequently in rural places, but all other crashes occur more frequently in urban areas. The interstate system has been shown to be safer than other road types.

Road conditions. Most motor vehicle crashes occur on dry road surfaces. If there is an object near a roadway, sooner or later it will be struck. The streets and highways are dotted with them—bridge abutments, guardrails designed for strength rather than safety, and sign and light poles embedded in concrete are only a few examples.

Vehicle size. In every type of crash situation, the occupants of small vehicles fare worse than the occupants of large vehicles. For example, ejections from vehicles during crashes happen substantially more often in small cars than in larger vehicles due to the small vehicles' structural inadequacies to keep occupants contained. Small vehicles involved in fatal crashes are far more likely to roll over than large vehicles. Even if all vehicles were the same size, the death rate would be greater if all vehicles were small because smaller cars simply have less room for energy to be absorbed and occupants to decelerate in a crash. Small vehicles are not less dangerous because of their maneuverability; subcompacts have more insurance claims than larger cars.

Alcohol-Impaired Driving

Alcohol-impaired drivers are involved in about 40 percent of U.S. traffic-related fatalities (National Safety Council, 2007). Alcohol-impaired drivers decreased since 1982 for many reasons. Substantial public attention, the growth of grassroots organizations such as MADD, increased federal funding, state task forces, tougher laws, increased enforcement, and intensive publicity all combined to help address this critical traffic safety problem.

Other traffic safety interventions help reduce alcohol-related crashes. Behavioral strategies, such as those that increase safety belt use and reduce speeding, improved vehicle structures, and centerline rumble strips also contribute to reducing crashes.

Deterrence

Deterrence means enacting laws that prohibit driving while impaired, publicizing and enforcing those laws, and punishing the offenders. Deterrence works by changing behavior through the fear of punishment. If drivers believe that impaired driving is likely to be detected and that impaired drivers are likely to be arrested, convicted, and punished, many will not drive while impaired by alcohol. This strategy is sometimes called general deterrence because it influences the general driving public through well-publicized and highly visible enforcement activities and subsequent punishment. In contrast, specific deterrence refers to efforts to influence drivers who have been arrested for impaired driving so that they will not continue that behavior.

Deterrence works when consequences are swift, sure, and severe (with swift and sure being more important in affecting behavior than severe).

Deterrence: Laws

ADMINISTRATIVE LICENSE REVOCATION OR SUSPENSION

Administrative license revocation or administrative license suspension laws allow law enforcement and driver licensing authorities to revoke or suspend a driver's license if the driver fails or refuses to take a blood alcohol concentration (BAC) test. The license revocation or suspension occurs very quickly; usually the arresting officer takes the license at the time that a BAC test is failed or

Testing for drunk driving.

refused. The driver typically receives a temporary license that allows the driver time to make other transportation arrangements and to request and receive an administrative hearing or review. In most jurisdictions, offenders may obtain an occupational or hardship license during part or all of the revocation or suspension period.

These laws provide for swift and certain penalties for DWI, rather than the lengthy and uncertain outcomes of criminal courts. They also protect the driving public by removing some DWI offenders from the road.

BAC TEST REFUSAL PENALTIES

A driver's BAC is a critical piece of evidence in any alcohol-impaired driving action. A positive BAC provides evidence of alcohol presence that supports the basic driving while intoxicated (DWI) charge. All states have enacted laws under which it is illegal to drive with a BAC of .08 or greater, with no other evidence required. Many states have established more severe penalties for drivers with BACs that exceed a specific higher BAC level, typically .15 or .16. Administrative license revocation or suspension laws are based entirely on the driver's BAC level.

However, many drivers refuse to provide a breath or blood sample for a BAC test. All states have established separate penalties for BAC-test refusal, typically involving administrative license revocation or suspension. If the penalties for refusal are less severe than the penalties for failing the test, many drivers will refuse. All states except Nevada impose administrative sanctions for test refusal. Test refusal rates are lower in states where the consequences of test refusal are greater than the consequences of test failure.

HIGH BAC SANCTIONS

Many states increase penalties for the standard DWI offense for two classes of drivers. Almost all states increase the penalties for repeat offenders. Recently, some states also have increased the penalties for drivers with a high BAC, typically .15 or .16 or higher.

OPEN CONTAINERS

Open-container laws prohibit the possession and consumption of alcoholic beverages by drivers or passengers. These laws typically exempt passengers in buses, taxis, and the living quarters of mobile homes. The U.S. Congress requires states to enact open-container laws or have a portion of their federal and highway construction funds redirected to alcohol-impaired driving or hazard elimination activities.

Deterrence: Enforcement

SOBRIETY CHECKPOINTS

At a sobriety checkpoint, law enforcement officers stop vehicles at a predetermined location to check whether the driver is impaired. They either stop every vehicle or stop vehicles at some regular interval, such as every third or tenth vehicle. The purpose of checkpoints is to deter driving after drinking by increasing the perceived risk of arrest. To do this, checkpoints should be highly visible, publicized extensively, and conducted regularly. Checkpoints reduce crashes.

Checkpoints are permitted in most states. Checkpoints are permitted under the U.S. Constitution, but some state courts have held that checkpoints violate their state's constitution. States where checkpoints are not permitted may use saturation patrols.

SATURATION PATROLS

A saturation patrol (also called a blanket patrol, "wolf pack," or dedicated DWI patrol) consists of a large number of law enforcement officers patrolling a specific area for a set time to detect and arrest impaired drivers. The purpose of saturation patrols is to arrest impaired drivers and also to deter driving after drinking

Sobriety checkpoints involve law enforcement officers stopping vehicles to check whether the driver is impaired.

by increasing the perceived risk of arrest. To do this, saturation patrols should be publicized extensively and conducted regularly. A less-intensive strategy is the "roving patrol" in which individual patrol officers concentrate on detecting and arresting impaired drivers in an area where impaired driving is common or where alcohol-involved crashes have occurred. Saturation patrols can be very effective in arresting impaired drivers.

INTEGRATED ENFORCEMENT

Impaired drivers are detected and arrested through regular traffic enforcement and crash investigations as well as through special impaired driving checkpoints and saturation patrols. Another approach is to integrate impaired driving enforcement into special enforcement activities directed primarily at other offenses such as speeding or safety belt nonuse, especially since impaired drivers often speed or fail to wear safety belts.

PRELIMINARY BREATH TEST DEVICES

A preliminary breath tester (PBT) is a small handheld alcohol sensor used to estimate or measure a driver's BAC. Law enforcement officers use PBTs in the field to help establish evidence for a DWI arrest. The driver blows into a mouthpiece and the PBT displays either a numerical BAC level, such as .12, or a BAC range, such as a red light for BACs above .08. Law enforcement officers generally agree that PBTs are useful.

PASSIVE ALCOHOL SENSORS

A passive alcohol sensor is a device to detect alcohol presence in the air. The sensor usually is integrated into a flashlight or clipboard. Officers hold the flashlight or clipboard near the driver's mouth where it measures alcohol presence in the air where the driver is breathing. The PAS can be used without the driver's knowledge and without any probable cause because the PAS is considered "an extension of the officer's nose" and records information that is "in plain view." The PAS displays its results using light of different colors to indicate different alcohol concentration levels.

Deterrence: Prosecution and Adjudication

SANCTIONS

The standard court sanctions for DWI offenses are driver's license suspension or revocation, fines, jail, and community service. All states use some combination of these sanctions. DWI offenders also may have their driver's licenses revoked or suspended administratively and may have sanctions imposed on their vehicles or license plates.

DIVERSION AND PLEA AGREEMENT RESTRICTIONS

Diversion programs defer sentencing while a DWI offender participates in some form of alcohol education or treatment. In many states, charges are dropped or the offender's DWI record is erased if the education or treatment is completed satisfactorily.

Negotiated plea agreements are a necessary part of efficient and effective DWI prosecution and adjudication. However, plea agreements in some states allow offenders to eliminate any record of a DWI offense and to have their penalties reduced or eliminated.

DWI COURT

A dedicated DWI court provides a systematic and coordinated approach to prosecuting, sentencing, monitoring, and treating DWI offenders. A DWI court's underlying goal is to change offenders' behavior by identifying and treating their alcohol problems and by holding offenders accountable for their actions.

Prosecutors and judges in DWI courts specialize in DWI cases. Probation officers monitor offenders closely and report any probation infraction to the judge immediately for prompt action. DWI courts can reduce recidivism because judge, prosecutor, probation staff, and treatment staff work together as a team to assure that alcohol treatment and other sentencing requirements are satisfied.

Deterrence: DWI Offender Treatment, Monitoring, and Control

ALCOHOL PROBLEM ASSESSMENT AND TREATMENT

It is widely recognized that many DWI first-time offenders and most repeat offenders are dependent on alcohol or have alcohol use problems. They likely will continue to drink and drive unless their alcohol problems are addressed. A DWI arrest provides an opportunity to identify offenders with alcohol problems and to refer them to treatment.

Alcohol problem assessment can take many forms, from a brief paper-and-pencil questionnaire to a detailed interview with a treatment professional. Alcohol treatment can be even more varied, ranging from classroom alcohol education programs to long-term inpatient facilities.

Alcohol ignition interlocks allow a car to be
started by sober drivers but not by alcohol-
impaired drivers.

DWI OFFENDER MONITORING

The most successful methods for controlling
convicted DWI offenders and reducing recidivism have the common feature that they
monitor offenders closely. Close monitoring
can be accomplished at various levels and in
various ways, including a formal intensive su-
pervision program, home confinement with electronic monitoring, dedicated
detention facilities, and individual oversight by judges. These methods can result
in substantial reductions in DWI recidivism.

ALCOHOL INTERLOCKS

An alcohol ignition interlock prevents a car from starting unless the driver provides a breath sample with a BAC lower than a preset level, usually .02 grams
per deciliter. Interlocks typically are used as a condition of probation for DWI
offenders to prevent them from driving while impaired by alcohol after their
driver's licenses have been reinstated.

Interlocks are highly effective in allowing a car to be started by sober drivers,
but not by alcohol-impaired drivers. A "running retest" requires the driver to
remain sober while driving. A data recorder logs the driver's BAC at each test and
can be used by probation officers to monitor the offender's drinking and driving
behavior. Interlocks can cut DWI recidivism at least in half—and sometimes
more—compared to similar offenders without interlocks.

VEHICLE AND LICENSE PLATE SANCTIONS

In recent years, many states have implemented sanctions affecting a DWI offender's license plate or vehicle. These sanctions both prevent the offender from
driving the vehicle while the sanctions are in effect and also deter impaired driving
by the general public. Vehicle and plate sanctions include:

▶ Special license plates for drivers whose licenses have been revoked or suspended. The plates allow family members and other people to drive the
  offender's car, but permit law enforcement to stop the car to verify that
  the driver is properly licensed.

- ▶ License plate impoundment. Officers seize and impound or destroy the license plate.
- ▶ Vehicle immobilization. Vehicles are immobilized on the offender's property with a "boot," "club," or similar device.
- ▶ Vehicle impoundment. Vehicles are stored in a public impound lot.
- ▶ Vehicle forfeiture. Vehicles are confiscated and sold at auction.

LOWER BAC LIMITS FOR REPEAT OFFENDERS

All states now have an illegal BAC limit of .08. All states also have a BAC limit of .02 or lower for drivers under the age of 21. These laws reinforce the minimum drinking age laws in all states that prohibit people under 21 years of age from purchasing or possessing alcohol in public.

Prevention, Intervention, Communications, and Outreach

Prevention strategies seek to reduce drinking, especially drinking associated with driving, or to prevent driving by people who have been drinking. Prevention and intervention measures are especially important for those under 21 years of age.

Communications and outreach strategies seek to inform the public of the dangers of driving while impaired by alcohol and to promote positive social norms of not driving while impaired. As with prevention and intervention, education through various communications and outreach strategies is especially important for youth under 21. Education may occur through formal classroom settings, news media, paid advertisements, public service announcements, and a wide variety of other communication channels such as posters, billboards, and Web site banners.

RESPONSIBLE BEVERAGE SERVICE

Responsible beverage service covers a range of alcohol sales policies and practices that prevent or discourage restaurant and bar patrons from drinking to excess or from driving while impaired by alcohol. Server training programs teach servers how to recognize the signs of intoxication and how to prevent intoxicated patrons from further drinking and from driving. Management policies and programs include limits on cheap drinks and other promotions, support for designated driver programs, strong commitment to server training, and strong support for servers who refuse alcohol to intoxicated patrons. Intensive, high-quality, face-to-face server training—when accompanied by strong and active management support—is effective in reducing the levels of intoxication in patrons.

ALTERNATIVE TRANSPORTATION

Alternative transportation describes methods by which people can get to and from places where they drink without having to drive. Alternative transportation supplements normal public transportation provided by subways, buses, taxis, and other means.

Ride service programs transport drinkers home from, and sometimes to and between, drinking establishments using taxis, private cars, buses, trucks, and even police cars. Some will drive the drinker's car home along with the drinker. Most operate only for short periods of the year, such as the Christmas and New Year's holidays. Many are free, but some charge users a minimal fee, and some are operated commercially on a for-profit basis.

DESIGNATED DRIVERS

Designated drivers are individuals who agree not to drink so they can drive their friends who have been drinking. Formal designated driver programs in drinking establishments provide incentives such as free soft drinks for people who agree to be designated drivers. Usually, though, designated driver arrangements are completely informal.

ALCOHOL SCREENING AND BRIEF INTERVENTIONS

Alcohol screening is a quick form of estimating whether a person has an alcohol problem. Brief interventions refer to short, one-time encounters with people who may be at risks of alcohol-related injuries or other health problems. Alcohol screening is a quick form of estimating whether a person has an alcohol problem. The combination of alcohol screening and brief intervention is most commonly used with injured patients in emergency departments or trauma centers. Patients are screened for alcohol use problems and, if appropriate, counseled on how alcohol can affect injury risk and overall health and referred to a follow-up alcohol treatment program. Brief interventions take advantage of a "teachable moment" when a patient can be shown that alcohol use can have serious health consequences.

MASS MEDIA CAMPAIGNS

A mass media campaign consists of intensive communications and outreach activities regarding alcohol-impaired driving that use radio, television, print, and other mass media. Mass media campaigns are a standard part of every state's efforts to reduce alcohol-impaired driving. Some campaigns publicize a deterrence or prevention measure such as a change in a state's DWI laws or a checkpoint program. Others promote specific behaviors, such as the use of designated drivers, illustrate how impaired driving can injure and kill, or simply urge the public not to drink and drive. Campaigns vary enormously in quality, size, duration, funding, and every other way imaginable. Effective campaigns identify a specific audience and communications goal, and they develop messages and delivery methods that are appropriate to and effective for the audience and goal.

Underage Drinking and Alcohol-Related Driving

Some interventions are directed specifically to those under 21 years of age.

MINIMUM DRINKING AGE 21 LAW ENFORCEMENT

The minimum legal drinking age is 21 years of age in all states. There is strong evidence that these laws reduce drinking, driving after drinking, and alcohol-related crashes and injuries among youth. Drinking and driving has become less socially acceptable among youth, and more youth have separated their drinking from their driving. The specific laws implementing the minimum legal drinking age of 21 for alcohol vendors, adults, and youth differ substantially from state to state.

Minimum drinking age law enforcement is very limited in many communities. Enforcement can take several forms:

▶ Actions directed at alcohol vendors: compliance checks to verify that vendors will not sell to youth.
▶ Actions directed at youth: "use-and-lose" laws that confiscate the driver's license of an underage drinker, "Cops in Shops" directed at underage alcohol purchasers, law enforcement "party patrols," and penalties for using false identification.
▶ Actions directed at adults: beer keg registration laws, enforcement of laws prohibiting purchasing alcohol for youth, and programs to limit parties where parents provide alcohol to youth.

ZERO-TOLERANCE LAW ENFORCEMENT

Zero-tolerance laws set a maximum BAC of .02 or less for drivers under 21 years of age. Violators have their driver's licenses suspended or revoked. There is strong evidence that zero-tolerance laws reduce alcohol-related crashes and injuries. However, zero-tolerance laws often are not actively enforced or publicized.

SCHOOL EDUCATION PROGRAMS

Elementary and secondary schools often include education on alcohol, impaired driving, and traffic safety as regular topics in health and driver education courses.

YOUTH PROGRAMS

States and communities have conducted extensive youth drinking-and-driving-prevention programs. These programs seek to motivate youth not to drink, not to drink and drive, and not to ride with a driver who has been drinking. They use positive messages and methods: educating youth on the crash and injury risks of drinking and driving, informing on the effects of alcohol use and abuse, providing positive role models that discourage alcohol use, promoting positive norms that do not involve alcohol, and encouraging youth activities that do not involve or lead to alcohol use.

The most well-known youth program is SADD, founded in 1981 as Students Against Driving Drunk, later renamed Students Against Destructive Decisions. MADD's Youth In Action is found in most states.

Seat Belt Use

Wearing a seat belt is the single most effective way to save lives and reduce injuries in crashes. The NHTSA estimates that seat belt use in passenger cars reduces serious injuries by 69 percent and fatalities by 45 percent. In comparison, air bags without seat belts reduce serious injuries by 30 percent and fatalities by 14 percent. Seat belts are similarly effective for pickup truck and other light-truck occupants. The challenge is to convince all passenger vehicle occupants to buckle up.

All new passenger cars had some form of seat belts beginning in 1964. Shoulder belts were added in 1968 and the integrated lap and shoulder belt systems in 1974. However, few occupants wore the belts (10 percent). New York enacted the first belt use law in 1984. The national belt use rate currently is over 80 percent (National Safety Council, 2007). As of October 2006, all states except New Hampshire required adult passenger vehicle occupants to wear seat belts. The basic strategy

Wearing a safety belt is the single most effective way to save lives and reduce injuries in crashes.

for achieving and maintaining high seat belt use is highly publicized high-visibility enforcement of strong belt-use laws. The strategy's three components—laws, enforcement, and publicity—cannot be separated; effectiveness decreases if any one is weak or lacking.

Seat Belt Use Laws

STATE PRIMARY ENFORCEMENT BELT-USE LAWS

Primary enforcement belt-use laws permit non–seat belt users to be stopped and cited independently of any other traffic behavior. Secondary enforcement laws allow nonusers to be cited only after they first have been stopped for some other traffic violation. Belt use averaged 85 percent in states with a primary law and average 75 percent in secondary law states.

In most states, there is substantial opposition to changing a secondary to primary belt use law. Opponents claim that primary laws impinge on individual rights and provide opportunities for law enforcement to harass minority groups. Studies have found that minority groups were ticketed at similar or lower rates than others after a primary law was implemented. States that changed their law from secondary to primary show that belt use increased.

LOCAL PRIMARY ENFORCEMENT BELT-USE LAWS AND ORDINANCES

In some states with secondary enforcement belt use laws, individual communities have enacted and enforced community-wide primary laws or ordinances. These laws differ from statewide laws only in that they are enacted, publicized, and enforced locally.

INCREASED BELT-USE LAW PENALTIES: FINES AND DRIVER'S LICENSE POINTS

Penalties for most belt-use law violations are low. In some states, the typical fine is $25 or less. Low fines may not convince nonusers to buckle up. They also may send a message that belt-use laws are not taken seriously.

Most states penalize serious traffic law violations by assessing demerit points against a driver's license. Drivers lose their licenses if they accumulate more than a specified number of points within a specified period of time.

BELT-USE LAW COVERAGE: SEATING POSITIONS, VEHICLES, AND AGES

Belt-use laws do not cover rear seat passengers in more than half of the states. Most states' laws exempt some vehicles, such as those designed for more than 10 passengers, taxis, postal delivery vehicles, farm vehicles, or vehicles not required to have safety belts.

Most state belt use laws cover passengers over a specified age and are designed to work in combination with child passenger safety laws covering younger passengers, usually up to the minimum driving age. Some states exempt passengers for specified medical or physical reasons. Many states make belt use mandatory under their graduated driver licensing laws for beginning drivers.

Seat Belt Law Enforcement

SHORT-TERM, HIGH-VISIBILITY BELT-USE LAW ENFORCEMENT

The most common high-visibility belt-use law enforcement method consists of short-term (typically lasting for 2 weeks), intense, highly publicized periods of increased belt-use law enforcement, frequently using checkpoints, saturation patrols, or enforcement zones. These periods are sometimes called blitzes.

COMMUNICATIONS AND OUTREACH SUPPORTING ENFORCEMENT

Effective, high-visibility communications and outreach are an essential part of successful seat belt law high-visibility enforcement programs. Paid advertising can be a critical part of the media strategy.

COMMUNICATIONS AND OUTREACH STRATEGIES FOR LOW BELT-USE GROUPS

The large majority of drivers and passengers use their belts on every trip. The challenge is to reach the minority who still do not buckle up regularly. Lower use is found for males than females, for drivers aged 16 to 24 than those 25 to 69, for rural drivers compared to urban and suburban drivers, and for passengers than for drivers. Belt use is lower for pickup truck drivers than passenger car drivers.

Employer and School Programs

Employers, schools, and similar institutions provide well-defined and somewhat controlled audiences for seat belt use programs. Education and other communications strategies can be tailored to a specific audience. Seat belt use policies can be implemented and enforced in certain settings. Incentive programs can be conducted. Employer and school programs in a low seat belt use environment with no use law have increased seat belt use substantially.

Incentive Programs

Incentive programs use rewards of some sort as an inducement to wear seat belts. Incentive programs have been implemented by employers, schools, and entire communities. Rewards have included cash, coupons for merchandise or food, T-shirts or other promotional items, and raffle tickets for valuable prizes. Rewards typically have been given to people observed wearing their belts, but sometimes have been given for a pledge to buckle up. Incentive programs usually are accompanied by seat belt communications and outreach and may also be combined with seat belt use policies.

Aggressive Driving and Speeding

Aggressive driving generally is understood to mean driving actions that markedly exceed the norms of safe driving behavior and that place the driver or other road users in unnecessary danger. Aggressive behaviors may be directed at other drivers or pedestrians through actions such as following too closely or erratic and unsafe lane changes. In addition, aggressive behaviors may violate the established traffic control system through speeding or running red lights. All aggressive driving violates some traffic laws, but not every moving violation is considered aggressive driving. Aggressive driving should not be confused with road rage, which is defined as an intentional assault by a driver or passenger, with a motor vehicle or a weapon, on the roadway or precipitated by an incident on the roadway.

The legal definition of speeding is exceeding the posted speed limit. Speeding becomes aggressive driving when a vehicle's speed is too high for conditions or substantially exceeds the prevailing travel speeds of other vehicles. Speeding is common— and on some roads almost universal. Speeding can be dangerous on all roads. Half of the speed-related traffic fatalities occur on roads posted at 50 mph or less and one-fifth happen on roads posted at 35 mph or less.

With public acceptance and enforcement, lower speed limits can reduce travel speeds and casualties.

Laws

SPEED LIMITS

Speed limits are only one part of the system that attempts to control driving speeds, but without broad public acceptance and active enforcement, they have little effect. With public acceptance and enforcement, lower speed limits can reduce travel speeds and casualties.

AGGRESSIVE DRIVING LAWS

Aggressive driving actions are covered by specific traffic laws such as speeding, improper lane changes, following too closely, or by general laws such as reckless driving. Aggressive drivers often can be identified as those who violate traffic laws repeatedly or whose violations lead to crashes producing serious injury or death.

HIGH-VISIBILITY ENFORCEMENT

High-visibility enforcement campaigns have been used to deter aggressive driving and speeding. They are based on the same principles as high-visibility safety belt and alcohol-impaired driving enforcement to convince the public that speeding and aggressive driving actions are likely to be detected and that offenders will be arrested and punished.

AUTOMATED ENFORCEMENT

Automated enforcement is used in some jurisdictions to reduce red light running and speeding. At intersections with traffic lights, automated cameras take photographs of vehicles entering the intersection on a red light. Citations are sent to vehicles' registered owners.

TRAFFIC VIOLATOR SCHOOL

In many jurisdictions, drivers who accumulate enough demerit points on their driver's licenses are allowed to attend a traffic violator school. In most instances, drivers who complete traffic violator school have their traffic offenses dismissed or removed from their driving record.

COMMUNICATIONS AND OUTREACH SUPPORTING ENFORCEMENT

Effective, high-visibility communications and outreach are an essential part of successful speed and aggressive-driving enforcement programs. Most campaigns have not used paid advertising. The success of paid advertising in seat belt use campaigns suggests that it is worth considering for speed and aggressive driving enforcement campaigns. However, communications and outreach programs urging drivers to behave courteously or not to speed are unlikely to have any effect unless they are tied to vigorous enforcement.

Distracted and Fatigued Driving

Distracted and fatigued driving are common—though both are difficult to define, observe, and measure. Both distracted and fatigued driving result in large part from lifestyle patterns and choices: They are societal issues rather than just driving and transportation system issues.

Laws

CELL PHONE LAWS

Cell phones have become an essential feature of modern life. About two out of three drivers now have cell phones, and, before long, almost all of them will. Cell phones are involved in 1 to 4 percent of crashes.

Although cell phone use occurs less frequently than other driver distractions, it has been singled out for special attention for several reasons. Cell phone use is a multisensory distraction, requiring a driver's eyes to locate a ringing phone, hands to hold or dial the phone, hearing to listen to the call, and attention to carry on a conversation. In response to these concerns, the District of Columbia, New Jersey, New York, and several communities prohibit handheld cell phone use while driving. Several states prohibit all cell phone use by drivers under the age of 18 or 21, drivers with a graduated driver's license, and school bus drivers. No

Several states and communities prohibit handheld cell phone use while driving.

A learner's permit allows supervised driving by teenagers under certain restrictions.

state or community restricts hands-free phone use for all drivers. Many European countries and all Australian states prohibit handheld phone use.

GRADUATED DRIVER LICENSING REQUIREMENTS FOR BEGINNING DRIVERS

Graduated driver licensing (GDL) is a three-phase system for beginning drivers consisting of a learner's permit, then a provisional license, and finally a full license. A learner's permit allows driving only while supervised by a fully licensed driver. A provisional license allows unsupervised driving under certain restrictions. GDL helps beginning drivers acquire their initial driving experience in lower-risk situations. During the provisional phase, this is accomplished by restricting driving under certain high-risk circumstances. Some of these restrictions are directly linked to fatigue and distractions. Driving at night is more dangerous overall than during the day and also may pose greater risks of drowsy driving. Passengers, especially teenage passengers, are a major source of distraction. Cell phones also can distract drivers, as previously discussed.

Communications and Outreach

COMMUNICATIONS AND OUTREACH ON FATIGUED DRIVING

Fatigued or drowsy driving occurs when drivers do not get enough sleep. States and national organizations, such as the National Sleep Foundation, have conducted drowsy driving communications and outreach campaigns directed to the general public. Campaign goals usually include:

▶ Raising awareness of the dangers of drowsy driving
▶ Motivating drivers to take action to reduce drowsy driving

Stopping at a rest area to get out of the car for fresh air can reduce the chances of having an accident.

▶ Providing information on what drivers can do, either before they start out on a trip or if they become drowsy while driving

The NHTSA identified three groups that are over-involved in drowsy driving crashes: drivers in their teens and 20s, shift workers, and people suffering from sleep apnea or narcolepsy. Their report to Congress on drowsy driving recommended that communications and outreach on drowsy driving be directed to these groups, especially to young drivers. This information can be delivered in several ways. Driver education programs can include information on both drowsy and distracted driving, and the model curriculum developed by the NHTSA and the American Driver and Traffic Safety Education Association (ADTSEA) includes both.

Communications and outreach campaigns can be delivered in high schools, colleges, military training programs and bases, and other locations where there are many young drivers. Many young drivers have part-time jobs, which place them at even higher risks for drowsy driving.

Communications and outreach by themselves rarely change driving behavior. Stand-alone campaigns must have careful planning, good target audience identification, good message development, and substantial funding.

An additional barrier is that drowsy driving is a byproduct of busy lifestyles that do not include enough sleep. The only truly effective method to prevent drowsy driving crashes is to get enough sleep. Traffic safety messages urging enough sleep may be overwhelmed by the other demands on a driver's time that are responsible for insufficient sleep.

COMMUNICATIONS AND OUTREACH ON DISTRACTED DRIVING

Distracted driving communications and outreach campaigns for the general public face different, but equally difficult, obstacles than drowsy driving campaigns. All drivers "know" at some level that they should be alert. Distractions outside the car are not under the driver's control. Many distractions inside the car also cannot be controlled easily (e.g., conversations, children) or are intentional (e.g., listening to the radio or CD player, eating). However, some of these distractions may in fact be useful to keep drivers alert on a long trip.

As discussed previously, communications and outreach by themselves rarely change driving behavior. To have any chance, stand-alone campaigns must have careful planning, good target audience identification and research, good message development and placement, and substantial funding. A broad "stay alert" message may be too general to have any impact.

Other Strategies

EMPLOYER PROGRAMS

Driver fatigue and distractions are critical issues for commercial drivers. Shift workers are another employment group at high risk for drowsy driving crashes. Young male drivers with part-time jobs especially are at high risk because they satisfy two of the three high-risk conditions identified by NHTSA, which are shift workers, young drivers (especially males), and drivers with medical conditions of sleep apnea or narcolepsy. Shift workers include people who work long or irregular hours or who work at night. The NHTSA has produced a comprehensive workplace education program for shift workers. It includes information on sleep habits in general and drowsy driving in particular. Program material includes a video, posters, brochures for workers and their families, tip cards, a PowerPoint training session, and an administrator's guide.

MEDICAL CONDITIONS AND MEDICATIONS

Two medical conditions can cause drivers to fall asleep at the wheel:

1. Sleep apnea is a breathing disorder characterized by brief interruptions of breathing during sleep, perhaps as many as 20 to 60 per hour. By fragmenting nighttime sleep, sleep apnea produces daytime sleepiness. The National Sleep Foundation estimates that about 4 percent of men and 2 percent of women are affected by sleep apnea. It can be treated by physical or mechanical therapy or by surgery.
2. Narcolepsy is a disorder of the central nervous system's sleep-wake mechanism that can cause narcoleptics to fall asleep suddenly at any time. It is quite rare, affecting about one person in 2,000. It can be treated with medications.

The number of crashes resulting from sleep apnea or narcolepsy is not known. Most cases of sleep apnea or narcolepsy are undiagnosed and untreated. Falling asleep at the wheel may be one of the main ways to raise the possibility of a sleep disorder and motivate a driver to seek medical care. Even without treatment, drivers who are aware that they have one of these disorders can take precautions to avoid falling asleep at the wheel.

Many common prescription and over-the-counter medications can cause drowsiness. Warning labels on the medications note this and caution users against driving or other activities that could be affected by drowsiness. As with sleep apnea and narcolepsy, the number of crashes resulting from or affected by drowsiness produced by medications is unknown.

The principal strategies to address sleep apnea, narcolepsy, and medication effects are:

1. Communications and outreach on sleep disorders to increase overall awareness of their symptoms, consequences, and treatment.
2. Efforts with driver licensing medical advisory boards to increase their awareness of these conditions as they review driver fitness for licensing.
3. Efforts with physicians to increase their awareness of these conditions and their potential effects on driving, to treat these conditions as appropriate, and to counsel their patients to take steps to reduce the risk of drowsy driving.

Motorcycle Safety

A two-wheeled motorcycle is inherently more difficult to operate and more unstable than a four-wheeled passenger vehicle. A motorcycle offers riders almost no protection in a crash. The NHTSA estimates that 80 percent of motorcycle crashes injure or kill a motorcycle rider, while only 20 percent of passenger car crashes injure or kill an occupant.

Motorcycle Operator Training and Licensing

OPERATOR EDUCATION AND TRAINING

Motorcycle operator education and training has been thoroughly integrated into all aspects of motorcycle safety. The NHTSA's motorcycle safety program guideline states that "safe motorcycle operation requires specialized training by qualified instructors" and recommends that states conduct education and training. Many states encourage training either by requiring it for all motorcycle operators under a specified age or by waiving some licensing or testing requirements for motorcycle operators who complete an approved training course. Education and training enjoys broad support from the motorcycle industry, motorcycle user organizations, and motorcyclists. The Motorcycle Safety foundation offers instructor training.

OPERATOR LICENSING

All states require motorcyclists to obtain a motorcycle operator license or endorsement before they ride on public highways. The goal of licensing is to assure that motorcyclists have the minimum skills needed to operate a motorcycle safely.

Motorcycle Helmets

STATE MOTORCYCLE HELMET USE LAWS

Motorcycle helmets are highly effective in protecting motorcycle riders' heads in a crash. Helmets reduce motorcycle rider fatalities by over 37 percent.

State helmet use laws are effective in assuring that almost all motorcycle riders wear helmets. Helmet use is 80 percent in states with a universal helmet law that covers all riders and about 46 percent in states with no law or a law covering only young riders. States that repeal universal helmet laws have use rates dropped from well above 90 percent to about 50 percent.

The first universal helmet law was enacted in 1966. Universal laws were in force in 47 states and in the District of Columbia by 1975. After federal penalties were eliminated in 1975 for states failing to have a universal law, about half the states repealed their laws. Several states have enacted or repealed helmet laws since then.

Helmet law opponents claim that helmet laws impinge on individual rights. They also claim that helmets interfere with motorcycle riders' vision or hearing, though research shows that these effects are minimal.

State helmet use laws are highly effective in assuring that almost all motorcycle riders wear helmets.

MOTORCYCLE HELMET LAW ENFORCEMENT: NONCOMPLIANT HELMETS

Law enforcement officers in universal helmet law states can easily observe and cite motorcycle riders who are not wearing a helmet. This likely explains why helmet use rates are well above 90 percent in universal helmet law states. However, some helmets are noncompliant in that they do not meet the FMVSS 218 performance requirements. State helmet laws require motorcycle riders to wear helmets that comply with FMVSS 218. Almost one-fifth of the helmets worn are noncompliant. Motorcycle riders wearing these helmets are no safer than if they wore no helmets at all.

In addition to flimsy construction, noncompliant helmets often cover only a portion of the rider's head and have inadequate chin straps. Compliant helmets are formally identified by a DOT sticker on the back of the helmet. However, counterfeit DOT stickers are easily available and are found on many noncompliant helmets.

MOTORCYCLE HELMET USE PROMOTION PROGRAMS

A few states with no motorcycle helmet use laws have attempted to promote helmet use through communications and outreach campaigns. These campaigns can be expensive to develop and implement.

Alcohol Impairment

DETECTION AND SANCTION

Alcohol impairment is a substantial problem for motorcycle operators, more so than for drivers of other motor vehicles. Law enforcement officers on traffic patrol use characteristic driving behaviors, or cues, to identify drivers who may be impaired by alcohol. An example of this might be in having trouble maintaining balance at a stop.

Vehicle impoundment or forfeiture can be an effective deterrent to drinking and driving for all drivers. It may be even more effective for motorcyclists. Cyclists have strong concerns for the safety and security of their motorcycles.

Motorcyclist groups likely will object strenuously to any enforcement activities that are perceived to target motorcyclists unfairly. The best strategy is to assure that motorcyclists, rider organizations, and motorcycle dealers are included in planning and publicizing impaired riding enforcement.

MOTORCYCLE COMMUNICATIONS AND OUTREACH

Many states have conducted communications and outreach campaigns directed at drinking and motorcycling. Various organizations have produced campaigns and material on drinking and motorcycling. The experience of drinking and driving campaigns directed at all drivers suggests that they are unlikely to have any effect unless: they are carefully researched and planned, are well-funded and well-executed, achieve high levels of target audience exposure (perhaps using paid advertising), use high-quality messages that are pre-tested for effectiveness, and are conducted in conjunction with other activities directed at impaired motorcyclists.

Rider groups can play a critical role in planning and implementing activities to reduce drinking and motorcycling. Some state and local rider groups sponsor alcohol-free events or adopting alcohol-free policies.

Communications and Outreach

PROTECTIVE AND CONSPICUOUS CLOTHING

Motorcycle riders should wear clothing that provides both protection and visibility. FMVSS 218 helmets with face shields protect the eyes from wind and foreign objects in addition to protecting the head in a crash. Well-constructed jackets, pants, boots, and gloves can prevent abrasions and bruises. If made of impact-resistant material, the clothing even may prevent arm and leg fractures or serious torso and spinal cord injuries.

A common cause of motorcycle crashes involving other vehicles is that other vehicle drivers do not see the motorcycle. One easy way to increase motorcycle conspicuity is through lighted headlights. Most motorcycles on the road have their headlights always on, because most motorcycles manufactured since 1979 have this feature and because half the states require daytime headlight use for all motorcycles manufactured since 1980.

A second way to increase conspicuity is to wear brightly colored clothing (for increased visibility during daylight) incorporating some retro-reflective material (for increased visibility at night). Motorcyclists wearing conspicuous clothing or helmets are less likely to be involved in a crash.

There is no data on how many motorcycle riders wear various types of protective clothing other than helmets. Only a minority wears brightly colored clothing; in fact, the predominant color of motorcycle clothing is black. Helmet manufacturers and distributors report that more than half the helmets sold for street use are black.

AWARENESS OF MOTORCYCLISTS

When motorcycles crash with other vehicles, the other vehicle driver usually violates the motorcyclist's right-of-way. Motorcycles and motorcyclists obviously are a smaller visual target than cars or trucks. Also, drivers may not expect to see motorcycles on the road and may not anticipate how motorcycles are likely to be driven.

Several states have conducted communications and outreach campaigns to increase other drivers' awareness of motorcyclists. Typical themes are "Share the Road" or "Watch for Motorcyclists."

Young Drivers

Young drivers under 21 years of age are substantially involved in crashes.

Young drivers have high crash risks for two main reasons. First, they are inexperienced, just learning to drive. The mechanics of driving require much of their attention, so safety considerations frequently are secondary. They do not have experience in recognizing potentially risky situations or in reacting appropriately and controlling their vehicles in these situations. Second, they are immature, sometimes seeking risks for their own sake, often not able or willing to think ahead to the potentially harmful consequences of risky actions.

Inexperience and immaturity combine to make young drivers especially at-risk in these circumstances:

▶ At night: Driving is more difficult and dangerous at night for everyone, and young drivers have less experience driving at night than during the day. Also, they may be tired and may have been drinking.

▶ After drinking alcohol: Young drivers' inexperience with both driving and drinking means that they have a higher crash risk at all BAC levels than older drivers.

▶ With passengers: Passengers can distract young drivers and encourage them to take risks.

▶ When unbelted: Safety belts reduce the risk of injury or fatality in a crash, but teenage drivers and passengers have lower belt use rates than older drivers and passengers.

Graduated Driver Licensing

GDL is a three-phase system for beginning drivers, consisting of a learner's permit, a provisional (or intermediate) license, and a full license. A learner's permit allows driving only while supervised by a fully licensed driver. A provisional license allows unsupervised driving under certain restrictions. These usually include limits on driving at night or with teenage passengers. The learner's permit and the provisional license each must be held for a specified minimum period of time.

GDL serves two functions: reducing risk and reducing exposure. GDL allows beginning drivers to acquire driving experience in less-risky situations, under direct supervision during the learner's permit phase. It helps young drivers avoid dangerous conditions such as late-night driving or driving with teenage passengers in the vehicle during the provisional phase. GDL delays full licensure by requiring a minimum time in both the learner's permit and provisional phases. Compared to earlier requirements in many places, where beginning drivers could receive a full license at age 16 (and sometimes earlier) by passing a minimal driving test, GDL reduces the amount of driving by 16-year-old drivers. GDL also assures that young drivers are more mature when they receive their first unrestricted license. Most states now have some form of GDL in place.

GDL LEARNER'S PERMIT LENGTH AND SUPERVISED HOURS

With a learner's permit, a beginning driver can drive when supervised by a fully licensed driver at least 21 years of age. The learner's permit allows and encourages beginning drivers to acquire substantial driving experience. To aid this, most states require the learner's permit to be held for a minimum period of time and most require a minimum number of supervised driving hours.

GDL PROVISIONAL LICENSE NIGHTTIME RESTRICTIONS

Driving at night increases the fatal crash risk per mile of travel for all drivers, especially for teenage drivers. Night driving is more difficult, driver fatigue is more common, and alcohol is more likely to be used. For these reasons, a night driving restriction or prohibition is the most common provisional license restriction. The restricted hours vary widely, from "sunset to sunrise" or 6 PM to 6 AM in the most restrictive states to 1 AM to 5 AM in the least restrictive. The most common hours are midnight to 5 AM.

GDL PROVISIONAL LICENSE PASSENGER RESTRICTIONS

Passengers increase the crash risk for teenage drivers, especially the youngest drivers. Each additional passenger produces an additional increase in crash risk. In contrast, passengers decrease crash risk for drivers 20 to 59 years old.

GDL PROVISIONAL SEAT BELT USE REQUIREMENTS

Teenage drivers and passengers have lower seat belt use rates than older drivers and passengers. All states except New Hampshire have belt-use laws covering passengers of all ages, though the laws in over half the states exempt passengers in some seating positions or in some passenger vehicles. New Hampshire requires belt use by all passengers under 18.

GDL PROVISIONAL LICENSE CELL PHONE RESTRICTIONS

Cell phones may distract drivers. Cell phone distractions may pose greater risks for beginning drivers than for experienced drivers. To reduce this risk, a few states include cell phone restrictions in their GDL laws.

Driver Education

PRELICENSURE/DRIVER EDUCATION

Driver education has long been advocated and used to teach both driving skills and safe driving practices. Driver education in high schools grew in popularity in the 1950s, using a standard curriculum of at least 30 hours classroom instruction and 6 hours on-the-road driving practice. By about 1970, about 14,000 high schools taught driver education to about 70 percent of all eligible teenagers. Many states and insurance companies encouraged driver education by allowing driver education graduates to be licensed at an earlier age, and insurance companies reduced auto insurance premiums. During the 1980s, driver education offerings decreased as state and federal funding for driver education decreased. By the early 1990s, fewer than half of all high schools offered driver education and the majority of beginning drivers did not take driver education.

The evaluations to date find that driver education does not improve safety. Driver education lowers the age at which teenagers become licensed but does not affect their crash rates once they do become licensed. The net effect of driver education is to increase crashes because it puts more young drivers on the road.

The NHTSA dropped driver education from its list of priority highway safety program areas for states, but concluded that driver education should be integrated into a GDL program. It also concluded that driver education should be "distributed over time." NHTSA proposed a two-stage driver education system, both prelicensure and postlicensure.

As of July 2006, most states encouraged driver education by lowering the minimum learners, intermediate, or unrestricted licensing age for driver education graduates or by reducing the required number of supervised driving hours. These driver education "discounts" will likely increase crashes rather than reduce.

POST-LICENSURE OR SECOND-TIER DRIVER EDUCATION

As previously discussed, standard prelicensure driver education leads to earlier licensure, but does not reduce crash rates. Based on this conclusion, recent driver education research sought to develop post-licensure driver education curricula and to integrate driver education with GDL. These "second-tier" postlicensure courses teach safety-related information, building on the on-road experience that the students have acquired in their initial months of driving. They should not be confused with advanced driving performance courses that teach driving skills such as panic braking, skid control, and evasive lane-changing maneuvers.

Previous postlicensure driver education courses were remedial, directed at drivers who had accumulated enough violations or crashes to warrant some attention. For this audience, driver education had no effect. Postlicensure driver education is still under development and is not in regular use in any state.

Parents

PARENTAL ROLE IN TEACHING AND MANAGING YOUNG DRIVERS

Most parents are heavily involved in teaching driving skills to their beginning teenage drivers and supervising their driving while they have a learner's permit. Parents are in the best position to enforce GDL restrictions for provisional drivers, and many parents impose additional driving restrictions on their teenagers. Some parents strongly support GDL, but many parents do not understand the dangers of high-risk situations, such as driving with teenage passengers.

Older Drivers

As drivers age, their physical and mental abilities, driving behaviors, and crash risks all change, though age itself does not determine driving performance. Many features of the current system of roads, traffic signals and controls, laws, licensing practices, and vehicles are not designed to accommodate older drivers. Older Americans are increasingly dependent on driving to maintain their mobility, independence, and health. The challenge is to balance mobility for older drivers with safety for all road users. Certain changes, however, are inevitable as drivers age. These include:

- ▶ Physical capabilities diminish. Hearing, muscle tone, reaction time, and vision (especially at night) all decline, though at very different rates for different people.
- ▶ Fragility increases. The same force produces more serious injuries to a 70-year-old than to a 20-year-old. Injuries take longer to heal.
- ▶ Older drivers use more medications, which may be necessary to control disease or health conditions but also may cause drowsiness or otherwise affect driving. Older drivers are less likely than younger people to be impaired by alcohol or recreational drugs.
- ▶ Older drivers rarely drive aggressively or speed, but they may exhibit other risky behaviors such as driving more slowly than prevailing traffic or not accurately judging the speed of an oncoming vehicle while making a left turn.

Some courses designed for senior citizens focus on how to adjust driving to accommodate age-related cognitive and physical changes.

▶ Most older drivers reduce their driving mileage as their lifestyles change. Many older drivers voluntarily do not drive in situations where they feel uncomfortable, such as at night, on high-speed roads, or in unfamiliar situations.

Formal Courses for Older Drivers

Formal courses specifically for older drivers are offered by organizations including the American Automobile Association (AAA), AARP (formerly the American Association of Retired Persons), and National Safety Council (NSC). AARP's Driver Safety Program, formerly called "55-Alive," is the oldest and largest. The courses typically involve 6 to 10 hours of classroom training in basic safe driving practices and in how to adjust driving to accommodate age-related cognitive and physical changes. In 2006, 34 states and the District of Columbia mandated automobile insurance discounts for graduates of accredited courses. None of the courses have shown to reduce crashes, but have reduced citations and, in some cases, changed driving behaviors.

General Communications and Education

Many organizations offer educational material for older drivers to inform them of driving risks, help them assess their driving knowledge and capabilities, suggest methods to adapt to and compensate for changing capabilities, and guide them in restricting their driving in more risky situations.

Licensing

LICENSE RENEWAL POLICIES: IN-PERSON RENEWAL, VISION TEST

Drivers licenses in most states are valid for 4 to 6 years, longer in a few states. To renew an expiring license, drivers in many states must appear in person, pay the license fee, and have new pictures taken for their licenses. Some states require a vision test for license renewal. Some states allow some drivers to renew by mail or electronically.

More than half the states change license renewal requirements for drivers older than a specified age, typically 65 or 70. These changes may include a shorter interval between renewals, in-person renewal (no renewal by mail or electronically), or a vision test at every renewal. A very few states require written or road tests for some older renewal applicants.

License examiners report that the driver's appearance at the motor vehicle office is the single most important criterion for identifying a person of any age whose driving skills may be impaired. Frequent in-person renewals and vision tests may be more useful for older drivers than for younger drivers because their abilities may change more quickly.

REFERRING OLDER DRIVERS TO LICENSING AGENCIES

Licensing agencies in all states accept reevaluation referrals for drivers of any age. A survey of state licensing agencies found that 85 percent of referrals came from three sources: 37 percent from law enforcement, 35 percent from physicians and other medical professionals, and 13 percent from family and friends. The remaining 15 percent came from crash and violation record checks, courts, self-reports, and other sources.

LICENSE RESTRICTIONS

If a state licensing agency determines through screening, assessment, medical referrals, road tests, or other means that a driver poses excessive risks in certain situations, the driver can be issued a restricted license. This process of graduated delicensing preserves the driver's mobility while protecting the driver, passengers, and others on the road. Drivers whose vision is adequate during daylight hours but not at night present an obvious example. Their licenses can be restricted to daylight driving only. Other common restrictions limit driving to a specific geographical area, such as the town or county where the driver lives or limiting driving only to low-speed roads.

Law Enforcement Roles

Law enforcement plays three overall roles in improving safety of older drivers:

- ▶ Enforce traffic laws. In particular, active publicized enforcement of seat belt use laws can help increase belt use for older drivers and occupants.
- ▶ Identify drivers with potential driving impairments and refer them to licensing agencies. Traffic stops and crash investigations provide officers excellent opportunities to observe and evaluate driving behavior.
- ▶ Provide information and education. Law enforcement officers have formed many partnerships with public and private organizations to give talks, teach safe driving courses, work with media on news stories and public service announcements (PSAs), and work on other communications and outreach initiatives.

Child Passengers

For children up to 4 years of age, correctly installed child safety seats reduce the risk of death by 70 percent for infants and by about 50 percent for toddlers (aged 1–4 years). If all children in this age group rode in safety seats, almost 140 lives could be saved each year.

Some groups of children are at greater risk than others. Child safety seat ownership and use are lower among rural populations and low-income families.

Child safety seat laws require children traveling in motor vehicles to be buckled into federally approved infant or child safety seats that are appropriate for the child's age and size.

Child Safety Seat Laws*

Child safety seat laws require children traveling in motor vehicles to be buckled into federally approved infant or child safety seats that are appropriate for the child's age and size. All states currently have child safety seat laws in place. The laws, which vary from state to state, specify the children they cover in terms of age, height, weight, or a combination of these factors. All the laws allow for primary enforcement, which means that a driver can be stopped, cited, or fined simply for not restraining child passengers properly. The laws apply to children of various ages; some apply to children up to 1 year old and others apply to children up to 5 years old. Most laws do not specify a seating position. The various laws allow for penalties ranging from an oral warning to a monetary fine. One barrier to strengthening or enhancing enforcement of these laws may be resistance to such changes by people who believe that the laws limit parental discretion.

Distribution and Education Programs

Distribution and education programs provide free or low-cost child safety seats to parents, along with education about proper use of the seats. The idea behind such programs is that parents who cannot afford a safety seat might be more likely to use it if they receive financial help in acquiring a safety seat and learn about the importance of using it. However, only new safety seats, not used or refurbished ones, should be distributed, because the safety of seats previously involved in crashes cannot be guaranteed.

Community-Wide Information and Enhanced Enforcement Campaigns

Community-wide information and enhanced enforcement campaigns provide information about child safety seats and child motor vehicle safety to an entire community (usually defined geographically). These campaigns use several approaches: mass media, publicity, safety seat displays in public places, and special law enforcement strategies, such as checkpoints, dedicated law enforcement officials, or alternative penalties (e.g., warnings instead of tickets).

Incentive and Education Programs

Incentive and education programs reward parents for obtaining and correctly using child safety seats or directly reward children for correctly using safety seats. These programs also include educational components of varying intensity.

---

*This section is adapted from Centers for Disease Control and Prevention. Motor Vehicle Occupant Injury. www.thecommunityguide.org/mvoi. Accessed: August, 2007.

In these programs, the rewards—ranging from inexpensive trinkets, stickers, or coupons for fast food meals or movies to relatively expensive prizes donated by community merchants—are distributed constantly over program periods ranging from 1 to 5 months. Parents are shown correct use of safety seats to receive rewards. The larger rewards are provided to randomly selected eligible participants. Some programs also give small rewards to all eligible participants.

Programs include educational components of varying intensity. Some programs simply provide information about the reward program itself, whereas others provide information about existing laws on safety seat use and the importance of using safety seats. Programs also vary in how they provide information. Some use only brochures or other printed materials; others use more interactive educational and behavioral techniques, such as supervised practice of correct safety seat use, signed pledge cards, and educational videos and DVDs.

Education Programs Used Alone

Education programs provide information to parents, children, or professional groups about the importance of child safety seats and how to use them properly. The goal of providing information is to give people knowledge, skills, and reasons for behavior change and for instituting new policies.

Pedestrians

A pedestrian is defined as any person not in or upon a motor vehicle or other vehicle. It includes persons injured while using a coaster wagon, child's tricycle, or roller skates. It excludes persons boarding, alighting, jumping, or falling from a motor vehicle in transport who are considered occupants of the vehicle (National Safety Council, 2007). During 2005, 6,200 pedestrians were killed and 70,000 injured in motor vehicle crashes in the United States. Most pedestrian fatalities occur in urban areas, at nonintersection locations, in normal weather conditions, and at night. More than two-thirds of the pedestrians killed are males (National Safety Council, 2007).

Epidemiological information identifies the factors involved in pedestrian injuries and deaths.

Age. Pedestrians over 70 years of age account for about 16 percent of all pedestrian fatalities. This age group has a higher fatality rate than for any other age group. Older persons often are hampered by reduced vision and hearing, slow walking, and reduced decision-making capabilities.

Nearly one-fifth of all children between the ages of 5 and 9 who are killed in traffic crashes are pedestrians. Children age 15 and younger account for 8 percent of the pedestrian fatalities.

Most pedestrain fatalities occur in urban areas, at non-intersection locations, in normal weather conditions, and at night.

Toddlers between ages 1 and 2 are more likely to be injured, usually in a driveway and when a vehicle is backing up. Most injuries involving preschool and school-age children occur as a child darts out midblock between parked vehicles.

Time of day and day of the week. Over 40 percent of under 16 years of age fatalities occur in crashes between 3 PM and 7 PM. Nearly one-half of all pedestrian fatalities occur on Friday, Saturday, or Sunday.

Alcohol involvement. Alcohol involvement—either for the driver or for the pedestrian—is reported in 44 percent of the traffic crashes that killed a pedestrian.

Socioeconomic. Pedestrians living in poor neighborhoods are at higher risk due to a lack of defined sidewalks.

Interventions

A variety of pedestrian interventions exist. Rather than implementing a single intervention for this injury problem, as with most injury problems, several interventions should be considered.

Young Children

CHILDREN'S SAFETY CLUBS

Very young children have limited abilities to perceive traffic hazards, little experience with which to anticipate and interpret, and limited abilities to reason and react. They are not developmentally capable of making the kinds of perceptions and judgments necessary to successfully negotiate motorized traffic. Motor vehicles crashes involving preschool children often involve slow-moving vehicles. Frequently backing up in driveways and parking lots. It is important to teach children age-appropriate lessons about traffic. It is even more important that parents and caregivers take direct responsibility and supervise young children carefully.

Safety clubs are a proven way to promote understanding and to teach a specific set of appropriate behaviors for young pedestrians. However, the knowledge and skill benefits have not been found to translate into crash and injury reductions. An equally important outcome of safety clubs is for parents and caregivers to recognize their charges' limits and to understand their own obligation to maintain supervisory control.

NHTSA has a number of brochures on child pedestrian safety, as does Safe Kids Worldwide. The main development of safety clubs took place in Europe a number of years ago, but they have not been adopted broadly in the U.S. There do not appear to be any national or statewide standards, models, or curricula.

CHILD SUPERVISION

Programs to increase the supervision of children when they are exposed to traffic, or when they are nearby with direct access to traffic, can be an asset to anyone responsible for supervising children. States can require such programs for teachers, day care workers, and others licensed to care for children. The programs can also be made available to parents, babysitters, or other caretakers through PTAs, churches, pediatricians, or even direct mail and Internet access.

One of the ways to "sell" these programs may be to point out that parents do not know how much their children need supervision. Parents consistently overestimate the ability of children to negotiate in traffic.

School Age

ELEMENTARY SCHOOL PEDESTRIAN TRAINING

A number of elementary school pedestrian training programs have been developed. "Willy Whistle" was developed in the 1970s as a film to teach K–3 children to look Left-Right-Left before crossing. It has been updated in a video format.

NHTSA-developed materials for grades 4–6, including two videos, "Keep on Looking" and "Walking with Your Eyes." These programs are useful to teach basic pedestrian concepts and safe behaviors at schools, churches, and other institutions with groups of elementary-age children.

SAFETY ROUTES TO SCHOOL

Safe Routes to School (SR2S) packages are available from NHTSA. The materials are effective in teaching young children and their parents how to evaluate and choose the best routes for walking or bicycling to and from school. See Safe Routes to School News at www.walkinginfo.org for information on SR2S programs around the United States.

"ICE CREAM VENDOR" ORDINANCE

One very specific hazard for children is the neighborhood ice cream truck. As children run to or from the truck, they may pay little attention to traffic. The truck may screen the children from drivers. The ordinance requires that drivers come to a complete stop before passing an ice cream truck that is stopped to vend. Drivers may proceed when it is safe at no more than 15 mph and must yield to all nearby pedestrians. The ice cream truck must be equipped with flashing signal lamps and a stop signal arm, similar to those found on school buses, which can be activated when the truck is stopped for vending. When tested in Detroit, crashes to pedestrians going to or from ice cream trucks were reduced by 77 percent.

CHILD SCHOOL BUS TRAINING

School buses are an extremely safe form of transportation, and children are far safer traveling to school on a school bus than in other ways. Approximately 800 children have died in traffic crashes in each recent year during normal school travel hours. On average, only 5 were school bus passengers and 15 were pedestrians near a school bus.

Basic training for children who ride school buses should be part of the normal school routine, if it is not already. Training should include behavior on the bus as well as getting on or off the bus at bus stops or school, obeying bus drivers and bus monitors, and any topics unique to the school.

Adults

MODEL ROAD WORK SITE LAWS

Road work sites are very hazardous. A number of countermeasures are common for work sites, including double fines, awareness campaigns (e.g., "Slow down.

My daddy/mommy works here!"), requirements for worksite signing, lighting, traffic control, and heightened enforcement.

PEDESTRIAN SAFETY ZONES

About 20 percent of all pedestrian fatalities and 8 percent of all pedestrian injuries occur to pedestrians age 67 and older. About one-third of their fatalities and two-thirds of their injuries occur at intersections. Countermeasures include signal retiming, providing communications and outreach for both drivers and pedestrians living near the zones, and enhanced enforcement.

Impaired Pedestrians

COMMUNICATIONS AND OUTREACH

About one-third of all fatally injured pedestrians have a positive blood alcohol concentration of .08 or higher. Most are young adult males. Some of the countermeasures for impaired drivers, such as responsible beverage service training and alternative transportation, are also appropriate for impaired pedestrians.

Communications and outreach to reduce impaired-pedestrian crashes can be directed at a wide variety of audiences. Recommended target audiences include drivers, alcohol servers and vendors, civic and neighborhood leaders, and friends and family of likely impaired pedestrians. Likely impaired pedestrians are also a target audience, of course. It is felt that reaching others who are in a position to prevent these crashes, or to alter the circumstances that lead up to such crashes, is the most effective way to achieve success.

PEDESTRIAN "SWEEPER" PATROLS

Pedestrians with high BACs are at high risk of injury due to motor vehicle crashes. A program of removing or "sweeping" inebriated pedestrians from the streets until they no longer have high BACs can be effective in reducing the exposure and thus the risk. There are some issues that need to be resolved when setting up sweeper programs, such as how to identify at-risk pedestrians (e.g., calls from bars or direct observers, observation by police or health professionals), who picks up the targets, where they are kept until they sober up, whether friends or family need to be notified at the time of the pickup, how the pedestrians are returned home after the intervention, and how the costs of the program are born.

Such programs typically reach only a fraction of those people who need the services. The sweeps typically deal with persons who are too drunk to walk or even know that they are being "swept." These same people are at risk while they are becoming intoxicated, and, in all likelihood, will be at risk again in the future as they start to sober up. These individuals need intensive treatment for alcoholism; sweeper programs may be useful in identifying potential treatment candidates.

All Pedestrians

REDUCED SPEED LIMITS

Higher vehicle speeds produce more and more serious pedestrian crashes and casualties. Reducing speeds through lowering speed limits is a time-honored countermeasure. For maximum effectiveness, speed limit reductions need to be accompanied by communications and outreach, which inform the public and make the case for the reduction and by heightened, visible enforcement. Just changing the speed limits is of limited, though positive, effectiveness. Some reasons for this include drivers simply not noticing if just old signs are updated, drivers not understanding any reason to reduce speed, or drivers continuing to keep up with the speeds maintained by other drivers.

DAYLIGHT SAVING TIME

Daylight saving time shifts an hour of daylight from the morning, when pedestrian traffic, crashes, and injuries are lighter, to the afternoon, when pedestrian traffic, crashes, and injuries are heavier. In daylight, pedestrians and drivers can see each other better. Shifting the hour of daylight by means of daylight saving time reduces afternoon crashes by many more than it adds in the morning.

CONSPICUITY ENHANCEMENT

Pedestrians who are more visible are less likely to be struck. Retro-reflective materials are built into many shoes. Other materials, such as arm or leg bands, gloves, vests, and caps are available. Light sources, including strobes and other flashing lights, are also available. Many have been designed for bicyclists but are equally applicable to pedestrians. The difficulty with most of these devices is that the user must decide in advance to take and use them. Because of this extra step, and because most of the conspicuity enhancements do not look like "normal" clothing, they are very much underused. Light-colored clothing, long a recommended solution, does virtually nothing to improve conspicuity.

DRIVER TRAINING

Training for new drivers typically includes relatively little information on other road users. Information on pedestrians can be significantly strengthened by including specific information on right of way requirements for driver and pedestrian and key ways drivers can avoid being involved in pedestrian crashes.

TARGETED ENFORCEMENT

Once pedestrians and drivers are informed of the changes needed in walking or driving actions and habits, and why they are important, enforcement often is necessary to encourage compliance. Enforcement is most effective when it is highly visible and publicized, to reinforce the message of the required behavior and to raise the expectation that failure to comply may result in legal consequences.

ROAD ENGINEERING

To help pedestrians get safely across intersections or crosswalks, these interventions are available:

▶ Increase lighting at pedestrian crosswalks. Nighttime pedestrian activity is inherently dangerous, and pedestrians who can be illuminated by street lights are less likely to be hit by a motor vehicle.
▶ "No turn on red" signs that prohibit turns during a red light when pedestrians are using the intersection. More stringent are "right-turn-on-red" laws prohibiting all right turns at intersection regardless of a pedestrian's presence.
▶ Red light photo enforcement cameras. A red light camera is a system that automatically detects whether a vehicle has run a red light, and if so, photographs the car's license plate. The vehicle's owner is sent a ticket or warning.
▶ Push buttons. Pedestrian push buttons actuate the walk signal where pedestrian activity is infrequent.
▶ Flashing crosswalk lights. These are a series of lights embedded in the pavement adjacent to the crosswalk and facing oncoming vehicles. The lights shine toward approaching traffic to warn drivers of a pedestrian's presence.
▶ Countdown signs. A countdown signal is a visible timer incorporated into a standard "Walk/Don't Walk" signal that counts down the total crossing time remaining before the red light.
▶ Parking. Banning the parking of vehicles near crosswalk locations so that drivers and pedestrians can see each other.

Bicyclists

The estimated number of deaths from bicycle-motor vehicle collisions was about 1,000 bicyclists in 2005 with an estimated 51,000 nonfatal disabling injuries (National Safety Council, 2007).

The first motor vehicle crash in the United States occurred in New York City in 1896, when a motor vehicle collided with a bicycle rider. Bicyclist deaths account for 2 percent of all traffic fatalities. Bicyclist fatalities occur more frequently in urban areas, at nonintersection locations, between the hours of 5 PM and 9 PM, and during the months of June, July, and August. Epidemiological data identifies other factors involved in bicyclist injuries and deaths.

Age. The average age of those killed is around 38. Bicyclists under age 16 accounted for 18 percent of all bicyclists killed. Bicyclists 25 years of age and older have made up an increasing proportion of all bicyclist deaths. Nearly one-fifth of the bicyclists killed in traffic crashes were between 5 and 15 years old.

Alcohol involvement. Alcohol involvement—either for the driver or the bicyclist—is reported in more than one-third of the traffic crashes that resulted in bicyclist fatalities.

Gender. Most (about 90 percent) of the bicyclists killed or injured are males, and most are between the ages of 5 and 44 years.

Pathophysiology

Most bicycle-related injuries occur to the upper or lower extremities, followed by the head, face, abdomen, and neck. Most involve superficial trauma such as abrasions ("road rash"), contusions, and lacerations. Road rash can range from superficial abrasions to those involving partial or full skin thickness requiring removal of embedded debris to prevent "traumatic tattooing." One of the most serious types of injury associated with bicycles is traumatic brain injury.

Brain Injuries

Traumatic brain injuries (TBI) can result in long-term, negative health effects (e.g., memory loss, behavioral changes). Increased awareness of TBI risks and prevention strategies is essential for reducing the incidence, severity, and long-term negative health effects.

Concussion. A blow to the head or face may cause a concussion. A concussion is a temporary loss or alteration of part or all of the brain's abilities to function without physical damage to the brain. A concussion may result in unresponsiveness.

Contusion. The brain can sustain a contusion or bruise. A contusion is far more serious than a concussion because it involves physical injury to the brain tissue, which may result in permanent damage. With contusions, there is associated bleeding and swelling from injured blood vessels. Injury of brain tissue or bleeding inside the skull will cause an increase of pressure within the skull.

Interventions

While much of the focus for bicyclist safety focuses upon helmet use, other interventions also play a major role in protecting the bicyclist.

Children

BIKE FAIRS AND BIKE RODEOS

Young children are just learning about traffic. They have limited abilities to perceive traffic hazards, little experience with which to anticipate and interpret what may happen, and limited abilities to reason and react. Their brains are still developing, and they lack the maturity and judgment needed to negotiate traffic safely and limit risk-taking behaviors. They also are less able to ride than adults. Their bicycles often are smaller and less stable, and most children are not able to maintain the same speeds that adults can. Bike fairs and rodeos cannot correct the physical shortcomings, but they can teach youngsters about traffic laws that apply to them and how to ride defensively in a number of typical traffic conditions.

A bike fair or rodeo is an event that provides children an opportunity to learn and practice bicycling skills. A rodeo typically has several stations for specific skills and also includes bicycle and helmet inspections. They are local events often run by the police, school personnel, or health educators. There may be permanent

Helmets have proved to offer protection in preventing brain injuries when a crash occurs, even those involving motor vehicles.

"neighborhood" layouts where the rodeos are conducted, and the events may be scheduled as part of the elementary and middle school curriculum.

BICYCLE EDUCATION IN SCHOOLS

A bicycle education curriculum offered in schools can teach traffic laws and how to ride on streets with traffic present. As part of the regular curriculum, the courses can reach every student. Most courses can include helmet fitting and wearing. In addition, the course could include pedestrian training, making it part of a comprehensive traffic safety program.

BICYCLE HELMET LAWS FOR CHILDREN

Head injury poses the greatest risk to bicyclists—resulting in almost 70 percent of the deaths due to crashes. Helmets have been proved to offer protection in preventing brain and face injuries when a crash occurs, even those involving motor vehicles. The Bicycle Helmet Safety Institute estimates that helmets reduce the risk of all head injuries by up to 85 percent and reduce the risk of brain injuries by as much as 88 percent.

The most common reasons given for not wearing a bicycle helmet include: "uncomfortable," "annoying," "it's hot," "don't need it," and "don't own one." Bicycle helmet use is significantly influenced by peer helmet use. Children are more likely to wear a bicycle helmet when their parents wear bicycle helmets.

A helmet use law is a significant tool in increasing helmet use. Its effectiveness is enhanced when combined with a supportive publicity and education campaign.

While helmets that meet safety requirements can be purchased for less than $10, programs may wish to provide free or discounted helmets to some children.

SAFE ROUTES TO SCHOOL FOR RIDERS

Safe Routes to School (SR2S) programs include identifying routes that are appropriate for bicycling and walking to school and improving the safety of those routes. The goal is to increase the amount of bicycling and walking trips to and from school while increasing the safety of those routes. SR2S packages are available from NHTSA that include student and instructor materials.

Adults

BICYCLE SAFETY IN DRIVER EDUCATION

Though driver education and state driver manuals address sharing the road with bicyclists, they spend relatively little time on the topic. Materials exist that could be used to increase the emphasis on driving around bicyclists.

BICYCLE HELMET LAWS FOR ADULTS

Bicycle helmets—when used properly—reduce head injuries and fatalities. Currently, no state requires adult bicyclists to wear helmets. About 40 communities, mostly in the state of Washington, require helmet use.

All Bicyclists

RIDER CONSPICUITY

A common contributing factor for crashes involving bicyclists in the roadway is the failure of the driver to detect and notice the bicyclist. New bicycles must be sold with reflectors meeting the Consumer Product Safety Commission requirements (though owners are free to remove them after the purchase). The reflectors significantly improve a bicycle's visibility when lit by vehicle lights. Even low beam headlights can illuminate figures hundreds of feet away, much farther than figures wearing normal clothing. Bright colored or white clothing is not detected much more readily than dark clothing.

Additional materials attached to bicyclists can increase their conspicuity day or night. For daytime, bright clothing, including vests, caps, and ankle and wrist straps, can make the bicyclist much more noticeable. At night, the same items can have retro-reflective materials incorporated in them, so that headlights can make the bicyclist visible and identifiable from much greater distances.

Use of bicycle reflectors is high. Use of retroreflective clothing is rare. Most, if not all, athletic shoes contain some retroreflective material. Some athletic clothing has retroreflective material. Bicycle helmets have retroreflective elements. Some bicyclists may be seen wearing additional retroreflective materials, such as vests, arm bands, or rear-mounted reflective triangles.

ACTIVE BICYCLE LIGHTING

In most places, bicycles ridden after dark are required to have active front and rear lights (i.e., devices that emit their own light, not just reflect light from automobile headlights or other external sources). Most bicycles do not have such lighting.

The laws for bicycle lightning typically specify lights on the bicycle. Though standard headlights and tail lights are continuously lit, bicycle lights that flash are more readily detected. Lights also may be strapped to the bicyclist's ankles, wrists, or elbows, where the motion of the rider makes them more detectable. Most active lights are not permanently mounted on bicycles, so they are often not available when needed.

TARGETED ENFORCEMENT

Enforcing laws concerning bicyclists requires focus on both motorists and bicyclists. While bicyclists often fail to follow the rules of the road as they are written for motor vehicles, motorists often fail to treat bicyclists as legitimate vehicles on the roads.

Bicyclists often take inappropriate paths, such as wrong-way riding, riding on sidewalks, and making left turns by creatively weaving through lanes and traffic. They also frequently ignore stop signs and red lights. Motorists may cut bicyclists off by overtaking and then turning through the bicyclist's path without allowing enough room, or by making a left turn in front of an oncoming bicyclist. Motorists also may pass without allowing enough space between the car and the bicycle or drive in or otherwise block a designated bicycle lane. All of these actions, and others, are enforceable offenses.

BICYCLE HELMET PROMOTIONS WITH EDUCATION

Bicycle helmet promotions are frequent, but all have been aimed at child bicyclists. Promotions can include sponsoring organizations and often involve police and schools to deliver helmets and teach their proper use. Promotions can be conducted through single events or extended campaigns to promote helmet distribution and use. Bicycle helmet promotions must include instruction on properly fitting and wearing the helmets.

BICYCLE LANES AND PATHS

Bicycle lanes are defined as portions of the roadway designated for the use of bicycles. Bicycle paths are defined as physically separated right of ways for the exclusive use of bicyclists and pedestrians.

Separating bicycles from motor vehicle traffic through dedicated bicycle paths reduces the risk of injury from collisions. There is some evidence that bicycle riding with the flow of traffic reduces the likelihood of a collision with a motor vehicle, and therefore riding should be restricted to the direction of motor vehicle travel.

References

Centers for Disease Control and Prevention. (2002). Guide to Community Preventive Services, *Motor Vehicle Occupant Injury.* http://www.thecommunityguide.org/mvoi. Accessed: August 2007.
National Highway Traffic Safety Administration, U.S. Department of Transportation. (2007). Countermeasures that work: A highway safety countermeasure guide for state highway safety offices. http://www.ghsa.org/html/publications/pdf/CountermeasuresThatWork_2007.pdf. Accessed: August 2007.

National Safety Council. (2007). Injury facts. Itasca, IL: National Safety Council.

Thygerson, A.L. (1992). Safety, 2nd edition. Sudbury, MA: Jones and Bartlett Publishers.

CHAPTER 10 ▶

Poisoning

There is no single agreed-upon definition of a poisoning. Each organization collecting data or providing services has its own definition. The implication of inconsistent definitions is profound for the measurement of the magnitude of poisonings and for the implementation of interventions. For this book, a poison is any substance with a chemical action that causes harm if it gets into the body. Harm can be mild (e.g., headache, nausea) or severe (e.g., seizures, high fever), and severely poisoned people may die.

Almost any chemical can be a poison if there is enough in the body. Some chemicals are poisonous in very small amounts (e.g., a spoonful by mouth); others are only poisonous if a large amount is taken (e.g., several cupfuls). The amount of a chemical substance that gets into the body at one time is called a dose. A dose that causes poisoning is a poisonous dose or toxic dose. The smallest amount that causes harm is the threshold dose. If the amount of a chemical substance that gets into the body is less than the threshold dose, the chemical will not cause poisoning and may even have good effects. For example, medicines have good effects if people take the right doses, but some can be poisonous if people take too much.

When people are in contact with a poison, they are *exposed* to it. The effect of exposure depends partly on how long the contact lasts and how much poison gets into the body. Exposures may be acute (single contact lasting for seconds, minutes, or hours, or several exposures over a day or less) or chronic (contact lasts for many days, months, or years and may be continuous or broken by periods when there is no contact). This book focuses on acute exposures and not chronic.

No single data source fully captures the total number of poisonings. Poison data in the United States come from:

▶ Poison control centers
▶ Emergency departments

- ▶ Hospital admissions
- ▶ Physician office visits
- ▶ Death certificate data

Magnitude of Poisoning

The vast majority of poison exposures are unintentional in all age groups. Therapeutic errors account for about 10 percent of exposures (Lai, 2005). Poisoning deaths are a major cause of unintentional death and remain an important cause of emergency department visits and hospitalizations.

Data about the number of people exposed to poisons come from the Toxic Exposure Surveillance System (TESS). The American Association of Poison Control Centers (AAPCC) compiles TESS data on poison exposure from phone calls received at U.S. poison control centers (American Association of Poison Control Centers, 2007). These poison control centers record about 2.5 million poisoning telephone calls annually. This number includes both unintentional and intentional poisonings (e.g., suicide). Not all poison exposures come to the attention of poison control centers (e.g., from private physicians or emergency departments).

Death statistics are derived from a national file of death certificate–derived data maintained by the National Center for Health Statistics. This data file is designed to capture all deaths on a yearly basis. This is the "universe" of observations, not a selected sample from which estimates of incidence are derived. This database indicates that unintentional poisoning deaths number over 19,000 annually (Lai, 2005).

The best data may be from the Institute of Medicine (2004), which makes a conservative estimate that the annual incidence of poisoning episodes in the United States is four million cases. Of these, about 300,000 cases may be hospitalized and an estimated 24,000 deaths (includes intentional and unintentional deaths).

Pathophysiology

Poisons can be classified into four types, according to how they enter the body (see Figure 10-1):

1. Inhalation
2. Absorption
3. Ingestion
4. Injection

Figure 10-1 Sources of poisons.

Inhaled poisons (breathed in). These poisons take the form of gases, vapors, and sprays. Many of these substances are in common use in the home, industry, and agriculture. Such poisons include carbon monoxide (from motor vehicle exhaust, wood-burning stoves, furnaces), ammonia, chlorine, insect sprays, and the gases produced from volatile liquid chemicals (including many industrial solvents). Some, such as carbon monoxide, are odorless and produce severe hypoxia without damaging or even irritating the lungs. Others, such as chlorine, are very irritating and cause airway obstruction and pulmonary edema.

Poison that gets into the lungs passes into the blood vessels very quickly because the air passages in the lungs have thin walls and a good blood supply.

Absorbed poisons (contact through the skin). Poisons that come in contact with the surface of the body can affect the victim in many ways. Many corrosive substances will damage the skin, mucous membranes, or eyes, causing chemical burns, rashes, or lesions. Acids, alkalis, and some petroleum products are very destructive. Other substances are absorbed into the bloodstream through the skin and have systemic effects, just like medications or drugs that are swallowed or injected.

Ingested poisons (swallowed). Between 75 and 80 percent of all poisoning is by mouth (ingestion) (Lai, 2005). Ingested poisons include medications, household and industrial cleaners, plants, petroleum products, and agricultural products made specifically to control rodents, weeds, insects, and crop diseases.

When poisons are swallowed, they go to the stomach. Some poisons can pass through the intestinal wall and into the blood vessels. The longer a poison stays in the digestive system, the more that will get into the blood and the worse the poisoning will be.

Injected poisons (inserted through the skin). Poisoning by injection is usually the result of drug abuse, such as heroin, cocaine, or methamphetamine—all are intentional actions that are not covered in this book. Unintentional injections include snakebite, insect stings, spider bites, and scorpion stings.

Poisons Inside the Body

Once a poison gets into the blood, it is carried through the whole body as the blood is pumped around the body by the heart. Some poisons are changed by the body into other chemicals called metabolites, and may be less or more poisonous than the original substance. The metabolites are more easily passed out of the body than the original chemicals. These changes take place mostly in the liver. Unchanged poisons or their metabolites usually leave the body in the urine, feces, sweat, or respiration.

The effects of a chemical substance on the body may be described as either local or systemic. A local effect is limited to the part of the body in contact with the chemical: the skin, the eyes, the airway, or the digestive system. Examples of local effects are skin rashes, skin burns, watery eyes, and irritation of the throat causing coughing.

A systemic effect is a more general effect. Systemic effects only happen when the amount of poison in the body is greater than the amount the body can get rid of, and the poison builds up and reaches the threshold level. Usually, when contact with a poison lasts only a short time (acute exposure), the effects happen soon after exposure and do not last very long.

Ways in which poisons can cause harm:

▶ Stopping the body from working properly (e.g., blocking the oxygen supply)
▶ Blocking messages between nerves
▶ Damaging the organs such as the brain, nerves, heart, liver, lungs, kidneys, or skin

Risk Factors for Ingested Poisoning

Risk factors include anything that increases a person's chance of becoming poisoned.

Age. Children younger than 6 years are involved in about 50 percent of exposures to poison (National Safety Council, 2007). When exposed to poison, children are more likely to suffer serious consequences because they are smaller, have faster metabolic rates, and their bodies are less capable of handling toxic chemicals.

However, the majority of poisons cause only minor symptoms and major health effects are uncommon.

All poisonings in young children are unintentional (Lai, 2005). However, with increasing age into the adolescent years, the likelihood increases that a poisoning is intentional where intentional and unintentional poisonings are equally divided. A profile of poisoned children shows that they are more likely to be impulsive and overactive, and may be discipline problems for their parents. Children are most susceptible to unintentional poisoning when family patterns are interrupted (e.g., moving, pregnancy, illness, death, marital problems).

In order to understand how unintentional poisoning occurs, it is essential to explore how poisoning is related to normal childhood development and behavior. Children under 1 year of age are relatively immobile and exist in a controlled environment. Once they begin to walk, however, their environment dramatically expands and becomes far less controlled. Young children become hungry and thirsty much more frequently than do older children and adults. They are attracted to objects that have a pleasant odor, are brightly colored, or are in familiar shapes. These same characteristics are used by manufacturers to make their products more marketable. Thus, many attractive objects that are potential toxins are available in the home. Because a young child's primary method of sampling is to taste, he or she is prone to ingest some of these potential toxins.

Pica, an abnormal craving for nonfood or unnatural food substances, is not fully understood. There are various theories as to why a child will eat a nonfood item (e.g., dirt, crayons, chalk, grass, soap, paper, plaster, twigs). Nutritional deficiencies, especially iron deficiency, were formerly thought to be responsible for the habit, but this theory has been challenged. A high level of anxiety in a child seems to be related to pica. At any rate, children will eat nonfood items—some more than others. The problem with eating nonfood items is that some of them may be poisonous.

By age 3, a child is adventurous. A dangerous time is prior to meals while children are hungry and are waiting to be fed. Thirst is another problem; in the warm months, the ingestion of poisonous liquids increases as children drink such substances as petroleum products, paint solvents, and pesticides.

Children over 3 years tend to be more selective in what they eat or drink, preferring things that taste good (e.g., flavored children's aspirin, vitamins).

Another factor in poisoning is parents calling medicine "candy" to induce children to take them during a sickness. To a child, this description seems reasonable because many drugs taste sweet and resemble familiar candies. Furthermore, parents often take products out of the original containers and keep them in food containers.

Still another factor that often leads to unintentional poisoning of young children is the strong influence of imitation. They see parents taking a certain substance and want to be like mom or dad, so they too swallow whatever the parent did.

Nonreaders are the most likely victims. The written words "caution," "warning," and "poison" mean nothing to the preschool child. It is thought that the traditional skull and crossbones may even attract children with its pirate connotation.

Children younger than 6 years old are involved in approximately 50 percent of poisonings.

Adults often do not recognize the capabilities of small children. There are three basic stages of development in young children from 6 months to 5 years of age in which natural tendencies to explore and experiment create situations that lead to unintentional poisonings. These three stages are:

1. The *Crawler*, age 6 months to 1 year. Everything goes into his or her mouth. His or her world is the floor and storage areas under the floor. The products he or she is most likely to find are household cleaners.
2. The *Toddler*, age 1 to 3 years. They have the highest poisoning rate of any age group. Their world includes the closet, tops of tables, stoves, and counters. Many cleaning products, medications, and cosmetics often are found in these places.
3. The *Climber*, age 3 to 5 years. It is at this stage of development that the child most often surprises his parents with his or her capabilities. Intrigued by high storage areas he or she has never been able to reach, the child can be most ingenious in creating ways to reach them.

Gender. Male children under age 13 are more likely than females of the same age to suffer unintentional poisoning exposures and death (National Safety Council, 2007). A profile of poisoned children shows that they are more likely to be impulsive and overactive and may be discipline problems for their parents; these characteristics may be found more often in male than female children.

Race. Black children ages 14 and under have a poisoning death rate more than one and a half times that of white children. Living in low-income communities and large metropolitan areas are contributing factors. Because the North American population is becoming more ethnically diverse, an increased proportion of ethnic groups in the population may result in increased poisonings (Institute of Medicine, 2004).

Location and time. About 90 percent of all poison exposures occur in a residence. Just over half of all poisoning deaths occur in the home. It can be generally concluded in cases of unintentional poisoning that the substances ingested were not only easily accessible, but also were not in their proper locations (e.g., left on cabinet tops). The kitchen exceeds all other areas in the home as the place for accessible poisons. Calls to poison control centers peak between 4 PM and 10 PM and during warmer months. The items in Table 10-1 can be found in most residences.

Interventions

Poison Prevention Packaging Act

This legislation, passed in 1970, requires toxic, corrosive, or irritative substances to be placed in child-resistant packaging so that children less than 5 years of age have difficulty opening them, but it is not too difficult for adults to open. It has been very successful in reducing unintentional poisoning (Hingley, 1997).

Poison Control Centers

Poison control centers are cost efficient and economical because more than 70 percent of cases are resolved over the telephone while the victim remains at home. This avoids unnecessary emergency department visits, ambulance use, and hospital admissions. Most of the victims fully recovered, and billions of dollars did not have to be spent on medical treatment (Lai, 2005).

Physicians, hospitals, public health departments, and the public depend on poison control centers to provide state-of-the-art emergency advice and treatment information 24 hours a day, 365 days of the year. The national telephone number is 1-800-222-1222.

A study by Wigder et al. (1995) found that the advice given by hospital emergency rooms was correct 64 percent of the time. In contrast, poison control centers gave correct advice 94 percent of the time.

Table 10-1 Ten Most Frequently Involved Substances in Child Exposures (Children Younger Than 6 Years)

Rank	Substance
1	Cosmetics/personal care products
2	Cleaning substances (household)
3	Analgesics
4	Foreign bodies/miscellaneous
5	Topical preparations
6	Cold and cough preparations
7	Plants
8	Pesticides
9	Vitamins
10	Antihistamines

Source: Lai, M.W., et al. Annual report of the American Association of Poison Control Centers' national poisoning and exposure database. Clinical Toxicology 44(6):821.

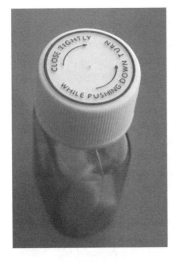

Child-resistant packaging has been very successful in reducing unintentional poisoning.

Poison Container Labels

Cautions and warnings on products play an important role in the prevention and treatment of poison exposures. Frequently those exposed will follow the directions before calling the poison control center, a physician, or the emergency department. A label review of 200 commercial products was conducted to determine if the medical treatment advice was correct, if the general public was able to comprehend the warning statements, and if the warnings were adequate. It was concluded that there are products available that provide precise, correct information. However, there are many that contain incorrect, misleading, and often dangerous information (Mrvos, 1986).

Several self-adhesive labels are available and frequently distributed in connection with poison control center activities. The stickers are meant to be placed on containers or hazardous materials in the home. One of the most widely used is "Mr. Yuk" (a pale green picture of a frowning face and a protruding tongue). Other stickers include the traditional skull and crossbones and "Officer Ugg" (a policeman with his hands over his mouth). Studies have shown that the stickers are not effective; as a matter of fact, children appear attracted to the stickers (Vernberg et al., 1984). Do not confuse these stickers with those on or near telephones with the poison control center's telephone number.

Community-Based Education Programs

Community-based educational efforts are designed to change the poison storage habits of parents of young children. Community-based programs need to be targeted to specific age groups and specific substances.

Storage of Poisonous Substances

Installing cabinet and drawer locks or latches have been highly recommended. However, they may not be widely accepted due to the cost, trouble to install, and inconvenience when opening a cabinet.

A study (Coyne-Beasley et al., 2005) found that poisons were stored less securely in homes with visiting young children compared to homes with resident young children. In 55 percent of homes where young children lived and in 74 percent of homes where young children were only visitors, household chemicals were stored unlocked. This study found that adults keep medicines out in the open (33 percent), in an unlocked drawer or cabinet (82 percent), and in their purse (42 percent). Strategies are needed to improve the storage practices of poisons to minimize these hazards to young children.

Ipecac Syrup–Induced Emesis

For decades, ipecac syrup–induced emesis (vomiting) has been used for ingested poison victims. However, its use plummeted after the American Academy of Clinical Toxicology and the European Association of Poison Centres and Clinical Toxicologists published a joint position statement on ipecac syrup that concluded that ipecac does not have a positive impact on a victim's outcome. These groups do not support the routine stocking of ipecac in households with young children. The American Academy of Pediatrics (AAP) published a policy statement that affirmed, "ipecac should no longer be used routinely in the home" (AAP, 2003).

The American Academy of Clinical Toxicology (2004) made an even stronger statement against ipecac's use by saying that there is no evidence from clinical studies that ipecac improves the outcome of poisoned victims and its routine administration in the emergency department should be abandoned. Ipecac may delay the administration or reduce the effectiveness of activated charcoal, oral antidotes, and whole bowel irrigation.

Activated Charcoal

Activated charcoal is recognized as the treatment of choice for many ingested poisonings. Activated charcoal use in the home has been limited by concerns that parents would not administer it properly and that children would refuse to take it. Researchers (Spiller and Rodgers, 2002; Eldridge et al., 2007) concluded that activated charcoal can be given successfully by the lay public in the home.

Poisonous Plants

A surprisingly small number of plant species account for the majority of plant poisonings. Furthermore, plants are a leading household poison. Children who balk at spinach apparently have no hesitancy in sampling leaves from the family's potted plants. Small children do not have a highly developed sense of taste, so they are not able to recognize a bad-tasting plant and spit it out.

Although most plants are not deadly, many can cause discomfort. Only certain parts of some plants, often the berries or bulbs, concentrate the toxin in dangerous amounts and perhaps only during certain times of the year.

Although most plants are not deadly, many can cause discomfort such as this poinsettia plant commonly found during the Christmas season.

Table 10-2 identifies the most prevalent poisonous plants. If the plant was ingested more than 12 hours before and no symptoms appeared, there is no problem. Symptoms usually appear within 4 hours. Only with mushrooms are symptoms delayed for more than 12 hours.

Inhaled Poisoning: Carbon Monoxide

Carbon monoxide (CO) is the leading cause of unintentional poisoning death in the United States. Each year, about 500 U.S. residents die from nonfire-related carbon monoxide poisoning. An estimated 15,000 persons with confirmed or possible nonfire-related CO exposure or poisoning are treated annually in hospital emergency departments (CDC, 2005; Lai, 2005).

Carbon monoxide poisoning cases are often underreported or misdiagnosed by medical professionals. Therefore, the precise number of victims who have suffered from CO is not known. Victims who survive the initial CO poisoning may still face the prospect of delayed neuralgic (nerve pain) dysfunction.

Table 10-2 Top Ten Plants for Poison Exposures

Rank	Common name	Botanical name
1	Peace lily	*Spathiphyllum ssp*
2	Pokeweed, inkberry	*Phytolacca Americana*
3	Poinsettia	*Euphorbia pulcherrima*
4	Philodendron	*Philodendron ssp*
5	Holly	*Ilex spp*
6	Poison ivy	*Toxicondendron radicans*
7	Oleander	*Nerium oleander*
8	Christmas cactus	*Schlumbergera bridgesii*
9	Jade plant	*Crassula argentea*
10	Dandelion	*Taraxacum officinale*

Source: Lai, M.W. et al. Annual report of the American Association of Poison Control Centers' national poisoning and exposure database. *Clinical Toxicology* 44(6):832.

Pathophysiology

Carbon monoxide is a colorless, odorless, and tasteless gas produced by burning material containing carbon; a person cannot see it, smell it, or taste it.

When air is breathed into the lungs, oxygen is transferred from the air to the blood. Oxygen attaches to a component of blood called hemoglobin; the hemoglobin carries the oxygen to the body's tissues. CO also is capable of attaching to the hemoglobin in the blood. If air contains carbon monoxide, it attaches to the hemoglobin in place of the oxygen because it can quickly bind with the hemoglobin 200 times quicker than that of oxygen (Auerbach, 2007).

If there is a lot of CO in the air, the body may replace oxygen in the blood with CO. This keeps life-sustaining oxygen from reaching the body's tissues. This adversely affects the brain and heart, which are very sensitive to CO poisoning (other organs are also affected) and can result in death.

Blood levels containing less than 10 percent CO do not cause symptoms. At levels of 20 percent, mild effects can be mistaken for the flu. These symptoms include headaches, dizziness, disorientation, nausea, and fatigue. The effects of CO exposure can vary greatly from person to person depending on age, overall health, and the concentration and length of exposure. At 30 percent, victims become confused and lethargic. At levels between 40 percent and 60 percent, the victim lapses into coma, and levels much above 60 percent are usually fatal (Auerbach, 2007).

Risk Factors

Risk factors include anything that increases a person's chance of becoming poisoned by carbon monoxide.

Age. The CO poisoning death rate is highest among people over 65 and likely attributed to a higher risk for undetected CO exposure. Symptoms of CO exposure often resemble those associated with other health conditions that are common among the elderly and they may not seek prompt medical care for undetected CO exposures. In addition, children usually fare less well than adults with CO poisoning.

Gender. Although males and females are equally likely to visit emergency departments for CO exposure, males are over two times more likely to die from CO exposure. Males might be exposed to high CO levels during high-risk activities such as working in enclosed garages with generators or power tools. Women, because they are usually comparatively anemic, tend to fare less well than men when exposed to CO.

Location and time. Most CO exposures and poisonings occur more often during the fall and winter (highest occurs in December), when people are more likely to use gas furnaces, heaters, and generators in their residences.

The motor vehicle is probably the most potent producer of CO and accounts for about half of the CO deaths. People who drive long distances in older, often poorly maintained vehicles, such as college students on their winter vacations or migrant farm workers, are at increased risk. Rust is a major factor in damaging the exhaust system and creating holes in the body of the car through which carbon monoxide can enter. Usually these holes are in the muffler and the floor of the car.

Parking inside a garage with the engine running produces many deaths. Many deaths involve persons who are sleeping inside a car, often because of previous drinking. Sleeping may be caused by a combination of alcohol and CO, without real intent to fall asleep. Deaths also involve parking in remote areas for romantic purposes. In addition to parking, drivers also have been overcome by CO while the vehicles were in motion.

The majority of cases occur in residences. Sources of carbon monoxide poisonings include:

▶ Gas water heaters
▶ Kerosene space heaters
▶ Charcoal grills
▶ Hibachi grills
▶ Propane stoves
▶ Cigarette smoke
▶ Propane-fueled forklifts
▶ Gas-powered concrete saws
▶ Swimming behind a motor boat or houseboat
▶ Motor vehicle exhaust from attached garages, nearby roads, or parking areas (accounts for more than half of CO deaths)
▶ Fireplaces burning wood or natural gas
▶ Wood-burning stoves

Normally, the amount of CO produced by these sources is not a cause for concern. However, if they are not kept in good working order or, if they are used in a closed or partially enclosed space (e.g., indoors, garage), the CO can build to dangerous levels.

Activities. Exposure to carbon monoxide is high for these activities:

▶ Children riding in the back of an enclosed pickup truck (e.g., the truck exhaust system had a leak or a tail pipe that exited at the rear instead of the side)
▶ Industrial workers at pulp mills, steel foundries, and plants producing formaldehyde or coke
▶ Firefighters at fire scenes
▶ Using heating sources during power outages (e.g., hurricanes, winter storms)
▶ People working indoors with combustion engines or combustible gases

Medical conditions. All people are at risk for CO poisoning. Certain groups, however, such as unborn babies, infants, and people with chronic heart disease, anemia, or respiratory problems, are more susceptible to its effects.

Chronic CO Poisoning

Chronic CO poisoning involves an exposure to CO that occurs more than once and lasts longer than 24 hours. Accordingly, acute CO poisoning involves an exposure to CO that occurs only once and lasts no longer than 24 hours. Chronic CO poisoning usually involves lower levels of the gas in the air and lower blood CO levels; higher CO levels often end in death thus never becoming chronic. Exposure usually continues for many days, months, and even years.

Interventions

Various types of interventions have been used or warrant application for preventing carbon monoxide poisoning.

CARBON MONOXIDE DETECTORS

The U.S. Consumer Products Safety Commission recommends that every home have at least one CO detector located near sleeping areas. Plug-in and battery-powered models are available and should be certified by the Underwriters Laboratories; they generally cost between $35 and $80. Properly installed detectors monitor carbon monoxide levels over time and are designed to sound an alarm before an average, healthy adult would experience symptoms of poisoning.

However, detectors do have limitations. Some may not provide adequate warning if the CO increases rapidly to very high levels. Infants, the elderly, and people with breathing or heart problems are at increased risk for low-level poisoning and may experience symptoms before an alarm sounds. Thus, a CO detector is only a first-line defense and not a substitute for proper use and regular maintenance and inspection of all potential sources of carbon monoxide.

Every home should have at least one carbon monoxide detector.

PROPER INSTALLATION AND CHECKING OF GAS-OPERATED APPLIANCES

Gas-operated appliances (e.g., furnaces, hot water heaters) should be properly installed and periodically checked to determine that there is no buildup of carbon monoxide. Some health departments and utility companies who supply gas or deliver their product directly to the residence periodically have campaigns for checking for CO levels.

Conclusion

More than a quarter of a million different household products are used in and around the home. While useful, they can be dangerous. Unintentional poisonings can be prevented. Child-resistant packaging has greatly reduced the number of child poisonings. In addition to ingested poisoning, carbon monoxide can be lethal. The best protection is to install a CO alarm in residences.

References

American Academy of Clinical Toxicology. (2004). Position paper: Ipecac syrup. *Journal of Clinical Toxicology*, 42(2):133–143.

American Academy of Pediatrics. (2003). Poison treatment in the home. *Pediatrics* 112:1182.

American Association of Poison Control Centers. (2007). 2004 Poison Center Survey. www.aapcc.org. Accessed August 2007.

Auerbach, P.S. (editor). (2007). Wilderness medicine. St. Louis, MO: Mosby.

Centers for Disease Control and Prevention. (2005). Unintentional non-fire-related carbon monoxide exposures—United States, 2001–2003. *Morbidity and Mortality Weekly Report*. 54(02);36–39.

Coyne-Beasley. T., C.W. Runyan, L. Baccaglini, D. Perkins, and R.M. Johnson. (2005). Storage of poisonous substances and firearms in homes with young children visitors and older adults. *American Journal of Preventive Medicine* 28(1):109–115.

Eldridge, D.L., J. Van Eyk, and C. Kornegay. (2007). Pediatric toxicology. *Emergency Medicine Clinics of North America*, 25(2):283–308.

Hingley, A.T. (1997). Preventing childhood poisoning. *FDA Consumer Magazine*, 30(2):1–7.

Institute of Medicine of the National Academies, Committee on Poison Prevention and Control. (2004). Forging a poison prevention and control system. Washington, DC: The National Academies Press.

Lai, M.W. et al. (2005). Annual report of the American Association of Poison Control Centers' national poisoning and exposure database. *Clinical Toxicology* 44(6):803–932.

Mrvos, R., B.S. Dean, and E.P. Krenzelok. (1986). An extensive review of commercial product labels the good, bad and ugly. *Veterinary and Human Toxicology* 28(1):67–69.

National Safety Council. (2007). Injury facts. Itasca, IL: National Safety Council.

Penny, D.G. (2000). Carbon monoxide toxicity. Boca Raton: CRC Press.

Spiller, H.A. and G.C. Rodgers. (2002). Evaluation of administration of activated charcoal in the home. *Pediatrics*, 108(6):E100.

Thygerson, A.L. (1992). Safety, 2nd edition. Sudbury, MA: Jones and Bartlett Publishers.

Vernberg, K., P. Culver-Dickinson, and D.A. Spyker. (1984). The deterrent effect of poison warning stickers. *American Journal of Diseases of Children*, 138:1018–1020.

Wigder, H.N., T. Erickson, T. Morse, and V. Saporta. (2005). Emergency department poison advice telephone calls. *Annals of Emergency Medicine* 25(3):349–352.

CHAPTER 11 ▶

Fall Injuries

It may sound like a joke, but it is not the falling that hurts—it's the landing. To many people, falls seem to be insignificant occurrences because they do not realize that falls represent one of the most serious threats to life. Over 18,000 people in the United States die annually from injuries sustained in unintentional falls and over 8 million people are treated in hospital emergency departments for unintentional fall-related injuries yearly (National Safety Council, 2007). This number makes falls the leading cause of nonfatal unintentional injuries treated in hospital emergency departments.

Definitions

The Injury Surveillance Workgroup on Falls of the State and Territorial Injury Prevention Directors Association (STIPDA) developed these definitions for *fall* and *fall-related injury* (2006):

> *Fall*: An event that results in a person coming to rest on the ground or other lower level precipitated by a misstep such as a slip, trip, or stumble; from loss of grip or balance; from jumping; or from being pushed, bumped, or moved by another person, animal, or inanimate object or force.

> *Fall-related injury*: An injury precipitated by a fall (as defined above) and caused by striking an injury-producing surface.

The remaining sections of this chapter focuses on two age groups: older people and children—those most likely affected by falls because each group has different risk factors and interventions associated with falls.

Pathophysiology

The injury potential of a fall is related to the height from which the victim fell: In other words, the greater the height of the fall, the greater the potential for injury. A fall from more than 15 feet or three times the victim's height is considered significant. The victim lands on the surface just as an unrestrained passenger smashes into the interior of a vehicle. The internal organs travel at the speed of the victim's body before it hits the ground and stop by smashing into the interior of the body. It is these internal injuries that are the least obvious but pose the gravest threat to life.

Victims who fall and land on their feet may have less severe internal injuries because their legs may have absorbed much of the energy of the fall. However, as a result of landing on their feet, they may have severe injuries to the lower extremities and pelvis and spinal injuries from energy that the legs do not absorb. For example, heel bone fractures often are associated with this type of fall. After the feet land and stop moving, the legs are the next body part to absorb injury. Knee fractures, long-bone fractures, and hip fractures can result. If the victim falls forward onto outstretched hands, the result can be fractures of the wrists. Victims who fall onto their heads will likely have serious head and/or spinal injuries.

Many falls, especially those by older persons, are not considered "true" trauma, even though bones may be broken. Sometimes, these falls occur as a result of a fracture. Older persons often have osteoporosis, a condition in which the musculoskeletal system can fail under relatively low stress. Because of this condition, an older person can sustain a fracture while in a standing position and then fall as a result. Therefore, an older person may have actually sustained a fracture before the fall.

The proneness to fractures, especially in areas such as the hip, are associated with osteoporosis and commonly connected to postmenopausal women and older persons of both sexes. In older persons, the spine stiffens as a result of shrinkage of disk spaces, and vertebrae become brittle, making people susceptible for spine fractures.

Head and Brain Injuries

Deaths from falls often evolve from injuries to the head. With a head injury, the crucial question is the state of the brain rather than the state of the skull. The two main types of brain injury are: (1) bruising when the head forcibly strikes a blunt object (e.g., the ground or floor) and (2) lacerations of the brain tissue from skull fragments being depressed inward into the brain. When the head strikes a blunt object, the resulting contusion causes swelling, which in turn causes pressure on the brain. The pressure disrupts the brain's normal functions.

Older persons can have closed head injuries, such as subdural hematomas. These hematomas can go unnoticed because the blood has a space (due to brain

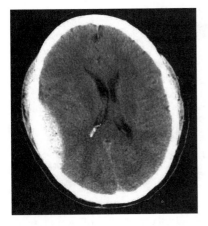

Falls can cause skull and brain injuries.

shrinkage associated with aging) to fill before it produces pressure on the brain showing the familiar signs of head trauma, such as headache, drowsiness, vision problems, mobility, speech, seizures, nausea, and vomiting.

Death may not be a direct result of the fall, but instead may result from complications of the fall. For example, while recovering from bruised ribs sustained in a fall, an older woman may not breathe as deeply as normal because of the pain related with inhalation. As a result of not being able to breathe normally or to cough, as well as other changes in the aging lungs, if this woman comes down with pneumonia, she is more likely to die from it.

When children are hurt in the same type of fall as an adult, the location of their injuries may differ because they are smaller. Children's bones and soft tissues are less developed than those of adults.

Head injuries are common in children because the size of a child's head, in relation to the body, is larger than that of an adult. Greater stress on the neck structures occur during a fall. The center of gravity is higher for young children than for older ones, promoting easy toppling over. In addition, children's bones bend more easily than do adults' bones. As a result, incomplete or greenstick fractures can occur.

Hip Fractures

Ninety percent of the more than 352,000 hip fractures in the United States each year are the result of a fall. By the year 2050, there will be an estimated 650,000 hip fractures annually—nearly 1,800 hip fractures a day (AAOS, 2007).

Women have two to three times as many hip fractures as men, and white, postmenopausal women have a one in seven chance of hip fracture during a lifetime. The rate of hip fracture increases at age 50, doubling every 5 to 6 years. Nearly one-half of women who reach age 90 have suffered a hip fracture (AAOS, 2007).

Older persons of both sexes are prone to fractures, especially in the pelvic and hip areas.

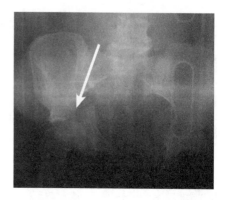

The risk of hip fracture for women 5'8" or taller is twice that of women who are under 5'2". Studies show that women who have broken their arm in the past have an increased risk of breaking a hip. Among people age 50 and older who fall, women have two to three times as many hip fractures as men (AAOS, 2007).

Hip fractures are extremely serious as indicated by this data (AAOS, 2007):

- ▶ Only 25 percent of hip fracture patients will make a full recovery; 40 percent will require nursing home care; 50 percent will need a cane or walker; and 24 percent of those over age 50 will die within 12 months.
- ▶ Nearly one in four hip fracture victims will die within 12 months after the injury because of complications related to the injury and the recovery period.

Older Persons

Falls are among the most common and serious problems facing older people. The Centers for Disease Control and Prevention reports (2006):

- ▶ For people ages 65 and older, falls are the leading cause of injury-related death.
- ▶ Among older people, falls are the underlying cause of a large proportion of fatal traumatic brain injuries.
- ▶ The incidence and the severity of fall-related injuries rise steadily after age 60. About 35 to 40 percent of older people living at home fall at least once a year. After age 75, the rates are higher. For those in nursing homes and hospitals, the rates are almost three times higher.
- ▶ Falls are a common reason for admission of previously independent older persons to long-term care institutions.
- ▶ Older adults who have fallen previously or who stumble frequently are two to three times more likely to fall within the next year.

- ▶ For people ages 65 and older, two-thirds to one-half of falls occur in or around the home.
- ▶ At least 95 percent of hip fractures among older people are caused by falls.
- ▶ Fall-related death rates and hip fracture hospitalization rates have been increasing.

Additional statistics from the Centers for Disease Control and Prevention (2006) show the severity of the issue among the elderly:

- ▶ Nearly 14,000 persons over the age of 65 years die yearly from falls.
- ▶ More than one-third of adults ages 65 years and older fall each year.
- ▶ Nearly two million older people age 65 and older receive hospital emergency department care for fall-related injuries and more than 400,000 are hospitalized.

Risk Factors

A number of risk factors have been identified. These can be classified as either intrinsic or extrinsic.

Intrinsic Factors

Intrinsic or personal factors originate inside the body.

AGE-RELATED FACTORS

Changes in vision. The ability of the eyes to adjust to different levels of light and darkness diminishes as people age. Glare from sunlight, bright light, or floor surfaces can lead to visual difficulties. The loss of visual acuity makes objects

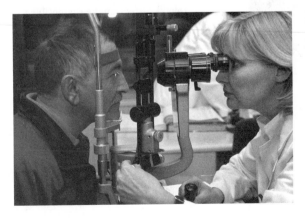

Vision diminishes as people age.

more difficult to detect. Depth perception declines and can make the detecting of certain surfaces appear as elevations or depressions.

Changes in gait and balance. Gait-and-balance disorders (walking and standing) are common among older people. Both of these impairments are found to be a significant risk factor for falls. Most of those in nursing homes require assistance with walking or are unable to walk.

Changes in the musculoskeletal system. Older people experience muscle atrophy, calcification of tendons and ligaments, and an increased curvature of the spine due to osteoporosis. Weakness in the lower extremities, which is very common in older people, is a major risk factor associated with falls.

Changes in the cardiovascular system. Aging is associated with regulation of blood pressure, which can predispose older people to falls. Episodes of low blood pressure (hypotension) can result from dehydration or medication side effects. The aged heart is less able than a younger heart to compensate for any hypotensive effects.

Fear of falling. As people age, they become afraid of falling. This fear can affect self-esteem, daily activities, mental health, and quality of life (Brown, 1999). Half of the older adults with hip fractures cannot return home or live independently after their injuries.

GENDER

With increasing age, both sexes have increased death rates from falling, but men are consistently higher than women. Perhaps this is due to men engaging in

Older people experiencing changes in the musculoskeletal system can be susceptible to falling.

risky behaviors (e.g., climbing on ladders) or having a greater number of chronic medical conditions than women of the same age.

Older women are disproportionately affected by nonfatal falls compared to older men. Of the adults aged 65 and older who were treated in hospital emergency departments in 2001, 70.5 percent were women. Fractures were 2.2 times more likely among women compared to men and hospitalization was 1.8 times more likely (Stevens and Sogolow, 2005).

PATHOLOGICAL CONDITIONS

Falls can be markers for an underlying acute disease or chronic diseases.

Acute diseases. Illnesses most often identified as a cause of falls include syncope, hypotension, cardiac arrhythmias, electrolyte disorders, seizures, stroke, and febrile conditions (e.g., urinary tract infections, pneumonia).

Chronic diseases. Diseases of the eye (e.g., cataracts, macular degeneration, glaucoma) impair vision. Dementia, especially of the Alzheimer's type, can lead to errors in judgment between safe and hazardous conditions. Neuropathy is a disease of the nerves—the results of conditions such as diabetes and vitamin B12 deficiency—and is associated with lower extremity weakness. Parkinson's disease can lead to a displaced center of gravity and loss of balance. Osteoarthritis of the knees and hips and foot disorders (e.g., calluses, bunions) can cause an unsteady gait, resulting in falling.

MEDICATIONS

A number of body changes take place that affect how the body handles a drug. The medications most commonly associated with falls include diuretics, sedatives, antidepressants, psychotropics, and antihypertensives. Any of these drugs may affect gait and balance and cause a fall. The risk of falling increases with the number of medications a person consumes (Stevens, 2005; Rao, 2005).

ALCOHOL

There has been a misrepresentation that drunks never get hurt when they fall because they are so relaxed. This does not mean that people can avoid an injury if they are relaxed. In fact, "drunks" will fall more often due to their drunkenness and therefore have a greater likelihood for being injured.

Extrinsic Factors

Extrinsic or environmental factors originate outside the body.

Older persons' residences should have grab-bars in bathroom areas.

PHYSICAL ENVIRONMENT

Obviously, older people fall in areas where they spend the most time—the bedroom, bathroom, and dining areas. The following features are associated with falling: sitting on and rising from low-seated, unstable, armless chairs and low-seated toilets lacking grab-bar support; walking in poorly lit areas and tripping over objects or floor coverings (e.g., thick-pile carpet, upended linoleum, tile flooring); slipping on highly polished or wet surfaces; and sliding rugs.

FOOTWEAR

Improper footwear can change gait and balance and cause falls. High-heeled shoes and poorly fitting shoes (especially loose shoes) are associated with falls. Loose shoes can cause people to shuffle and then trip when they walk. Leather-soled shoes and wearing socks without shoes promote slipping. Rubber soles may stick to linoleum floors and cause a loss of balance.

Children

Fatal falls are not common in children when compared with the high rate of fall-related deaths among older persons. However, nonfatal falls of all kinds account for over half of all nonfatal injuries in children (STIPDA, 2006). In the United States, between 100 and 200 deaths from falls occur annually in children younger than 15 years. Three million children require emergency department care for fall-related injuries (National Safety Council, 2007).

Risk Factors

The problem of fall-related injuries can often be related to risk factors. This is particularly true of children.

AGE

For infants and toddlers, falls are most often associated with nursery products such as furniture and walkers. Infants fall from beds, from other furniture, and on the stairs. Toddlers (ages 1–4 years) fall from beds and furniture, from buildings, and from playground equipment (STIPDA, 2006). A study of children receiving hospital emergency department care because of a fall found that falls from an object was the most common type. Those younger than 2 years most commonly fell from a bed or chair and sustained a head injury. Children 5 to 12 years old were likely to fall from playground equipment resulting in a fractured arm (Pitone and Attia, 2006).

Older children experience more slipping and tripping, often in sports or recreational activities as well as on playgrounds. Most of these injuries occur at public or school playgrounds (e.g., slides, swings) (STIPDA, 2006).

GENDER

Males predominate among children suffering fall-related injuries. Boys are more than twice as likely as girls to die from fall-related injuries (National Safety Council, 2007).

SOCIOECONOMIC

Children of low-income families are more likely to be injured from falls related to lack of adult supervision and deficiencies in the environment.

LOCATION AND ACTIVITY

Falls in children tend to be from balconies, windows, and trees, and most frequently tend to occur in homes, followed by schoolyards and playgrounds. Most fall deaths among children occur when a child falls from a height of two or more stores, often from upper-level windows or when the head of a child hits a hard surface (e.g., concrete). Falls from heights are a major problem in urban areas where children living in multiple-story and possibly low-income housing. Falls from heights tend to cluster during the summer months perhaps because windows are more likely to be open. Injuries include fractures, internal injuries, concussions, intracranial hematomas, and intracranial bleeding.

Injuries associated with falls from shopping carts and carts tipping over are common and can result in severe injury (e.g., head injuries, fractures) or even death. Other injuries from these types of falls include contusions, abrasions, and lacerations.

Trampoline-related injuries occur mainly on home trampolines—often involving backyard trampolines—and are on the rise. Many injuries occur when there are simultaneous multiple users. The most likely injuries include fractures to the upper and lower extremities. While catastrophic cervical spine injuries are rare, head and neck injuries constitute a notable number of the more serious injuries requiring hospitalization (American Academy of Pediatrics, 1999).

Falls account for about 80 percent of all playground equipment–related injuries and one-fifth of deaths. Factors in playground injuries are that children lack skills, strength, and judgment. Although most falls are from a height are 5 feet or less, the nature of the object or surface struck in the incident is important. For example, falls onto asphalt have higher injury rates compared with falls into sand.

When children are involved in skateboarding and in-line skating–related falls, they often are injured severely. Skateboarding and in-line skating are special risks for children because they have (1) a higher center of gravity, less development, and poor balance; (2) slower reaction times and less coordination than adults; and (3) often less skill and ability than they think. These factors make children more likely to fall and experience an injury. In addition, children are less able to break their falls and have a tendency to overestimate their skills and abilities. They are inexperienced in judging speed, traffic, and other risks, which can lead to accidents.

Interventions

Older Persons

Exercises can increase muscle strength and balance (e.g., Tai Chi, weight training, gait and balance training). Exercise is among the best single interventions (Stevens, 2005; Rao, 2005). Older persons should have their medications reviewed and changed if they may have side effects associated with increased risk of falls (Stevens, 2005). Symptoms of chronic diseases, such as Parkinson's disease, stroke, and arthritis, should be identified and treated.

Older persons should be taught about osteoporosis, a condition involving bone brittleness. This condition is attributed to several factors: decrease in physical activity, nutritional deficiency, and hormonal changes. An increase in calcium and vitamin D supplements and exercise may help to protect against the loss of bone mass and therefore fractures.

Individual stair steps should have a consistent height and length and should not have too steep an angle. Risers should not be greater than 8 inches and treads not less than 10 inches. Protruding nosings (the front edge) on steps can trip people. If possible, handrails should be continuous and on both sides of a staircase.

Residences should have securely mounted grab-bars in the bathroom's tub and shower areas. Tub and shower surfaces, if not slip resistant, should be fitted with slip-resistant applications. Safety mats are available, but can pose problems in cleaning and wearing out.

Lighting should be adequate with switches at the top and the bottom of stairs, and reflections should be minimal. Vision correction with eyeglasses can help avoid objects capable of tripping. Stairs should be kept clean of obstructions (e.g., toys, pets).

Wearing proper shoes also can help keep a person's balance. Hip protectors may reduce hip fractures in those susceptible to falling.

It is important for older people to keep in daily contact with relatives, friends, or neighbors who can take away the worry about someone who have fallen and have been unable to alert anyone about their plight. Alarm systems allow people to call if they need help.

Children

The goal of fall prevention strategies is to design interventions that minimize fall risk by eliminating contributing factors while still allowing a child freedom to develop and mature. Potential strategies are based on known risk factors.

Parents should select high chairs, infant seats, and carriages that have a wide base and low center of gravity. They should install protective gates or self-closing doors to prevent crawling infants from reaching and falling down stairs. Parents should have nonslip surfaces on tubs and avoid using baby walkers.

Window bars represent the most effective method for preventing children from falling out of windows. Parents should install protective bars or grates on windows that young children might be able to reach and place furniture away from windows so that children cannot crawl from the furniture onto the window. When bars are used in windows, however, they should be designed for rapid and easy removal by an older child or adult to permit escape in case of fire. The American Society for Testing and Materials have voluntary safety standards for window guards, which ensure that guards designed for homes or the lower floors of apartment buildings have emergency release mechanisms for use in case of fire.

Some playground surface materials produce a greater number—and more serious—injuries than others. Concrete and asphalt surfaces in playgrounds should not be used. Protective playground surfaces (e.g., wood chips) are highly recommended over the harder surfaces such as sand, synthetic matting, asphalt or concrete. The U.S. Consumer Product Safety Commission and the American Society for Testing and Materials have developed guidelines.

The rapid increase in the number of trampoline-related injuries to children during recent years is evidence that current prevention strategies are inadequate. Children should not use trampolines at home, and the sale of trampolines for private recreational use should be discontinued (Smith, 1998). The American Academy of Pediatrics (1999) makes these recommendations:

- The need for supervision and trained personnel at all times makes home use extremely unwise. Therefore, the trampoline should not be used at home, inside or outside.
- The trampoline should not be part of routine physical education classes in schools.
- The trampoline has no place in outdoor playgrounds and should never be regarded as play equipment.

Conclusion

Falls are the leading cause of unintentional fatal and nonfatal injuries in the United States. They can happen anytime and anyplace to people of any age, but most falls occur in the home. The severity and number of falls increases as people get older.

Certain factors increase the risk of falling for older adults. Some are personal risk factors and others are environmental. Personal risk factors include lower-body weakness, problems with gait and balance, use of psychoactive medications, and visual impairment. These may be mitigated by exercise, medication management, identification and treatment for symptoms of chronic diseases such as Parkinson's, stroke, and arthritis. Environmental factors may include tripping hazards, lack of stair railings or grab-bars, unstable furniture, poor lighting, and inappropriate footwear (Stevens, 2005).

Prevention of falls affecting children largely rests with their parents and caretakers.

References

American Academy of Orthopaedic Surgeons. Falls and hip fractures. http://orthoinfo.aaos.org/fact/thr_report.cfm?Thread_ID=77&topcategory=Hip. Accessed July 2007.

American Academy of Pediatrics (1999). Trampolines at home, school, and recreational centers: Policy statement. *Pediatrics* 103(5):1058–1056.

Brown, A.P. (1999). Reducing falls in elderly people: A review of exercise interventions. *Physiotherapy Theory and Practice* 15, 59–65.

Centers for Disease Control and Prevention. (2006). Fatalities and injuries from falls among older adults—United States, 1993–2003 and 2001–2005. *Morbidity and Mortality Weekly Report* 55(45):1221–1224.

National Safety Council. (2007). Injury facts. Itasca, IL: National Safety Council.

Pitone, M.L. and M.W. Attia. (2006). Patterns of injury associated with routine childhood falls. *Pediatric Emergency Care* 22(7):470–474.

Rao, S.S. (2005). Prevention of falls in older patients. *American Family Physician* 72(1):81–88.

Smith, G.A. (1998). Injuries to children in the United States related to trampolines, 1990–1995: a national epidemic. *Pediatrics*, 101(3 Pt1):406–412.

State and Territorial Injury Prevention Directors Association (STIPDA), Injury Surveillance Workgroup on Falls. (2006). Consensus recommendations for surveillance of falls and fall-related injuries. Atlanta: STIPDA.

Stevens, J.A. (2005). Falls among older adults—risk factors and prevention strategies. *Journal of Safety Research*, 36(4):409–411.

Stevens, J.A. and E.D. Sogolow. (2005). Gender differences for non-fatal unintentional fall related injuries among older adults. *Injury Prevention* 11(2):115–119.

Thygerson, A.L. (1992). Safety, 2nd edition. Sudbury, MA: Jones and Bartlett Publishers.

CHAPTER 12 ▶

Choking, Suffocation, and Strangulation

Between 5,000 and 6,000 people of all ages suffocate, choke, or strangle to death annually. These incidents are among the leading causes of unintentional death and are especially tragic because they largely affect young children.

Definitions

Definitions are critical to the understanding of an injury problem. Not only are definitions essential for correct understanding, they are also essential for communicating with other people. Unless clear definitions are provided when we attempt to communicate about injuries, it makes it difficult to solve an injury problem. This chapter focuses on three conditions necessitating definitions because they are sometimes confused and used interchangeably.

Choking: blocking the airway internally by a foreign body or object (e.g., food, balloons)

Suffocation: obstruction of the airway from an external object that blocks the nose and mouth (e.g., plastic bag)

Strangulation: external compression of the airway from an object (e.g., a cord around the neck)

Pathophysiology

Breathing is essential to life. When a person inhales, he or she breathes in air that contains 21 percent oxygen. In the lungs, oxygen enters the bloodstream to travel to the rest of the body. The body uses oxygen as a fuel source to make energy from the food that is eaten. Carbon dioxide, a waste product, enters the bloodstream and travels back to the lungs. When exhaling, a person breathes out 16 percent oxygen. When someone is choking, suffocating, or being strangled—causing a completely blocked airway—no oxygen can enter the lungs. The brain is extremely sensitive to this lack of oxygen. Without oxygen, the brain begins to die within 4 to 6 minutes.

Choking

Between 3,000 and 4,000 people of all ages choke to death annually, and death rates are higher for males than females. Most (90 percent) are children under 5 years of age, and 65 percent of those victims are infants. Older people in the seventh decade of life also have high choking death rates (National Safety Council, 2007).

Choking is caused when a foreign body or object gets stuck in the upper airway. In the back of the mouth are two openings. One is the esophagus, which leads to the stomach. Food goes down this pathway. The other is the trachea, which is the opening that air must pass through to get to the lungs. When swallowing occurs, the trachea is covered by a flap called the epiglottis, which prevents food from entering the lungs. The trachea splits into the left and right main stem bronchus. These lead to the left and right lungs. They branch into increasingly smaller tubes as they spread throughout the lungs. Any object that winds up in the airway will become stuck as the airway narrows. Many large objects get stuck just inside the trachea at the vocal cords.

The four kinds of choking are identified by the location of the foreign body or object that is stuck or located (Thygerson, 1992):

1. Type 0: Everyone has experienced this type of choking—the sensation of something in the airway that is relieved by coughing. This situation is not life threatening, but potentially could be if the object becomes dislodged and aspirated.
2. Type 1: Obstruction is on the mouth side of the epiglottis (also known as the "lid" type because it may hold the epiglottis down over the larynx like a lid); it is life threatening.
3. Type 2: Obstruction is on the lung side of the epiglottis (also known as the "plug" type because the obstruction closes up the trachea like a plug). A reflex laryngospasm may complicate the situation; it is life threatening.
4. Type 3: Subacute choking—a foreign body or object resides in the bronchi, but is not acutely life threatening.

In adults, choking most often occurs when food is not chewed properly. Talking or laughing while eating may cause a piece of food to go into the airway. Normal swallowing mechanisms may be slowed if a person has been drinking alcohol or taking drugs and if the person has certain illnesses such as Parkinson's disease. In older people, risk factors for choking include poorly fitting dental work, not chewing food completely, and alcohol consumption. The stereotype of an adult choking is an older man having a steak dinner combined with alcoholic beverages and often wearing dentures. The term *café coronary* was once used to describe cases of these sudden deaths in restaurants. At first the deaths were attributed to heart attacks, but later, at autopsy, they were shown to be the result of food obstructing the airway.

BEFORE

Food and nonfood substances present a choking hazard for children, especially younger children. Between 150 and 200 children under 14 years of age die from inhaling or ingesting a foreign body into the airway (National Safety Council, 2007). Food accounts for about 40 percent of these deaths; nonfood substances 60 percent. In children, choking is caused by chewing food incompletely, attempting to eat large pieces of food, attempting to eat too much food at one time, or eating hard candy. Children also put small objects in their mouths, which may become lodged in their throat. Nuts, pins, or coins, for example, create a choking hazard.

The chances of choking can be reduced by not feeding children younger than 4 years of age any round, firm food unless it is chopped completely. Small, round, firm foods are common choking dangers. The American Academy of Pediatrics (2007) recommends avoiding the following foods in children under the age of 4 because they can be choking hazards:

- ▶ Hot dogs
- ▶ Nuts and seeds
- ▶ Chunks of meat or cheese
- ▶ Whole grapes
- ▶ Hard, gooey, or sticky candy
- ▶ Popcorn
- ▶ Chunks of peanut butter
- ▶ Raw vegetables
- ▶ Raisins
- ▶ Chewing gum

Foods such as grapes can be a choking hazard.

Nonfood hazards are round or pliable objects such as coins, marbles, balloons, small balls, and jewelry. Uninflated balloons have been found to be one of the primary causes of choking among young children, especially toddlers. National Electronic Injury Surveillance System-All Injury Program data estimated that more than 17,000 children under age 14 years were treated in hospital emergency departments for choking-related episodes; many of these episodes were associated with candy, gum, and coins (CDC, 2002).

Physical and developmental factors put children at risk for choking on food and nonfood substances. Children choking run the risk of death, permanent brain damage caused by lack of oxygen, or other complications associated with airway blockage.

The Centers for Disease Control and Prevention (2002) reported on nonfatal choking-related episodes of children under the age of 14 years and found that:

▶ Choking-related episodes are highest for infants less than 1 year of age and decreased with age; the rate for boys and girls are similar.
▶ Of the 17,000 children treated in emergency departments—more than 100 visits occurred for every choking-related death—about 60 percent were treated for choking on a food substance, 30 percent were associated with nonfood objects including coins, and in about 10 percent the substance was unknown.
▶ Candy is associated with about 20 percent of all choking-related emergency department visits by children 14 years and younger. Of these cases, 65 percent were related to hard candy and about 12 percent were related to other specified types (e.g., chocolate candy, gummy candy, chewing gum); the type of candy is not always reported.
▶ Of those aged 14 and younger treated in an emergency department for choking, about 10 percent are admitted to the hospital.

Suffocation

Child deaths due to suffocation result when the child is in a place or position where he or she is unable to breathe. Most of the unintentional child suffocations are caused by:

▶ *Overlay*: a person who is sleeping with a child rolls onto the child and unintentionally smothers the child. Researchers from the CPSC and the National Institute of Child Health and Human Development report that infants sleeping in adult beds are 20 times more likely to suffocate than infants who sleep alone in cribs (CPSC, 1999).
▶ *Positional asphyxia*: a child's face becomes trapped in soft bedding or wedged in a small space, such as between a mattress and a wall or between couch cushions.

(a)

(b)

(c)

(d)

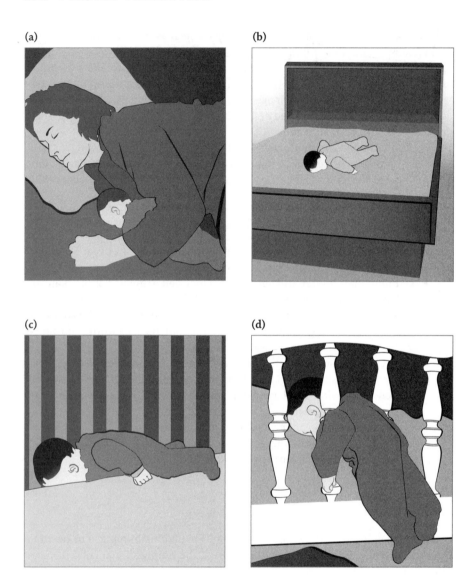

Figure 12-1 There are four types of hazards for child suffocation: (a) overlay (associated with cosleeping of adult and baby), (b) covering face (airway obstruction of excessive padding), (c) positional asphyxia (involving being caught between objects), and (d) strangulation/entrapment.

▶ *Covering of face or chest*: an object covers a child's face or compresses the chest, such as plastic bags, heavy blankets, pillows, comforters, sheets, or furniture.
▶ *Confinement*: a child is trapped in an airtight place such as an unused refrigerator or freezer, coolers, or toy chest.

Strangulation

Lives can be threatened if the human neck with its lack of bone protection and close association of the airway, and major blood vessels is compressed externally (e.g., by a cord or rope around the neck).

Although this book differentiates suffocation from strangulation, strangulation deaths are categorized as suffocation under the e-code classification system, which identifies the external cause of injury data.

When the neck is compressed, one or more mechanisms interfere with the normal flow of oxygen into the brain:

▶ Compression of the carotid arteries and/or jugular veins, which causes lack of blood to the brain leads to insufficient oxygen (hypoxia)
▶ Compression of the larynx and/or trachea, which results in a lack of oxygen (asphyxia)
▶ Stimulation of the carotid sinus reflex, which causes a slowing of the heart rate

Young children, especially toddlers, are at risk if placed in an older crib with bars too far apart. The distance between the bars allows the children to be caught by the neck and strangled as they push their heads out between the bars.

Unintentional strangulation often results from strings on clothing or pacifiers that catch on a household piece (e.g., crib post, furniture, doorknob) or playground equipment and tightly wrap around the child's neck. Cords, ribbons, and necklaces around necks cause several deaths each year. Children also can be strangled when a heavy hinged toy chest lid shuts and catches their necks between the lid and the toy chest.

An estimated 25 children strangle in window blind and drapery cords yearly, but, according to the U.S. Consumer Product Safety Commission (2006), it is estimated that about half of the deaths of children who strangle in window cords have not been reported. Almost all of these deaths (93 percent) are children 3 years old and under.

Interventions

Public Education

Education efforts have focused on two activities: counseling parents and caregivers about hazards and teaching the public how to manage a choking victim. Safe Kids Worldwide (2007) offers these precautions against choking, strangulation, and suffocation for parents and caregivers:

- **Supervise.** There is no substitute for active supervision. Pay attention to product labels. If a toy is labeled ages 3 and up, that doesn't refer to the child's intelligence or maturity—it means a younger child could choke to death on small parts.
- **Test small objects in your child's surroundings.** If an object can fit through a standard 1.5-inch toilet paper tube or a store-bought small parts tester, don't let your child play with it.
- **Remove drawstrings from children's clothing and remove bike helmets while using playground equipment**. In the past 20 years, at least 22 children have been strangled by drawstrings in clothing, mostly as a result of drawstrings getting tangled in playground equipment.
- **Install safety tassels for the ends of curtain pulls,** or cut the loops at the end. Since 1991, at least 130 children have been strangled by the cords of window blinds or curtains.
- **Inspect your baby's crib**. A safe crib has no more than 2-3/8 inches of space between slats, is not placed near a window and does not have anything hanging above it on a ribbon or string longer than seven inches. Kids under 6 should not sleep in the top bunk of a bunk bed, and the bed frame and guardrails should not be more than 3.5 inches apart.
- **Avoid thick, soft bedding for babies and toddlers.** To reduce the risk of Sudden Infant Death Syndrome, **always** lay babies down on their backs to sleep until they know how turn themselves over.

Additional precautions and hazards include:

- Plastic: Keep thin plastic sheets and bags from young children
- Foods: Certain foods (e.g., hot dogs, grapes, peanuts) become choking hazards because infants cannot chew sufficiently and the size, shape, and consistency of certain foods is conducive for choking
- Balloons: The hazard of letting children blow up latex balloons or allowing children to suck on balloons because the balloons can be aspirated
- Appliances: Discarding abandoned refrigerators and freezers and removing their doors to avoid entrapment
- Bedding: The potential for an infant becoming wedged between a bed and mattress or wall, and obstruction of the nose and mouth
- Co-sleeping: The danger of an infant being laid on (the adult on top of the child) while sharing a bed

Nonfood choking hazards include uninflated balloons.

Everyone should learn how to provide CPR and manage choking (for example, using the Heimlich maneuver). Classes can be provided to offer opportunities for training. The Emergency Care and Safety Institute, sponsored and endorsed by the American Academy of Orthopaedic Surgeons and the American College of Emergency Physicians, offers classroom and online training. See www .ecsinstitute.org for further information.

Legislation and Product Modification

Enacted laws deal primarily with modifying products that expose children to the risk of choking, suffocation, or strangulation. Examples of legislation include:

Consumer Product Safety Act. The U.S. Consumer Product Safety Commission (CPSC) is charged with protecting the public from unreasonable risks of

Everyone should learn how to perform the Heimlich maneuver for choking victims.

serious injury or death from more than 15,000 types of consumer products. Many of these products are potential choking hazards. Examples of other products with potential choking, suffocation, and strangulation risks include outerwear (jackets and sweatshirts) with drawstrings, mandatory standards for bunk beds to restrict opening size of guard rails and reduce entrapment, and mandatory standards for slats that does not allow an infant to get its head caught in cribs and play pens.

Hazardous Substances Act. The act gives the CPSC the authority to ban by regulation any toy or other article intended for use by children that presents a hazard. The CPSC has issued regulations under this provision relating to specific products with potential choking, suffocation, or strangulation hazards such as toys, cribs, rattles, pacifiers, and children's bunk beds.

Child Safety Protection Act. This legislation bans toys intended for children under age 3 that pose an obstructed airway hazard and requires warning labels for items with small parts when intended for children ages 3 to 6.

Refrigerator Safety Act. The Refrigerator Safety Act was enacted in 1956. The act requires a mechanism (usually a magnetic latch) that enables the door to be opened from the inside in the event of unintentional entrapment. The entrapment hazard occurs when children, during play, climb inside an old abandoned or carelessly stored refrigerators to hide. Many of the refrigerators manufactured before the legislation may still be in use, and when they are carelessly discarded or stored where they are accessible to children, they become a danger.

References

American Academy of Pediatrics. (2007). Choking prevention. http://www.aap.org/publiced/BR_Choking.htm. Accessed August 2007.

Centers for Disease Control and Prevention. (2002). Nonfatal choking-related episodes among children—United States, 2001. *Morbidity and Mortality Weekly Report* 51(42):945–948.

Consumer Product Safety Commission. (1999). CPSC warns against placing babies in adult beds. www.cpsc.gov/CPSCPUB/PREREL/PRHTML99/99175.html. Accessed August 2007.

Consumer Product Safety Commission. (2006). CPSC warns older window coverings pose strangulation risk to children. www.cpsc.gov/cpscpub/prerel/prhtml07/07002.html. Accessed August 2007.

Safe Kids Worldwide Media Center. Airway safety: Protecting kids from choking, suffocation, and strangulation. www.usa.safekids.org. Accessed August 2007.

National Safety Council. (2007). Injury facts. Itasca, IL: National Safety Council.

Thygerson, A.L. (1992). Safety, 2nd edition. Sudbury, MA: Jones and Bartlett Publishers.

CHAPTER 13 ▶

Drowning

Drowning is a major cause of death, disability, and lost quality of life. Between 3,000 and 4,000 yearly unintentional drowning deaths make it a significant public health problem. Drowning is the fifth leading cause of unintentional injury death in the United States and is a leading cause of death among children (National Safety Council, 2007). Any statistics cited probably underestimate the problem since many incidents are unreported or classified in other categories, such as motor vehicle crashes or acute illnesses (e.g., heart attack). Drowning rates, however, have declined steadily during the past century.

Drowning victims usually have been determined as those who seek medical care or die following their submersion. Lifeguard or layperson rescues may represent the real drowning population because their lives were seen at risk due to the lack of breathing. Even this figure does not give the whole picture because, in instances when the victim recovers at the scene, the incident may not be reported.

Definitions

One review found a total of 33 different definitions to describe drowning incidents: 20 for drowning and 13 for near-drowning (Papal and Edris, 2005). This variability in definitions makes it very difficult to assess and analyze the drowning problem. Therefore, experts associated with the first World Congress on Drowning 2002 (WCOD) held in Amsterdam, Netherlands, believed that a new definition should include both cases of fatal and nonfatal drowning. A consensus of these experts adopted the following definition of drowning (Bierens, 2006):

> *Drowning is the process of experiencing respiratory impairment from submersion/immersion in liquid.*

This definition means that drownings can be fatal or nonfatal. The WCOD definition includes all types of liquid, except body fluids (e.g., vomitus, saliva). The definition does not describe causes nor classify the outcome of the drowning process. The WCOD also determined that the terms wet, dry, active, passive, silent, and secondary drowning should no longer be used.

Immersion means to be covered in water. For drowning to occur, usually at least the face and airway are immersed. During submersion, the entire body, including the airway, is under water (ILCOR Advisory Statements, 2003).

Risk Factors

Identifying risk factors associated with drowning is essential for developing effective interventions.

Age. Age appears to be one indicator of risk because drowning appears to be a young person's event. Drowning is a leading cause of unintentional injury deaths for all ages and the second leading cause of all injury deaths in children aged 1 to 14 years (MMWR, 2004; National Safety Council, 2007). This may reflect a greater degree of exposure to the hazard and for longer periods of time than other age groups. A sizable percentage of the victims are children under the age of 4. Risk-taking and alcohol and drug use among adolescent boys while engaged in recreational sports and watercraft increase their susceptibility for drowning (Bierens, 2006).

Because the characteristics of drowning incidences vary by age, different interventions may be needed for different age groups (Quan, 2003).

Gender. Drowning occurs more often among males, as is the case for almost all types of unintentional injury. Males experience drowning three to five times more frequently than females in all age groups (Bierens, 2006). For males, the peak drowning incidence occurs at age 2 years, decreases until the age of 10, and then rises rapidly to a peak at age 18 (Baker et al., 1992). The incidence in females peaks at age 1 year, then falls off and does not rise again (Baker et al., 1992). Males may be more at risk because of higher exposure to aquatic activities, higher alcohol consumption while at the waterfront, and more risk-taking behavior (Howland et al., 1996).

Race. In the United States, Native Americans have the highest drowning rates and Asians and Caucasians the lowest. Some drownings by Native Americans may be due to low water temperatures or the dangers of fishing, such as in Alaska. In addition, many have few or no opportunities to learn to swim. This may also explain why African Americans have almost 50 percent higher drowning rates than that among whites. In the United States, unsupervised swimming or unintentional

Parents who can swim are more likely to have children who can swim.

falls into unattended canals or quarries account for a large percentage of deaths in black males (Saluja, et al., 2006).

Swimming ability. The ability to swim does not appear to be consistently related to drowning rates unless gender differences are considered. White males have a higher incidence of drowning than white females but reportedly have a better swimming ability (Schuman, 1976). On the other hand, black females are reported to have the lowest swimming ability but a very low rate of drowning (Schuman, 1976). In Florida, nonswimmers or beginners accounted for almost three-fourths of drownings in home swimming pools and over 80 percent of incidents in canals, lakes, and ponds (Rowe et al., 1977).

Parental example is an important determinant of whether children can swim. Children whose parents can swim are most likely to be strong swimmers; those with parents who cannot swim are likely to be nonswimmers. In addition, parents of white children are much more likely to be swimmers than are the parents of black children (Schuman, 1976).

Alcohol and drugs. Alcohol use has been estimated to be involved in about 25 to 50 percent of adolescent and adult deaths associated with water recreation (Howland and Hingson, 1988; Doll et al, 2007). Because alcohol intoxication affects judgment, it makes water recreation (e.g., boating, water skiing, swimming) more dangerous. Incidences of intoxicated individuals going swimming at night in deep water or jumping off a bridge indicate that alcohol is a significant factor in some drowning cases. In addition, alcohol increases heat loss and increases the incidence of vomiting—all factors that worsen the chances of survival.

Drugs such as PCP, LSD, and marijuana increase the risk of drowning. Although the incidents of these drugs and others are not known, it can be assumed that intoxicants play a role in drowning (Bierens, 2006).

Alcohol use affects judgment, making water recreation more dangerous.

Hyperventilation. Intentionally breathing more deeply than normal is known as hyperventilation and is used by some swimmers trying to increase their length of time under water. Some think that by hyperventilating, they get more oxygen into their blood, but this is not the case. Carbon dioxide in the blood provides the major stimulus to breathing, and, while those five to six deep breaths do not significantly increase the amount of oxygen normally present, they do reduce the carbon dioxide, which may block the built-in warning signals that tell a swimmer to surface for air. The result can be a blackout from lack of oxygen resulting in drowning. Hundreds, and possibly thousands, of good swimmers have drowned because they have not understood the effects of deep breathing before underwater swimming for distance.

Exhaustion/fatigue. Exhaustion and fatigue are among the most frequently reported factors involving drowning. Exhaustion most often occurs in swimmers and skin- and scuba divers, as well as among those attempting to rescue another person.

Fatigue and exhaustion leads to poor judgment, which causes victims to endanger themselves further by swimming away from help, leaving an overturned boat, or misjudging the distance to shore.

Food in the stomach. Water safety experts have long advised a swimmer to wait at least 1 hour after eating before swimming. Most people assume the reason for this traditional advice is to avoid abdominal cramps that may disable a swimmer and cause drowning.

Despite reports of those eating prior to swimming in competition when no adverse effects occurred, avoiding food prior to any physical activity including swimming is recommended. Evidence indicates that if a person has eaten a great deal, is in poor health, or has a cardiovascular problem, eating just prior to swimming presents a potential problem. After food is eaten, the stomach muscles need an adequate supply of oxygen-carrying blood. If strenuous exercise is begun shortly after eating, the heart may not be able to pump enough blood to both the stomach and skeletal muscles.

It takes 1 to 4 hours for the stomach to digest a meal and empty it into the intestines. Food that remains in the stomach during physical activity such as swimming may cause stomach upset, nausea, vomiting, and cramping.

Underlying disease or injury. An underlying injury or illness can account for loss of life in the water. Hypoglycemia, cardiac arrest, seizure, and syncope predispose some to drowning. Those who suffer from seizure disorders especially are vulnerable to drowning. Physician counseling for every person who experiences periodic lapses of unconsciousness due to seizures and acute circulatory ailments should be advised about the special hazards posed by aquatic environments. Such people should be advised to bathe in the smallest possible amount of water because it is in the bathtub that exposure is most frequent and the danger least evident. Cervical spine injuries and head injuries, which impair the ability to swim or float, may be involved when a victim dives into shallow water and strikes the bottom of a swimming pool or other body of water.

Swimming aids. Swim rings, inner tubes, and air mattresses are referred to by some as "drowning equipment." Flotation equipment usually are no threat to the capable swimmer who slides off a wet mattress or loses his or her hold on an inner tube. However, for the poor swimmer, such equipment allows the individual to have fun, but, by giving him or her a false sense of security, may cause the poor swimmer to go beyond a safe depth.

Place/location. The danger of drowning varies greatly in different parts of the country, depending on factors such as proximity and utilization of bodies of water and on the climate. Alaska has the highest drowning rate in the United States

Swim rings, inner tubes, and air mattresses can give a false sense of security.

because of the cold water and occupational (e.g., fishing) exposure (Bierens, 2006; Auerbach, 2007). See Figure 13-1 for more on drowning deaths by location. Drowning occurs not only in the backyard swimming pool and in the ocean, but also in the unsupervised bath and the cleaning bucket. Residential swimming pools are especially dangerous, particularly for young children.

Place. In water-oriented areas such as Florida and California, drowning incidents are common year-round and often occur in home swimming pools.

Location. The places where the largest numbers of drowning occur are rivers, lakes, ponds, and oceans. This list simply may reflect where the largest number of unsupervised exposures occur. Ocean drownings are not as frequent as those involving rivers and lakes, perhaps because of the more frequent supervision by lifeguards on ocean beaches.

For infants and children, the most frequent place is in the bathtub or in residential swimming pools. A similar proportion of drowning in bathtubs is found among the elderly. This may reflect the fact that the very young and the very old are less likely to be engaged in aquatic sports or recreational activities, or it may indicate that infants and children need more supervision in the bathtub and that the elderly are more prone to heart attacks, strokes, or falls (should this occur in a bathtub, drowning could be reported as the cause of death).

Of drownings where the location was specified, 52 percent occurred in natural bodies of water such as rivers, lakes, ponds, streams, and oceans; 22 percent occurred in swimming pools; and 14 percent occurred in bathtubs. Drowning while in a natural body of water was the most common location for all age groups except the youngest.

While the incidence of drowning tends to be greater in coastal communities with large bodies of water, drowning in salt water is relatively rare. This may be

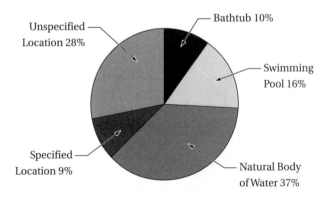

Figure 13-1 Drowning deaths by location.

the result of surveillance and rescue efforts at public beaches by lifeguards. The exceptions are in fishing communities in Alaska and Maine because of the cold water temperature and fishing industry.

Cold water. The body's responses to cold-water immersion can be divided into three phases: (1) initial immersion and the cold-shock response; (2) short-term immersion and loss of performance; and (3) long-term immersion and the onset of hypothermia (Auerbach, 2007).

> *Cold-shock phase.* This occurs within the first 1 to 4 minutes of cold water immersion and depends on the extent and rate of skin cooling. Rapid skin cooling causes an immediate gasp response, the inability to hold one's breath, and hyperventilation. The gasp response can cause death if the head is under water. Death can occur either immediately or within a matter of minutes after immersion.

> *Loss of performance phase.* For those surviving the cold-shock response, this phase develops during the first 30 minutes of immersion. Cooling of the extremities leads to finger stiffness, poor coordination, and loss of strength.

> *Hypothermia phase.* Most cold water deaths likely result from drowning during the first two phases of cold-water immersion. A large proportion of cold water drowning victims died too quickly for hypothermia to be involved. Hypothermia becomes a factor if immersion lasts more than 30 minutes.

Water below 91.4 degrees F (33 degrees C) is the point at which heat loss equals heat production for a person in water without clothes. Any water colder

Immersion in cold water may quickly lead to hypothermia-induced drowning.

than this will lead to ongoing heat loss. Thus, in very cold water, hypothermia may ensue rapidly and lead to drowning.

The effects of cold water is shown by the Rule of 50s: A healthy 50-year-old man has a 50/50 chance of surviving for 50 minutes in 50 degree water. However, survival time in cold water is not a precise calculation. Large individual variations among survivors and other variables affect the cooling rate. A core body temperature of 86 degrees F (30 degrees C) is the limit of survival in cold water (Auerbach, 2007).

The rate of body core cooling during cold water immersion depends on the following variables (Auerbach, 2007):

- ▶ *Water temperature*: water has a thermal conductivity of about 25 times that of air, and cold water has a high rate of heat transfer from the skin to water of at least 100 times greater than in air of the same temperature.

- ▶ *Clothing*: protective clothing diminishes the cold shock response from initial immersion in cold water, and clothing that limits the amount of water reaching a person's skin (e.g., wet suits) decreases the effects of sudden immersion in cold water. Protecting the arms and legs may be more important than the torso in the cardiac response to sudden cold water immersion.

- ▶ *Body size and composition*: children cool faster than adults because children have a greater surface area-to-mass ratio. Smaller adults generally cool faster than larger adults, and tall, lanky individuals cool faster than do short, stout individuals. Body composition is also important; subcutaneous fat is a very efficient insulator against heat loss.

- ▶ *Behavior* (e.g., excessive movement) *and posture* (e.g., HELP, huddle) *of the body in the water*: physical activity in cold water may increase heat loss through increased blood flow to the peripheral blood vessels. So, minimizing both physical activity and the exposure of major heat loss areas of the skin (e.g., groin, neck, chest) is the most effective way to minimize heat loss. Treading water and drownproofing (person floats with the head in the water, like a jellyfish, until a breath is needed when the person surfaces for the breath and then resumes floating) increases the cooling rate. Two well-known cold water survival techniques are: (1) HELP (Heat Escape Lessening Position) with the knees drawn up to the chest and the person wears a PFD to keep the head out of the water and (2) the group huddle (two or more people touching side-by-side and wearing PFDs) reduce core body cooling.

- ▶ *Shivering*: involuntary muscle contractions increases heat production in an effort to prevent or minimize body core cooling. Shivering intensity increases as core and skin temperatures decrease.

Interestingly, the colder the water, the better the chance of survival in case of a drowning. Hypothermia resulting from cold-water drowning may offer some degree of brain protection to hypoxia that warm water does not. Cases of surviving after 45 minutes submerged in cold water have been reported.

Time. Water activities are dictated by the warmth of the water, resulting in more people in or near the water and thus increasing the likelihood of drowning.

Month. More than half of all drownings take place during June, July, and August and less than 10 percent occur from December through February. This reflects the fact that a much larger number of persons are on or in the water during the summer months. In other words, the chance of drowning increases in warm weather because of the increase in aquatic activity.

Day and hour. About 40 percent of drownings occur on Saturdays and Sundays and about two-thirds in the afternoon or early evening hours. This pattern reflects the increase in recreational water activity and use of alcohol on weekends.

Pathophysiology

Every drowning victim is characterized by hypoxemia (decreased oxygen concentration in the blood). Victims can become hypoxic in several different drowning situations, which include:

- ▶ *Distressed nonswimmer*: Initially the victim stays on top of water for about 20 to 60 seconds before going beneath the water's surface. This is the most common type of victim and occurs near shallow water or near drop-offs in a lake or ocean. During this stage, the victim will make motions to try to reach or remain on the water's surface. Arm motions may approximate a rapid above-water breast stroke. Frantic hyperventilation occurs as long as the head can be held above water. The victims have their mouths open, but are unable to call out or wave for help, and often look as though they are playing in the water when they are actually drowning (Pia, 2007).
- ▶ *Immediate disappearance syndrome*: The victim enters the water and does not return to the surface. This is related to either: (a) diving from a height with the head striking an object or the bottom of a body of water, such as in a swimming pool, resulting in unconsciousness or paralysis either one resulting in the inability to swim, (b) hyperventilating before swimming underwater and while holding the breath underwater become unconscious, or (c) cold-induced cardiac arrest.
- ▶ *Sudden disappearance syndrome*: The victim can swim, is fully clothed, and disappears underwater after 5 to 10 minutes. Poor swimmers or cold persons can be supported by trapped air in the clothing. After attempting to swim or while struggling in the water, the trapped air is squeezed out of the clothing. After the trapped air escapes, they have *distressed nonswimmer* behavior (see above) and rapidly sink.

▶ *Hypothermia induced debility.* See the previous section on cold water and its relation to drowning.

Inhaling extremely small amounts of water can severely irritate the larynx, sending the muscles of the larynx and the vocal cords into spasm, called a laryngospasm. This is the body's attempt at self-preservation; laryngospasm prevents more water from entering the lungs. If the spasm does not relax, the victim cannot breathe. In the drowning victim, hypoxia will progress until the victim becomes unconscious. At this point, the spasm relaxes. If the victim is submerged, water will be aspirated into the lungs as the victim attempts to breath. In about 90 percent of cases, significant amounts of water enter the lungs of the drowning victim. In addition, there are no clinically relevant differences between submersion in salt- or freshwater. The amount of water aspirated, not the type, is of prime importance (Orlowski and Szpilman, 2001).

Interventions

Few drowning interventions have been properly evaluated. In fact, only isolation fencing of swimming pools have been well researched and proven effective (Doll et. al., 2006).

Adult Supervision

No single action will prevent all drownings. Childhood drowning usually occurs in bathtubs and swimming pools, and lapses in adult supervision are one of the major causes of these incidents. One measure, however, could prevent a large number of drownings: competent caregiver supervision. Caregivers should never leave a child unattended in order to attend to other things (e.g., answer the telephone). Small children can drown in a few seconds. Experts advise that children under 5 should not reside in homes that have swimming pools.

Boating Safety Education

Boaters frequently make mistakes. Novices frequently start their boats in gear, causing them to lurch forward; they also can anchor from the stern, instead of the bow, a maneuver that can drag the boat under. Boating safety courses are available from the U.S. Coast Guard, U.S. Power Squadrons, and many state and local boating programs.

Alcohol Restriction

Because alcohol consumption in water recreation activities predisposes a person to drowning, attempts to decrease alcohol consumption at water activities should be implemented with laws and enforcement. This may also include restricting the availability of alcohol at water recreation facilities. All 50 states prohibit boating under the influence of alcohol (Bierens, 2006; CDC, www.cdc.gov/ncipc/factsheets/drown.htm). Advertisements encouraging alcohol use during boating should be eliminated.

Lifeguards

Community and local government officials facing decisions about whether to begin, retain, or discontinue lifeguarding services typically want to know whether lifeguards are truly effective in preventing drowning and other aquatic mishaps, and whether the value of providing lifeguard protection outweighs the costs. Most drowning are preventable through a variety of strategies, one of which is to provide lifeguards in public areas where people are known to swim and to encourage people to swim in those protected areas.

Estimates indicate that lifeguards rescue more than 100,000 persons from drowning annually. Moreover, for every rescue, an effective lifeguard provides preventive actions, such as warning an individual away from a dangerous area and suggesting that poor swimmers stay in shallow water. Professional lifeguards have had a positive effect on drowning prevention (Branche and Stewart, 2001).

Personal Flotation Devices

In official U.S. Coast Guard language, there is no such thing as a "life jacket." Instead, there are personal flotation devices (PFDs). Studies show that 80 percent

Trained, professional lifeguards have had a positive effect on preventing drowning.

to 96 percent of those who drown while boating were not wearing a PFD (USCG, 2006).

Four types of PFDs are approved by the Coast Guard for use on recreational boats, and each type offers its own advantages. All wearable PFDs are designed to keep the person afloat and the head and mouth out of the water. Most PFDs are comfortable and durable, and some types can be worn with regular clothes.

> Type I PFDs are designed to turn an unresponsive person from a face-down to a vertical or slightly backward position. They provide at least 20 pounds of buoyancy (a typical adult weighs less than 15 pounds in water, depending on factors such as body fat and clothing worn). Type I PFDs are best for use in rough water.

> Type II PFDs also are designed to keep an unresponsive person's face out of water, but they provide less buoyancy (about 15.5 pounds). They are used most frequently in recreational settings where the chances of rescue are better. They come in a variety of models and are among the least expensive PFDs.

> Type III PFDs will keep a responsive person afloat with his or her face out of water. They provide the same range of buoyancy as Type IIs, but are designed so that a responsive person must place him- or herself in a vertical position. The Type III PFD then will hold the person that way with no tendency to turn face down. Type IIIs are lightweight, designed for ease of movement, and come in many colors and styles, including vests and jackets.

> Type IV PFDs are approved devices designed to be thrown to a person in the water, but not worn. These include flotation cushions and ring buoys. Type

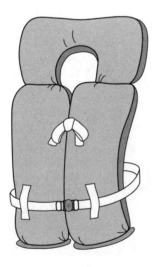

Figure 13-2 "Life jackets" are officially known as Personal Flotation Devices (PFDs).

IVs provide at least 16.5 pounds of buoyancy and are acceptable for use in canoes, kayaks, and boats less than 16 feet long. Type IVs are not intended for use by nonswimmers or children.

PFDs not only help keep people afloat, they also can help protect them from hypothermia while in the water. By rolling into the HELP position (Heat Escape Lessening Posture) while wearing a PFD, heat loss in water can be reduced by about 60 percent.

Fencing Around Pools

Evidence indicates that fencing around pools preventing children from reaching the pool unsupervised can prevent about three-quarters of all child drowning in pools. Fencing that completely encircles the pool and isolates it from the house is much more effective than methods where children can still gain access to the pool through the house or through an easily unlatched gate. Chain-link fences allows visibility of the pool, but are easily climbed by small children. Ornamental iron-bar fences reduce the chance of being climbed and offer visibility of the pool area.

The gate in the fence is the single most important part of the fence. It should be self-latching and self-closing, and it should open away from the pool and be checked frequently to ensure good working order.

The U.S. Consumer Product Safety Commission gives these minimum recommendations for fencing around a pool:

> Install a fence or other barrier, such as a wall, completely around the pool. If the house is part of the barrier, the doors leading from the house to the pool should be protected with an alarm or the pool should have a power safety cover. The barrier should be at least 4 feet high and should have no foot or handholds that could help a young child to climb it.

Pool fencing can prevent most child drownings.

Vertical fence slats should be less than 4 inches apart to prevent a child from squeezing through.

Use this as a guide when the release mechanism is located less than 54 inches from the bottom of the gate.

▶ If the horizontal members are equal to or more than 45 inches apart, vertical spacing shall not exceed 4 inches.
▶ If the fence is chain link, then no part of the diamond-shaped opening should be larger than 1-3/4 inches.
▶ Fence gates should be self-closing and self-latching. The gate should be well maintained to close and latch easily; the latch should be out of a child's reach. When the release mechanism of the self-latching device on the gate is less than 54 inches from the bottom of the gate, the release mechanism for the gate should be at least 3 inches below the top of the gate on the side facing the pool. Placing the release mechanism at this height prevents a young child from reaching over the top of a gate and releasing the latch. Also, the gate and barrier should have no opening greater than 1/2 inch within 18 inches of the latch-release mechanism. This prevents a young child from reaching through the gate and releasing the latch.

Swimming Ability

No universal, acceptable definition of swimming ability exists. Some have suggested that knowing how to swim places some swimmers in peril. They may be more likely to swim alone or in an unguarded remote location or take unnecessary risks. Also, learning to swim in calm water does not guarantee the ability to swim the same distance in water with currents, cold-water temperatures, and waves. In fact, a majority of drowning among good swimmers occur within a few yards of safety. Swimmers also may be less likely to wear PFDs. Another concern is that parents or caregivers may not be as vigilant when supervising children who can swim. In some instances, overestimating one's swimming ability or one's lifesaving ability (many die trying to save others) can result in drowning.

Nevertheless, knowing how to swim is a skill that can prevent drowning. The American Academy of Pediatrics (AAP) made this policy statement about when swimming lessons should start:

Infant and toddler aquatic programs provide an opportunity to introduce young children to the joy and risks of being in or around water. Generally, children are not developmentally ready for swimming lessons until after their fourth birthday. Aquatic programs for infants and toddlers have not been shown to decrease the risk of drowning, and parents should not feel secure that their child is safe in water or safe from drowning after participating in such programs. Young children should receive constant, close supervision by an adult while in and around water.

The YMCA and other organizations took issue and disagreed with the AAP statement. The AAP responded by saying:

> programs such as those developed by the YMCA and the American Red Cross emphasize aquatic readiness skills, other programs claim to make children safe in the water and thereby may raise unrealistic expectations among parents and guardians. ... Ultimately, the decision of when to start a child in swimming lessons must be individualized. We hope that our policy statement and recommendations can provide a guideline for these more individualized decisions.

The Harborview Injury Prevention and Research Center makes these important points (2007):

> Although a number of studies have shown that swimming lessons improve one's ability to dive, swim underwater, breathe correctly, and tread water, no study has examined the more important question of whether swimming lessons and/or drownproofing courses actually prevent drowning.

Parents can encourage young children to feel comfortable around water, beginning with carefully supervised bathtub play. This activity helps the child prepare for swimming readiness lessons.

Resuscitation

Cardiopulmonary resuscitation (CPR) serves as a temporary action used to maintain some degree of tissue perfusion prior to the arrival of an automated defibrillator (AED) and advanced life support (ALS). In most cases, CPR will not revive a person in cardiac arrest unless an AED and ALS arrive quickly. Nevertheless, CPR by bystanders, usually laypersons, can be a major factor in the successful

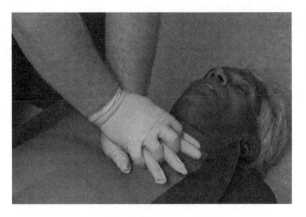

CPR can be a major factor in the successful survival of a drowning victim.

survival of a drowning victim. Not enough people know how to perform CPR. It is highly suggested that everyone should learn how to provide CPR.

References

American Academy of Pediatrics. (2004). Swimming programs for infants and toddlers. *Pediatrics* 105:868-870.
Auerbach, P.S. (editor). (2007). Wilderness medicine. St. Louis, MO: Mosby.
Baker, S.P., B. O'Neill, M.J. Ginsbury, and G. Li. (1992). The injury fact book, 2nd edition. New York: Oxford.
Bierens, J. and J.L.M. (editors). (2006). Handbook on drowning: Prevention, rescue, treatment. Heidelberg, Germany: Springer.
Branche, C.M. and S. Stewart. (editors). (2001). Lifeguard effectiveness: a report of the working group. Atlanta: Centers for Disease Control and Prevention, National Center for Injury Prevention.
Doll, L.S., S.E. Bonzo, J.A. Mercy, and D.A. Sleet. (2007). Handbook of injury and violence prevention. New York: Springer.
Harborview Injury Prevention and Research Center, University of Washington. www.depts.washington.edu/hiprc/index. Accessed August 2007.
Howland, J. and R. Hingson. (1988). Alcohol as a risk factor for drowning: A review of the literature (1950–1985). *Accident Analysis and Prevention* 20:19–25.
Howland, J., R. Hingston, T.W. Mangione, N. Bell, and S. Bak. (1996). Why are most drowning victims men? Sex difference in aquatic skills and behaviors. *American Journal of Public Health* 86:93–96.
ILCOR Advisory Statements. (2003). Recommended guidelines for uniform reporting of data from drowning. *Circulation* 180:2565.
Morbidity and Mortality Weekly Report. (2004). Nonfatal and fatal drownings in recreational water settings—United States, 2001–2002.
National Safety Council. (2001). Injury facts. Itasca, IL: National Safety Council.
Orlowski, J.P and D. Szpilman. (2001). Drowning: rescue, resuscitation, and reanimation. *Pediatric Clinics of North American* 48:627–646.
Papal, H.R. and A. Edris. (2005). Systematic review of definitions for drowning incidents. *Resuscitation* 65(3):255–264.
Pia, F. The reasons people drown video. www.pia-enterprises.com. Accessed April 2007.
Quan, L. and P. Cummings. (2003). Characteristics of drowning by different age groups. *Injury Prevention* 9(2):163–168.
Rowe, M.I., A. Arango, and G. Allington. (1977). Profile of pediatric drowning victims in a water-oriented society. *Journal of Trauma* 17(8):587–591.
Saluja, G., R.A. Brenner, A.C. Trumble, G.S. Smith, T. Schroeder, and C. Cox. (2006). Swimming pool drownings among U.S. residents aged 5–24 years: Understanding racial/ethnic disparities. *American Journal of Public Health* 96(4):728–733.
Schuman, S.H. (1976). The iceberg phenomenon of near-drowning. *Critical Care Medicine* 4:127.
Thygerson, A.L. (1992). Safety, 2nd edition. Sudbury, MA: Jones and Bartlett Publishers.
U.S. Coast Guard. (2006). Boating Statistics 2005, You're in command boat safety. www.uscgboating.org/statistics/Boating_Statistics_2005.pdf. Accessed August 2007.

CHAPTER 14 ▶

Residential Fire Injuries

The United States has one of the highest fire fatality rates in the developed world, and over 80 percent of these deaths occur in residential fires (U.S. Fire Administration, 2007). More than 4,000 Americans die each year in fires and more than 20,000 are injured (U.S. Fire Administration, 2007; U.S. Fire Administration/National Fire Data Center, 2004; Ahrens, 2006).

The U.S. fire death rate is high because the number of fires is high. During 1 hour, there is a statistical likelihood that more than 300 destructive fires will rage somewhere in the United States. At least one person dies in a home fire about every 2.5 hours (National Fire Protection Association, 2007).

Fire destroys or changes what is burned and usually produces heat, flame, light, and sometimes smoke. All fires require three basic ingredients and burn according to the same principle. Fires behave in different ways, however, depending on the nature of the ingredients involved.

The three components necessary for every fire are:

1. *Fuel.* Fuel, something that will burn, can be organic (such as wood), or inorganic (such as metal). It can be in the vapor or solid state, although many times only the vapor state is involved in the combustion process. For example, gasoline, a liquid, is commonly considered a fuel, but it is only the vapors that are involved in the burning process. Combustion of finely divided metals is a process that does not involve the vapor state. Steel wool, for example, will burn or oxidize rapidly in the presence of heat and oxygen.

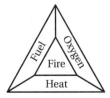 

Figure 14-1
The chemistry of fire.

2. *Heat.* Heat is necessary to initiate oxidation—enough to make the fuel burn. No matter where the heat originates, the combustion process cannot proceed without it.
3. *Oxygen.* Oxygen is almost always obtained from the surrounding atmosphere, which contains about 21 percent oxygen.

These three components—known as the Fire Triangle—can be used to simply explain the oxidation process and the basics of fire but it does not necessarily explain the entire fire process. Fire is rapid oxidation. By adding a fourth component, the fire is described as the Fire Tetrahedron, which more accurately shows the feedback of heat to the fuel to produce the gaseous fuel used in the flame. Another way to state this is to say that the chemical chain reaction provides the heat necessary to maintain the fire.

The process of burning can be described as follows. When a fuel becomes hot enough, its vapors mix with oxygen in the air, causing a chemical reaction that releases heat, flame, and smoke. The vapor, not the fuel itself, is what burns. A fire spreads because the heat feeds into new fuel and raises it to the ignition point. To extinguish a fire one removes one of the components—by cooling the hot fuel or by separating the fuel and the oxygen.

Each fuel has its own ignition temperature. The ignition temperature is the temperature to which a fuel must be heated in order for its vapors to combine with the oxygen and start to burn. The ignition temperature may also be called the kindling point.

Solid fuels (ordinary combustibles) do not produce vapors until they are heated to their ignition temperature. At this temperature, the vapors given off combine immediately with oxygen and burning begins. The ignition points of some solids: cotton sheets—464 degrees F (240 degrees C); newspaper—about 446 degrees F (230 degrees C); and wood—380–860 degrees F (193–466 degrees C). As a comparison of temperatures, a match flame has a temperature of about 2,000 degrees F (1,093 degrees C).

Flammable liquids are, by far, one of the most hazardous materials found. These include any number of solvents, ethers, alcohols, fuels, and cleaning solutions. It is important to minimize the use of, or preferably completely eliminate, flammable liquids wherever possible. For example, nonflammable liquids can be substituted in many cases for flammable cleaning solutions and solvents.

Flammable liquids give off vapors at temperatures lower than their ignition temperatures. For example, regular gasoline begins to give off vapors at about –45 degrees F, but its ignition temperature is 700 degrees F (371 degrees C). Although the vapors will not combine with oxygen and start burning on their own at these lower temperatures, they are capable of starting to burn when a flame or spark heats them to their ignition temperature. Often the vapors, though invisible, are present and can easily be ignited. The vapors usually travel near the floor.

Most common heat sources usually produce temperatures higher than the ignition temperatures of most common fuels; thus they can easily raise the fuel to its ignition temperature. For example, the heat produced by a match flame or an electric arc is about 2,000 degrees F, and the heat produced by a lighted cigarette ranges from about 550 degrees F to 1,350 degrees F. They are well above the ignition temperatures of paper, wood, cotton, and gasoline—the most common fuels.

Plastics exhibit a wide range of reactions when exposed to fire. Almost all plastics are somewhat flammable because they are petroleum-based products.

Burning begins in different ways, depending on the ingredients involved. Ordinary burning begins when heat—usually from friction, a flame, a spark, or a heat surface—is high enough to ignite the vapors of a fuel. Electrical current is another way. Spontaneous heating occurs when a fuel increases its own temperature without drawing heat from its surroundings. In other words, it heats by itself. This usually happens through fermentation or a chemical action. Spontaneous heating of a material to its ignition temperature results in spontaneous ignition. The fire literally starts by itself. Fuels that have a high spontaneous ignition include oily clothing or rags, silk and many other fabrics, and damp hay.

Explosion and fire occur when something is ignited in a confined space such as a container, room, or building, causing quick chemical changes that make the fuel gases expand rapidly with great force. Some examples are firecrackers, rockets, and blasting caps. Aerosol cans also may explode if heated.

Flammability

Flammability (how easily and how fast something burns) depends on the ingredients involved including the kind of fuels. Some fuels have lower ignition temperatures than other fuels and, therefore, burn more easily. For example, paper is easier to burn than metal. Some fuels burn very slowly (e.g., asbestos and cement), sometimes only smoldering and never really flaming, while others burn very quickly (e.g., soft wood and paper). The shape and form of the fuel also affects flammability. Usually a light, "airy" form burns more easily than a heavier, more solid form. For example, a crumpled-up newspaper sheet burns more easily than a folded sheet of newspaper. The rate and period of heating is another influence. Long exposure time to heat increase the possibility of burning. For example, a log surrounded by heat from paper and kindling is much more likely to ignite than a log that has a match held against it for a few seconds.

In general, fires spread very quickly. As a fire burns, it gives off heat. This heat warms other fuels in the area to their ignition temperatures and they begin to burn. As a fire grows, it can produce so much heat that it even heats fuels that are at a distance from the fire.

Cooking equipment is the leading cause of home structure fires and fire-related injuries. Smoking materials was the leading cause of fire deaths (see Table 14-1).

Table 14-1 Leading Causes of Home Structure Fires, 2000–2004 Annual Averages

Cause	Fires	Civilian deaths	Civilian injuries	Direct property damage; in millions of dollars
Cooking equipment fire	120,000 (32%)	220 (7%)	3,660 (25%)	362 (7%)
Heating equipment fire	59,000 (16%)	330 (11%)	1,250 (9%)	540 (10%)
Intentional	19,000 (5%)	310 (11%)	1,070 (7%)	487 (9%)
Candle	16,400 (4%)	200 (7%)	1,680 (12%)	450 (8%)
Smoking materials	14,000 (4%)	700 (24%)	1,340 (9%)	378 (7%)
Exposure to other fire	13,900 (4%)	30 (1%)	80 (1%)	319 (6%)
Electrical distribution or lighting equipment	13,100 (3%)	140 (5%)	580 (4%)	340 (6%)
Clothes dryer or washer	8,900 (2%)	10 (0%)	290 (2%)	85 (2%)
Playing with heat source	8,200 (2%)	170 (6%)	1,020 (7%)	225 (4%)
Confined or contained trash or rubbish fire	13,900 (4%)	0 (0%)	50 (0%)	3 (0%)

Risk Factors

Risk factor data should be used to assist in the development, targeting, and evaluation of interventions (Warda, 1999a).

Age. The very old and the very young are at highest risk of death from home fires. Children and older adults account for 45 percent of fire deaths and one-quarter of fire injuries (U.S. Fire Administration/National Fire Data Center, 2004). Young children are at higher risk for home fire death for a number of reasons: They may be more likely than older children to play with fire and then, in case of a fire, are unable to react appropriately and plan an escape; they may be left unattended; or they may be supervised and wake to the sounds of the smoke alarm, but are dependent on others for escape (McGwin et al., 1999).

The risk of dying for the elderly is 2.5 times higher than for the population as a whole (U.S. Fire Administration/National Fire Data Center, 2004). The elderly are at higher risk for home fire death for a number of reasons: They are known to have a lower prevalence of smoke detectors, they may be hearing impaired and cannot hear the smoke alarm; they are often physically impaired, which slows or prevents escape; and they may use older appliances, such as portable heaters or heating blankets, or live in older homes. Too, the elderly population is expected to increase in numbers with an assumed corresponding increase in fire deaths and injuries among older adults.

Gender. Like age, gender plays a role in the risk of death or injury from fire. For virtually all age groups, males are more likely to die in a fire-related incident. Males are about 1.5 times more likely to die in a fire than females. U.S. Fire Administration data show that males are also likely to suffer more injuries—from 1.5 to 2 times more (U.S. Fire Administration/National Fire Data Center, 2004). Why this is so is subject of speculation. Males may be more likely than females to try to extinguish a fire or try to rescue others from a fire, while females are more likely than males to attempt to escape. These actions could account for the differences between males and females.

Race. Race, which may be related to societal factors, cannot be ignored. African Americans and American Indians have noticeably higher death rates per capita than the national average. African Americans comprise a large and disproportionate share of total fire deaths, accounting for 25 percent of fire deaths—60 percent more than their share of the overall population. African Americans have twice the risk of dying than the general population. For American Indians, the risk also is elevated; 30 percent higher than the overall risk. By contrast, Americans of Hispanic origin have a lower risk of fire death than whites, and Asian Americans are much less likely than the overall population to die in a fire (U.S. Fire Administration/National Fire Data Center, 2004).

Socioeconomic. Socioeconomic studies repeatedly show income levels are tied to fire risk. There is an inverse relationship between fire risk and income. The poorer population groups have the highest risk of fire injury or death, while the wealthiest have the lowest (Istre, et. al., 2001). Many elderly people live alone on meager incomes, frequently in substandard housing. Closely tied to income is level of education. The groups living in poverty often are undereducated and lack a basic high school education (U.S. Fire Administration/National Fire Data

Center, 2004). Less safe behaviors can be due in part to gaps in knowledge, which may arise in part from a lack of formal education. Smoke detector use is known to be lower in poor, rural, remote, and central urban areas and in nonwhite populations. Mobile homes and substandard homes, more prevalent in these communities, are associated with a much higher risk of fire death. Methods of heating, such as wood stoves and kerosene, introduce additional risk.

Disability and alcohol-impairment. More than one-fourth (28 percent) of fatal home fire victims were reported to have some sort of disability, developmental limitation, or impairment before fire began. In two states where testing of blood alcohol levels was available for a large share of victims, the calculated share of adult fatal-fire victims with alcohol impairment (based on a 0.10 percent threshold, which is higher than the legal limit in many states) was 46–51 percent. A study of fire deaths in Alabama found a very similar 45 percent of victims aged 18 years and older had 0.10 percent or more blood alcohol concentration (McGwin, et al., 2000). Another report stated that alcohol use contributes to an estimated 40 percent of residential fire deaths (Smith, 1999).

Victim location at ignition. The majority of people fatally injured in U.S. home fires were not in the room of fire origin when fire began. The closer the victim was to the point of fire origin, the more likely it was that the fatal injury involved only a burn. For fatal victims who were in a different room or on a different floor, 25 percent of fatal injuries were smoke inhalation only and 1 percent were burns only (Hall, 2005b).

Victim activity when injured. Two of every five fatal home fire victims were asleep when injured. Only one-quarter of fatal victims are fatally injured while trying to escape. Two-fifths (40 percent) of nonfatal home fire injury victims were trying to fight the fire or rescue someone when they were injured. Males were more likely than females to be fighting the fire when injured, while females were more likely to be escaping the risk when injured (Hall, 2005b).

Escape difficulties. At least two-fifths to one-half of fatal and nonfatal victims had some problem interfering with their attempts to escape. The leading factor for fatal victims was fire blocking the exit. However, an exit blocked by flame and an exit blocked by smoke were the pair of factors most often reported together. Related factors, such as vision impaired by smoke or victim trapped by fire, also were cited with some frequency, but they often were reported in combination with fire blocking the exit. All these factors relate to the fire, while other factors relate more to the features of the building or the behavior of the individuals. Note that problems with door locks, security bars, or problem windows rarely are cited. Victims who were incapacitated before the fire began, moved too slowly, failed to follow escape procedures, or had burning clothing account for about 30 percent of fatal victims, but for 45 percent of victims aged 65 or older.

Smoking. The risk of home fire death is estimated to be twice as high for smokers as for nonsmokers. An average of 28 percent of home fire fatalities involve fires started by lighted tobacco products, nearly all of which were cigarettes; during the same period, roughly 23 percent of U.S. adults were current smokers (Hall, 2006a). A special study by the National Fire Protection Association (NFPA) estimated that 76 percent of home fire fatal victims of smoking-material fires were the smokers whose materials started the fire (Ahrens, 2003).

Many of the fires caused by lit tobacco products start in the bedroom or living room/family room areas of a home. Upholstered furniture and trash were the two items most often ignited in residential smoking fires. Fatalities are highest during the very early hours of the morning when the victims are asleep. Falling asleep is the highest contributor to smoking fires.

Although the relative number of residential fires caused by smoking materials is low, they do result in a high proportion of fire casualties.

Heating equipment. Fixed or portable space heating (i.e., units [not central furnaces] that heat entire housing), excluding electric-powered fixed units, poses a risk of death in home fire at least two to three times the risk for any type of central heating (Hall, 2006). However, any type of home heating equipment can be safely used. The heightened risk from space heating primarily is due to the close proximity of heating surfaces to combustibles and also to the greater role of typically untrained occupants in fueling, operation, placement, and maintenance of the unit. Natural gas and propane space heaters and portable electric heaters typically show a higher risk of home fire death relative to usage than fixed electric-powered space heaters and wood or coal stoves (Hall, 2006d).

Cooking equipment. Gas-fueled stovetops and ranges have a slightly higher risk of home fire death relative to usage than electric-powered stovetops and ranges but a much lower risk of fire incidents, nonfatal injuries, and property damage. Gas grills have a higher risk of home fire death than charcoal grills, though the risk for both is very low compared to other cooking equipment. However, if deaths due to unvented carbon monoxide with no hostile fire are included, then charcoal grills have a much higher risk (Hall, 2006a).

Consumer fireworks. The risk of fire death relative to exposure shows fireworks as the most risky consumer product. On Independence Day (July 4) in a typical year, more U.S. fires are reported than on any other day—fireworks account for half of those fires, more than any other cause of fires. From 2000 to 2004, 7 people per year were killed in fires started by fireworks, while 7 people per year were killed directly by fireworks. It is clear that fireworks can injure directly via a traumatic injury or indirectly via a fire injury from a fire initiated by fireworks. Structure fires can start with outdoor use of fireworks, similar to a bottle rocket when launched outside that lands on a roof.

The following five states have banned access by the public to all fireworks: Delaware, Massachusetts, New Jersey, New York, and Rhode Island. The National Fire Protection Association encourages people to enjoy public displays of fireworks. The NFPA is strongly opposed to any consumer use of fireworks (Hall, 2006c).

Place/location. Where injuries occur is of great importance. Clues can provide insights in determining what interventions might be successful.

Region. Geographic location comes into effect. There is a greater risk of dying in a fire in the South than other regions. This is attributed, in part, to the intermittent need for occasional heating. Rather than including central heating systems as in northern areas, many households in the South use portable heating devices for heat. By their nature, such heating strategies are more likely to lead to a fire problem. Conversely, the West, with the exception of Alaska, has a much lower risk of fire death. This reduction may also be due to the role of heating (or lack of) in fire deaths (U.S. Fire Administration/National Fire Data Center, 2004).

Location. Overall, the fire death problem seems more severe in rural communities than in mid-sized communities (50,000 to 100,000 population) or larger cities (Ahrens, 2003). Nonmetropolitan areas' high rates might be attributed to a lack of fire departments, local rather than central heating, and a shortage of emergency medical services.

More than 80 percent of the fatalities occur in residences (Karter, 2006). On an annual basis, roughly 1 percent of homes are damaged or destroyed by fire. Kitchens are the leading area of origin for home structure fires and third in fire deaths. Bedrooms ranked second for where fires started and also second for fire deaths (U.S. Fire Administration, 2007).

Most United States fire deaths occur in residences.

Time. The time pattern of death and injury occurrence offers extremely important information when selecting appropriate interventions.

Month. The majority of household fires and fire deaths occur from December through March, when the weather is cold, the hours of darkness long, and heating and lighting systems most utilized (CDC, 1998).

Day. Weekends have the highest rates, which is related to high blood alcohol concentrations in about half the adults who die in house fires. The relation between cigarettes and alcohol use is important because intoxication increases the likelihood that a lighted cigarette will fall unnoticed onto furniture or bed and remain undetected but after smoldering may erupt and rapidly spread.

Pathophysiology

Most fire victims die by inhaling smoke or toxic gases well before the flames have reached them. In fact, most fire victims never see the flames.

Sources vary in their estimates of what percentage (from 50 to 75 percent) of the fire deaths are related to smoke and/or toxic gases. Of the thousands admitted to hospitals every year, smoke or thermal damage to the respiratory system may occur in as many as 30 percent (Hall, 2005a).

The dominant modes of inhalation injury in a fire are: (1) asphyxia due to oxygen deficiency, (2) asphyxia due to carbon monoxide (CO) excess, (3) thermal damage, and (4) smoke poisoning.

Asphyxia Due to Oxygen Deficiency

The depletion of the oxygen supply can be extremely dangerous. Normally 21 percent by volume of the air humans breathe is oxygen. If that figure drops to 15 percent, breathing becomes labored, dizziness and headache set in, and muscular control is difficult. At 10 percent, extreme nausea is experienced and paralysis may be established. At 6 to 7 percent collapse and unconsciousness are inevitable, and below that figure, death will occur in a few minutes. Furthermore, at 12 to 15 percent, irreversible brain damage may result.

Asphyxia Due to Carbon Monoxide

Often called the silent killer, carbon monoxide is one of the most common and dangerous poisons. It is dangerous because it is a gas that is colorless, tasteless, odorless, and nonirritating; it can kill within minutes, depending on the concentration in the air. It is found in all fires. Generally a hot, fast fire, with plenty of oxygen, will produce a minimum of CO; a slow, relatively cool, fire with a limited amount of available oxygen, will produce greater amounts.

CO passes unchanged through the lungs and combines with hemoglobin (the oxygen-carrying pigment in red blood cells) producing carboxyhemoglobin. This deprives the cells of the body of necessary oxygen because CO's affinity for hemoglobin is about 200 to 250 times greater than that of oxygen. Thus, the red blood cell is unable to carry as much oxygen as it normally could.

Carboxyhemoglobin has a bright red color, and this has led people to say that it is possible to diagnose CO poisoning by noting the "cherry red" coloration of the victim's lips, nail beds, and skin. It has been shown, however, that the cherry red color occurs only with carboxyhemoglobin levels that are not compatible with life. In other words, it is only seen after death.

CO poisoning is not a minor incident that can be easily ignored. Even minor exposure can result in permanent central nervous system damage. Children fare less well than adults; it is not unusual for a child, especially an infant, to have severe symptoms including unconsciousness, while adults subjected to exactly the same exposure may show little effect. Women, because they have a greater tendency to be anemic, tend to fare less well than men.

Thermal Damage

Extremely high temperatures as a result of exposure to fire conditions can cause an immediate reaction in humans. Temperatures above 300 degree F (149 degree C) can cause death in minutes. The air temperature near the ceiling of a burning room may reach 1,000 degree F (538 degree C) or more, but most of the heat inhaled is dissipated in the nasopharynx and upper airway.

Thermal (heat) injury almost always is limited to the upper airway (nose, mouth, pharynx, larynx). Only those victims who inhale hot steam sustain actual lung damage from inhalation of heat. The upper airway damage is due to second- and third-degree burns that result in blisters, charring, and swelling due to capillary leakage and swelling.

Death can occur when the mucous membranes lining the respiratory system secrete fluids and thereby fill the lungs with liquid. A victim of heat inhalation can literally drown in his or her own liquid. Damage in the upper respiratory tract may cause swelling with gradual stoppage of the air passages, suffocation, and death.

Like burns of the skin, swelling does not occur immediately after the injury, and the risk of airway obstruction is greatest 12 to 24 hours after the damage first occurs.

Smoke Poisoning

Nearly 300 separate toxic products have been identified in wood smoke. The ever-present plastic products in today's homes produce these same types of toxins. The gases produced include: sulphur dioxide, nitrogen dioxide, hydrogen chloride, hydrogen cyanide, phosgene, and aldehydes. There is evidence that the combined hazard of two or more toxic gases is greater than the sum of the hazards of each.

The immediate effect of toxic gases is the loss of the bronchial epithelial cilia (hair-like projections) and decreased alveolar surfactant resulting in decreased lung volume. Surfactant is a chemical in the alveoli of the lung that is responsible for the stability of the alveoli (tiny air sacs in the lungs).

Panic

Though not a physical product of fire, panic often occurs when a fire breaks out and has been the cause of injuries and deaths due to trampling or jumping from windows too high off the ground. Several major fire disasters in the United States have had a high number of fatalities in a public building due to people trapped because of panic.

Burns

The most familiar aspect of fire damage to a human is a burn. The most common type of burn is the thermal burn. Soft tissue is damaged when it is exposed to temperatures above 111 degrees F (44 degrees C). The extent of damage depends on surface temperature and contact duration.

Burns are classified according to their depth. The three types of burns are:

- ▶ *First-degree* (superficial) burns involve only the top layer of skin, the epidermis. The skin turns red but does not blister or actually burn through the layer. Still, the burn site is painful. A sunburn is a good example of a superficial burn.
- ▶ *Second-degree* (partial-thickness) burns involve the epidermis and some portion of the dermis. These burns do not destroy the entire thickness of the skin, nor is the subcutaneous tissue injured. Typically, the skin is moist, mottled, and white to red. Blisters are common. These burns cause intense pain.
- ▶ *Third-degree* (full thickness) burns extend through all skin layers and may involve subcutaneous layers, muscle, bone, or internal organs. The burned area is dry and leathery and may appear white, dark brown, or even charred. Some third-degree burns feel hard to the touch. Clotted blood vessels or subcutaneous tissue may be visible under the burned skin. If the nerve endings have been destroyed, a severely burned area may have no feeling. However, the surrounding, less severely burned areas may be extremely painful. A pure full-thickness burn is unusual. Severe burns are usually a combination of first-, second-, and third-degree burns.

CAUSES OF BURNS

Various types of burn injuries exist, with each type depending on the source of the heat.

- ▶ *Flame burns* result from contact with an open flame that may ignite clothing. Although natural fibers tend to burn, synthetic fibers may melt or ignite.
- ▶ *Contact burns* result from direct contact with a hot object. Examples include burns from cigarettes and tools (e.g., cooking appliances).
- ▶ *Scalds* result from contact with hot liquids. The thicker the liquid and the longer the contact with the skin, the greater the damage.
- ▶ *Steam burns* most often occur in industrial incidents or result from motor-vehicle radiator incidents. Because of the pressurized steam and accompanying liquid, these burns produce extensive damage.
- ▶ *Electrical burns* produce heat damage by passing through tissue and most of the injury is deep in the skin.
- ▶ *Flash burns* are a result of rapid ignition of a flammable gas or liquid. Areas covered by clothing usually are spared while the face often may be involved. An example occurs when a person pours gasoline on a trash or leaf fire to increase the flame and is burned by the subsequent fireball.

Interventions

Numerous interventions have been used in an attempt to reduce residential fire-related death and injury (Warda, 1999b). However, the effectiveness of many of these interventions in reducing fire-related deaths and injuries remain unknown.

Public Education

Among the many measures that can be taken to reduce fire losses, perhaps none is more important than educating people about fire. People must be made aware of the magnitude of fire's toll and its threat to them personally. They must know how to minimize the risk of fire in their daily surroundings. They must know how to cope with a fire, quickly and effectively, once it has started.

Most fire service professionals agree that public education about fire has the greatest potential for reducing losses and that there is a need for public education in fire safety. Most of these professionals believe that many fires occur because of public apathy toward good fire prevention practices. The special target of educational efforts designed to prevent fire loss should be fires caused by human action. It is estimated that over 70 percent of building fires can be attributed to the careless acts of people.

The prevention of fires due to human carelessness is not all that fire safety education can hope to accomplish. Many fires caused by faulty equipment could be prevented if people were trained to recognize hazards; in addition, many injuries and deaths could be avoided if people knew how to react to a fire, whatever its cause.

Day in and day out, firefighters see the evidence of human failure. They see the tragic consequences of trash or flammable liquids stored near furnaces, overloaded electrical circuits, and gas heaters improperly vented. They find fire victims who have died in their sleep because they failed to take the routine precaution of always sleeping with bedroom doors closed. They find the charred bodies of those who took a fatal gamble with fire: who opened a hot door, who dashed through smoke instead of crawling along the floor, or who might have survived if they had held a wet cloth over their nose and mouth.

Educational messages about the prevention of fires are part of the work of the NFPA, the U.S. Fire Administration, and other organizations. The NFPA *Risk Watch* injury prevention curriculum, designed for children in preschool through grade 8 and their families, contains comprehensive fire prevention messages. The NFPA also offers the *Learn Not to Burn* and *Sparky the Fire Dog* programs for pre-school and elementary aged children and *Remembering When* for older adults, all focusing on fire prevention.

A 2-hour seminar focusing on fire and burn safety issues for a junior high school showed a significant improvement in burn and fire safety scores (Heinle et al., 1995). A statewide burn prevention program demonstrated a significant improvement in testable knowledge of burn prevention and fire safety among children and senior citizens as a result of an effective educational program (Victor et al., 1988).

While knowledge about fire prevention has been positively affected by educational programs, evidence is needed that such knowledge results in actual reductions in the number and the negative effects of fire. There is a need for more rigorous evaluation of educational programs, particularly those targeted at schools (Warda et al., 1999b).

Legislation

Several laws focus upon reducing the effects of fire. The most common legislation deals with the requiring smoke alarms to be installed in residences. States and communities vary considerably as to their smoke alarm requirements.

Another example of legislation is the Flammable Fabrics Act was passed in 1953 to regulate the manufacture of highly flammable clothing, such as brushed rayon sweaters and children's cowboy chaps. In 1967, Congress amended the Flammable Fabrics Act to expand its coverage to include interior furnishings as well as paper, plastic, foam, and other materials used in wearing apparel and interior furnishings. Under the Flammable Fabrics Act, the Consumer Product

Safety Commission (CPSC) can issue mandatory flammability standards. Standards have been established for the flammability of clothing textiles, vinyl plastic film (used in clothing), carpets and rugs, children's sleepwear, and mattresses and mattress pads.

Legislation requiring all cigarettes sold to be "fire-safe," which means they self-extinguish if left unattended too long, exists in most and have resulted in sharp reductions in the number of fires caused by cigarettes in those states.

Inspection

Many have found a checklist to be effective in inspecting a home for fire hazards. The CPSC has developed a checklist useful when checking for hazards. Go to www.cpsc.gov/cpscpub/pubs/556.pdf for a copy of the CPSC fire safety checklist. A computer search via Google or Yahoo can locate many other similar checklists.

Many fire departments offer a home fire inspection. Such an inspection should include testing of smoke detectors, inspecting the residence for fire hazards, and making recommendations about any hazards found.

Building Design and Codes

The two most important codes from the standpoint of fire safety are the building code and the fire prevention code. Typically, two-thirds to three-fourths of the provisions of a building code apply to fire safety, as do all the provisions of a fire prevention code. A problem with the codes is the diversity among cities.

A law is effective only to the extent that it is enforced, and so it is with a fire prevention or building code. Many serious building fires have been the result not of code deficiencies, but of lax enforcement. A fire-resistant floor, for example, is an insufficient barrier to smoke and fire if the architect allows gaps in the floor or a construction worker punches a hole in the floor to allow a pipe to pass through.

Vigilance is needed when reviewing plans and in inspection during construction. Once construction is finished, compromises in fire safety may be hidden from view. According to some experts, the training of building inspectors is, in many places, inadequate.

Product Design

It is not just the structures of the buildings that need improved design if fire losses are to be reduced. Many products also need design improvement. Heat and cooking equipment, faulty wiring, and electrical appliances are major causes of fire.

Upholstered furniture, bedding, and mattresses often are ignited in residences. Ignition resistance of these and other materials could reduce the risk of fires especially those fires related to smoking.

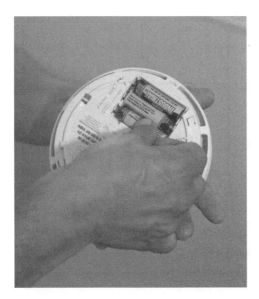

Smoke detectors are the single most important means of preventing fire-related deaths.

Smoke Alarms

Residential fires are especially dangerous at night when the occupants are asleep. Smoke alarms are effective, reliable, and inexpensive early warning devices that reduce injuries in residential fires. In the event of a fire, this early warning system can save lives. An estimated 890 lives could be saved each year if all homes had working smoke alarms (Ahrens, 2007b). Smoke alarms are the single most important means of preventing fire-related deaths by providing an early warning signal so the occupants can escape. Smoke alarms currently are in 95 percent of residences but should be present in every residence, including houses, apartments, and mobile homes. Unfortunately, about half of residential fire deaths occurred in homes without working smoke alarms (Ahrens, 2007b).

There should be one detector per level outside each bedroom area. More than half of the smoke alarm failures are due to missing or disconnected batteries, and 19 percent are due to dead batteries. Nuisance alarms were the leading cause of disabled alarms (Ahens, 2007b). Whenever possible, detectors should be located so that they avoid nuisance sources (e.g., avoiding areas near kitchens and bathrooms).

Ionization detectors are best for flaming fires, while photoelectric detectors are almost as good and still effective because they provide adequate warning of a fire. Photoelectric are best for smoldering fires, but ionization detectors are not effective since they will probably not provide adequate warning of a fire. A photoelectric sensor is the recommended type of smoke alarm because they respond more rapidly than ionization types and have fewer nuisance alarms.

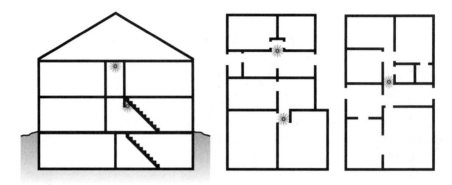

Figure 14-2 Smoke detector locations. *Source:* FEMA.

However, ionization alarms are the most common and battery-powered alarms the most popular.

Alarms should be installed, maintained, and tested according to the manufacturer's recommendations. Some experts suggest testing smoke alarms once a month; however, others recommend twice a year—during the spring and autumn when daylight saving time changes.

McDonald and Gielen (2006) found that "smoke alarm distribution programs that use the canvassing method of going to homes are an effective and efficient means of getting smoke alarms into people's homes but that smoke alarm functionality over time remains a problem." Increased smoke alarm use may be associated with community reduced price coupons and give away programs (DiGuiseppi and Higgins, 2000).

An automatic sprinkler system can reduce heat, flames, and smoke, which allows time to evacuate.

Home Sprinkler Systems

A sprinkler system is effective because it automatically reacts quickly to reduce heat, flames, and smoke thus allowing residents time to evacuate the home. In residences without sprinklers, fires become larger and more dangerous by the time the fire department arrives. However, the costs of sprinkler systems have deterred their widespread use, but that is changing with more economical technology being developed. The National Fire Protection Association says that automatic fire sprinklers and smoke alarms together cut the risk of dying in a home fire by 82 percent when compared to having neither.

Evacuation: Escape Planning

Two-thirds of Americans (66 percent) say they have developed a home fire escape plan, but only a third of those (35 percent) say they have practiced it (National Fire Protection Association, 2005). An escape plan includes drawing a floor plan and looking for two ways out of each room (including windows), testing all smoke alarms, practicing the plan at least twice a year, and agreeing on an outside meeting place.

Fire Extinguishers

A portable fire extinguisher can save lives and property by putting out a small fire or containing it until the fire department arrives. However, portable extinguishers have limitations. Before using a fire extinguisher, make sure that everyone has exited the building, the fire department has been or is being called, and the room is not filled with smoke.

A portable fire extinguisher can put out small fires.

There are three types of fires, and extinguishers are designed to fight particular classes of fires. Some fight only one class while some fight more. For a residence, select a multipurpose (Class ABC) extinguisher (can be used on all types of home fires).

- ▶ *Class A*: fire in ordinary combustible materials (e.g., paper, wood, cloth, plastics)
- ▶ *Class B*: fire in flammable liquids, gases, and greases
- ▶ *Class C*: fire in electrical appliances and equipment (faulty wiring)

To operate a fire extinguisher, remember the word PASS:

- ▶ **P**ull the pin. Hold the extinguisher with the nozzle pointing away and release the locking mechanism.
- ▶ **A**im low. Point the extinguisher at the base of the fire.
- ▶ **S**queeze the lever slowly and evenly.
- ▶ **S**weep the nozzle from side to side.

The person using the fire extinguisher should always keep a door behind them so that a quick exit can be made if the fire gets too large.

Conclusion

The United States has a severe fire problem. Nationally, there are millions of fires, thousands of deaths, tens of thousands of injuries, and billions of dollar lost through fires each year. Despite the availability of technology for detecting and suppressing residential fires, they remain a problem.

References

Ahrens, M. (2006). U.S. fires in selected occupancies. Quincy, MA: National Fire Protection Association.

Ahrens, M. (2007). U.S. experience with smoke alarms and other fire detection/alarm equipment. Quincy, MA: National Fire Protection Association.

Ahrens, M. (2003). The U.S. fire problem overview report: leading causes and other patterns and trends. Quincy, MA: National Fire Protection Association.

Centers for Disease Control and Prevention (1998). Deaths resulting from residential fires and the prevalence of smoke alarms—United States 1991–1995. *Morbidity and Mortality Weekly Report* 47(38):803–806.

DiGuiseppi, C. and J.P. Higgins. (2000). Systematic review of controlled trials of interventions to promote smoke alarms. *Archives of Disease in Childhood* 82(5):341–348.

Hall, J.R. (2005a). Characteristics of home fire victims. www.nfpa.org/assets/files/PDF/CharacteristicsOfHomeSummary.pdf. Accessed April 2007.

Hall, J.R. (2007b). Fireworks. www.nfpa.org/assets/files/pdf/os.fireworks.pdf. Accessed August 2007.

Hall, J.R. (2006c). Home cooking fire patterns and trends. National Fire Protection Association. www.nfpa.org/assets/files/MbrSecurePDF/cookingfull.pdf. Accessed August 2007.

Hall, J.R. (2006d). Home heating fire patterns and trends. www.nfpa.org/assets/files/PDF/HeatingExecutiveSummary.pdf. Accessed April 2007.

Heinle, J.A., R.W., Jensen, R.W. Lewis, and G.P. Kealey (1995). An effective method of educating junior high-aged children in fire and burn safety without disruption of the school curriculum. *Journal of Burn Care Rehabilitation* 16(1):91–95.

Istre, G.R., M.A. McCoy, L. Osborn, J.J. Barnard, and A. Bolton. (2001). Deaths and injuries from house fires. *New England Journal of Medicine* 344:1911–1916.

Karter, M.J. (2006). Fire loss in the United States during 2005. Quincy, MA: National Fire Protection Association, Fire Analysis and Research Division.

McDonald, E.M. and A.C. Gielen. (2006). House fires and other unintentional home injuries. From Gielen, A.C., D.A. Sleet, and R.J. DiClemente. (2006). *Injury and Violence Prevention: Behavioral Science Theories, Methods, and Applications.* San Francisco, CA: Jossey-Bass.

McGwin, G, V. Chapman, J. Curtis, and M. Rousculp. (1999). Fire fatalities in older people. *Journal of the American Geriatric Society,* 47(11):1307–1311.

McGwin, G., V. Chapman, M. Rousculp, J. Robison, and P. Fine. (2000). The epidemiology of fire-related deaths in Alabama, 1992–1997. *Journal of Burn Care & Rehabilitation* 21(1 Pt 1):75–83.

National Fire Protection Association. (2007). The U.S. fire problem. Available at www.nfpa.org. Accessed August 2007.

National Fire Protection Association. (2005). Young and older respondents are less likely to have developed and practiced a home fire escape plan. Available at www.nfpa.org/assets/files/PDF/Escapesurveyanalysis.pdf. Accessed August 2007.

National Safety Council. (2007). Injury facts. Itasca, IL National Safety Council.

Smith, G.S., C. Branas, and T.R. Miller. (1999). Fatal nontraffic injuries involving alcohol: a meta-analysis. *Annals of Emergency Medicine* 33(6):659-668.

Thygerson, A.L. (1992). Safety, 2nd edition. Sudbury, MA: Jones and Bartlett Publishers.

U.S. Fire Administration/National Fire Data Center. (2004). Fire risk. *Topical Fire Research Series* 4:7:1–6.

U.S. Fire Administration. (2007). Getting fire safety messages in the news. Available at www.usfa.dhs.gov/media. Accessed August 2007.

Victor, J., P. Lawrence, A. Munster, and S.D. Horn. (1988). A statewide targeted burn prevention program. *Journal of Burn Care and Rehabilitation* 9(4):425–429.

Warda, L., M. Tenenbein, and M.E. Moffatt. (1999a). House fire injury prevention update. Part I. A review of risk factors for fatal and nonfatal house fire injury. *Injury Prevention* 45(2):145–150.

Warda, L., M. Tenenbein, and M.E. Moffatt. (1999b). House fire injury prevention update. Part II. A review of the effectiveness of preventive interventions. *Injury Prevention* 5(3):217–225.

CHAPTER 15 ▶

Firearm Injuries

Guns are abundant in the United States. An estimated half of all American residences have a firearm (Wiley, 1993). While most firearm-related deaths involve suicide and homicide, this chapter focuses entirely on unintentional incidences.

In a recent year, there were 730 fatal unintentional deaths. This is 2.4 percent of firearm-related deaths (National Safety Council, 2007). Unintentional firearm death is often overlooked as a public health problem because they make up such a small percentage of all firearm injuries. Hospital emergency department surveillance data indicate about 19,000 unintentional nonfatal injuries occurred in a recent year (National Safety Council, 2007).

Pathophysiology

The seriousness of a gunshot wound usually is considered to be caused directly by the bullet. However, the wounding potential of bullets is exceedingly complex and is related to both the speed (velocity) and bullet mass. By greatly increasing the velocity, a bullet—despite its small size—contains extremely lethal amounts of energy. The speed of sound is the measure to which the speed of bullets is compared. Those that are slower than this are described as low velocity. They are fired from handguns and tend to be relatively large and round-nosed. High-velocity bullets travel faster than sound and can travel up to 3 miles in distance. Even a smaller .22-caliber bullet can travel a mile or more. The impact velocity depends on the ballistics of the ammunition and the distance of the victim from the muzzle.

Depending on its velocity, a bullet causes injury in the following ways:

▶ *Laceration and crushing.* When the bullet penetrates the skin, the tissue is crushed and forced apart. This is the main effect of low-velocity bullets. The crushing and laceration caused by the passage of the bullet usually is not serious, unless vital organs or major blood vessels are directly injured. The bullet merely damages tissues with which it comes into direct contact and the wound is comparable to those caused by weapons such as knives.

▶ *Shock waves and temporary cavitation.* When a bullet penetrates, a shock wave exerts outward pressure from the bullet's path. This pushes tissues away. This is much like a boat moving through water; the bullet disrupts not only the tissues that are directly in its path but also those in its wake. This has been described as a "blowing-out," resulting in the bursting of tissue. A temporary cavity is created that can be as much as 30 times larger than the diameter of the bullet. As the cavity is formed, a negative pressure develops inside creating a vacuum. This vacuum draws debris in with it.

This temporary cavitation occurs only with high-velocity bullets and is the main reason for their immensely destructive effect. The cavitation lasts for only milliseconds but can damage muscles, nerves, blood vessels, and bone.

In a *penetrating* wound, there is an entry of the bullet but no exit. In a *perforating* wound, there is both an entry and exit point. The exit wound of a high-velocity bullet is larger than the entrance wound, while the exit wound from a low-velocity bullet is about the same size of the entry wound. In a bullet wound that is made at very close range, the entrance wound may be larger than the exit because the gasses in the blast contribute to the surface tissue damage.

A bullet may flatten out, tumble, or even ricochet (bounce around) within the body. Bullets sometimes hit hard tissue (e.g., bone) and may ricochet in the body cavities and cause a great deal of damage to tissue and organs. Also, bone chips can be forced to other body areas, resulting in further damage. A split or misshapen bullet does greater damage because it tumbles, exerting its force over a greater diameter than a smooth bullet going in a straight line.

Shotgun Wounds

Shotguns are smooth-bore, long-barreled guns that are designed primarily for killing game birds and small animals. Another form of shotgun use not involved in the killing of animals is competitive shotgun shooting at clay targets, consisting of three types: skeet shooting, trap shooting, and sporting clays. A shotgun shell can contain (1) shot, also known as birdshot, which are round pellets, (2) buckshot, which is larger than birdshot and originally designed for hunting larger game such as deer, and (3) slug, which is a single solid projectile used to hunt large game.

An injury is determined by the type and amount of powder charge, the size of pellets, the constriction at the muzzle end of the barrel (choke), and especially the distance from the victim. At a range of 10 yards, about 95 percent of these pellets will be within a pattern 9 inches in diameter when fired from a full-choke bore. At

20 yards, these wound diameters are doubled. An effective shotgun range is about 40 yards, but pellets can travel 500 yards. Shotguns become ineffective at producing severe wounds at long ranges from loss of velocity and dispersion of the pellets.

Risk Factors

Few epidemiological studies of risk factors for unintentional firearm injuries have been published. Compared to firearm-related suicides and homicides, less is known about unintentional firearm injuries. However, it is believed that the easy availability of firearms is the main risk factor for unintentional firearm injuries.

The death rate from unintentional shootings is highest for males in all age groups. In fact, for those aged 0–14 years, 90 percent of the firearm-related deaths were males (National Safety Council, 2007).

Among children, most unintentional shootings occur to those left unsupervised at home. Unintentional shootings in rural areas are more likely to occur outdoors with shotguns or rifles, in contrast to urban areas, where they are more likely to be indoors with handguns. Handguns account for about 70 percent of unintentional firearm-related injuries and deaths (American Academy of Pediatrics, 2000).

Hunting. Hunting injuries have been studied much less that those occurring in residences. However, a profile of the typical hunting gunshot victim indicates that the victim is a male between 10 and 29 years of age and has had 1 to 5 years of

---

Guns are abundant in the United States.

hunting experience. Small-game hunters have more injuries (rabbit and squirrel versus deer hunters). Shotguns are involved in far more injuries than rifles. This is probably because there is more small-game hunting done with shotguns.

Hunting injuries most often occur between 6:00 AM and 9:00 AM on a Saturday, Sunday, Monday, or Tuesday. Hunting fatalities and injuries are, of course, related to the hunting seasons (usually the fall months).

Residence. Although men are the primary victims in hunting injuries, it is women and children who are getting unintentional shot in the home. Roughly half of the unintentional gunshot incidences occur in the home. This is a frightening aspect of the firearm injury problem because these injuries occurred in a situation where there was no intention of any shooting occurring at all. Most people think of hunting or target shooting when firearm injuries are mentioned. Most hunters spend just a few days a year in the field and the target shooters a day or two a month on the shooting range, but guns are kept in the home all year. Without question, there is more firearm handling in the home than on the shooting range and in the hunting field combined.

The problem of home gun safety becomes more complex when the number of untrained people who have access to firearms is considered. This is of particular concern for the million latch-key children who return every afternoon to a home that is unsupervised and contains an accessible gun. This partially explains why incidences tend to happen in the late afternoon.

Data shows that children are potentially exposed to firearms in many households (Stennies et al., 1999). This health threat illustrates the need for education about the child firearm injuries and for interventions to minimize the hazard.

When unsupervised young boys find a handgun, they are likely to handle it and even pull the trigger.

One-third of homes keep at least 1 firearm in the home and/or vehicle. Further-more, 21.5 percent keep at least 1 gun loaded and unlocked in the home, 30 percent stored all firearms unloaded and locked, and 48.5 percent stored firearms in a manner classified between these two practices. Households with children were more likely than households without children to store all firearms unloaded and locked (41.5 percent versus 20.9 percent); households without children were more likely than households with children to store at least one firearm loaded and unlocked (29.8 percent versus 11.1 percent).

Although it seems obvious, it is important to say that higher incidences of unintentional deaths occur where guns are more prevalent. This may explain why children living in the southern and western states have higher rates than those in the northeast.

Parents may believe that their guns in the home are safe from their children, but that often is not the case. A survey of parents who had firearms in their homes and who reported that their children had never handled firearms in their homes were contradicted by their children's self-reports. Parents who locked their guns away and discussed gun safety with their children were as likely to be contradicted as parents who did not take such safety measures (Baxley and Miller, 2006).

Another study determined how boys, aged 8 to 12 years old, behave when they find a handgun in a presumably safe environment. Many of them handled a handgun and one-fourth of them pulled the trigger. Boys who were believed by parental estimates to have a low interest in guns were as likely to handle the handgun or pull the trigger as boys who were perceived to have a moderate or high interest in guns (Jackman et al., 2001).

Nonpowder Guns

Nonpowder guns (e.g., BB guns, pellet guns, air rifles, paintball guns) continue to cause serious injuries to children and adolescents. The muzzle velocity of these guns can range from about 150 ft/second to 1,200 ft/second. Injuries include penetration of the eye, skin, internal organs, and bone. Each year, several deaths occur from injuries with these types of guns (Conn, 2004; Laraque, 2004; Nguyen, 2002).

Interventions

Safe storage. Guns kept in homes are more likely to be involved in a fatal or nonfatal unintentional shooting, criminal assault, or suicide attempt than to be used to injure or kill in self-defense (Kellermann, 1998).

The American Academy of Pediatrics and the American Medical Association recommend storing firearms unloaded and locked up to minimize the chance of injury (Miller, 2005). The four practices of keeping a gun locked, unloaded, storing ammunition locked, and in a separate location are each associated with

Gun locks can reduce
unintentional shootings.

a protective effect and appear to be a feasible strategy to reduce firearm injuries in homes with children and teenagers (Grossman, 2005).

A community-based handgun safe-storage campaign was conducted consisting of television and radio announcements, educational materials, billboards, and discount coupons for lock boxes. This educational campaign, combined with economic incentives to purchase lock boxes, did not seem to significantly change safe storage practices in homes with handguns and children (Sigman, 2005).

Safer firearms. Unintentional shootings can be reduced if firearms had loaded chamber indicators, grip safeties, and magazine-disconnects. A magazine disconnect device prevents the firearm from firing when the magazine is removed. Grip safeties require that the firearm be held properly and with a certain amount of strength (lacking in young children). A loaded chamber indicator shows that a bullet is in the chamber. Personalized guns require the owner to wear an electronic device or magnetic ring on the hand holding the gun.

Child access prevention (CAP) laws. CAP laws exist in some states that make it a crime if a child is shot with an adult's unsupervised access to a gun. The purpose of these laws is to promote the safe storage of guns. Most states that enacted CAP laws that allowed felony prosecution of offenders experienced greater declines in the rate of unintentional firearm deaths for children under the age of 15 compared with states not enacting the laws (Hepburn, 2006; Cummings, 1997).

Education. Programs exist that teach children how to behave safely around guns. Other programs exist for hunters and others programs on handling and shooting guns.

Few studies have evaluated the effectiveness of child-oriented programs designed to teach children gun safety skills. A study of two child gun safety skills programs found that children did not use the safety skills when tested in a

Gun safety classes involve handling and shooting guns.

naturalistic (outside of the training session) setting (Himle, 2004a). However, other research has shown that young children can learn important safety skills (e.g., fire safety skills) and use the skills when tested in naturalistic situations (Jones, 1981). Furthermore, another study demonstrated that more intensive behavioral skills training procedures were effective for teaching young children skills to prevent gun play and that the children used the skills when finding a gun in a naturalistic situation (Himle, 2004b).

Two studies investigated the effectiveness of skills-based firearm safety programs on reducing children's play with firearms. The studies found no difference between those in the program and those not in the program, which cast doubt on the potential effectiveness of skills-based gun safety programs for children (Hardy, 2002; Hardy et al., 1996). More research is needed to determine the most effective way to promote the use of the skills outside the training session.

Hunters' clothing color. "Hunter" orange (e.g., fluorescent or international orange) is worn by hunters to increase their visibility and to reduce their potential for being mistaken for game. Education courses for hunters promote the use of hunter orange, and most states require hunters to wear hunter orange. A New York study found that most injured hunters in shooting incidents were not wearing hunter orange (CDC, 1996).

Conclusion

When compared with homicides and suicides, unintentional firearm injuries are small but still important, especially for children. A multifaceted approach is best.

First, keeping guns out of the hands of children is important. This involves the proper storage of firearms and ammunition. It also includes parent education and legislation that makes parents criminally liable if their guns are accessed by a child who injures or kills another individual with it. There is evidence that such legislation can work. However, children will continue to find firearms and be at risk for injury. Therefore, teaching safety skills to children to prevent gun play minimizes the risk of injury. A child is best protected when the hazard has been reduced or eliminated and the child has learned skills to deal safely with the hazard should it ever be encountered.

References

American Academy of Pediatrics. (2000). Firearm-related injuries affecting the pediatric population. *Pediatrics* 105(4):888–895.

Baxley, F. and M. Miller. (2006). Parental misperceptions about children and firearms. *Archives of Pediatric and Adolescent Medicine* 160(5):542–547.

Centers for Disease Control and Prevention (CDC). Hunting-associated injuries and wearing "hunter" orange clothing—New York, 1989–1995. *Morbidity and Mortality Weekly Report.* 45(41):884–887.

Conn, J.M., J.L. Annest, J. Gilchrist, and G.W. Ryan. (2004). Injuries from paintball game related activities in the United States, 1997–2001. *Injury Prevention* 10(3):139–143.

Cummings, P., D.C. Grossman, F.P. Rivara, and T.D. Koepsell. (1997). State gun safe storage laws and child mortality due to firearms. *Journal of the American Medical Association* 278(13):1084–1086.

Grossman, D.C., B.A. Mueller, C. Riedy, M.D. Dowd, A. Villaveces, J. Prodziinski, J. Nakagawara, J. Howard, N. Thiersch, and R. Harruff. (2005). Gun storage practices and risk of youth suicide and unintentional firearm injuries. *Journal of the American Medical Association* 293(6):707–714.

Hardy, M.S., F.D. Armstrong, B.L. Martin, and K.N. Strawn. (1996). A firearm safety program for children: they just can't say no. *Journal of Developmental and Behavioral Pediatrics* 17(4):216–221.

Hardy, M.S. (2002). Teaching firearm safety to children: failure of a program. *Journal of Developmental and Behavioral Pediatrics* 23(2):71–76.

Hepburn, L., D. Azrael, M. Miller, and D. Hemenway. (2006). The effect of child access prevention laws on unintentional child firearm fatalities, 1969-2000. *Journal of Trauma* 61(2):423–428.

Himle, M.B., R.G. Miltenberger, B.J. Gatheridge, and C.A. Flessner. (2004a). An evaluation of two procedures for training skills to prevent gun play in children. *Pediatrics* 113(1):70–77.

Himle, M.B., R.G. Miltenberger, and C.A. Flessner. (2004b). Teaching safety skills for potential injury prevention and life saving. *Journal of Applied Behavior Analysis* 14:249–260.

Jackman, G.A., M.M. Farah, A.L. Kellermann, and H.K. Simon. (2001). Seeing is believing: What do boys do when they find a real gun? *Pediatrics* 107(6): 1247–1250.

Jones, R.T., A.E. Kazdin, and J.I. Haney. (1981). Social validation and training of emergency fire safety skills for potential injury prevention and life saving. *Journal of Applied Behavioral Analysis* 14:249–260.

Laraque, D. (2004). Injury risk of nonpowder guns. *Pediatrics* 114(5):1357–1361.

Kellermann, A.L., G. Somes, F.P. Rivara, R.K. Lee, and J.G. Banton. (1998). Injuries and deaths due to firearms in the home. *Journal of Trauma* 45(2):263–267.

Miller, M., D. Azrael, D. Hemenway, and M. Vriniotis. (2005). Firearm storage practices and rates of unintentional firearm deaths in the United States. *Accident Analysis and Prevention* 37(4):661–667.

National Safety Council. (2007). Injury facts. Itasca, IL: National Safety Council.

Nguyen, M.H., J.L. Annest, J.A. Mercy, G.W. Ryan, and L.A. Fingerhut. (2002). Trends in BB/pellet gun injuries in children and teenagers in the United States, 1985–1999. *Injury Prevention* 8(3):185–191.

Sidman, E.A., D.C. Grossman, T.D. Koepsell, L. D'Ambrosio, J. Britt, E.S. Simpson, F.P. Rivara, and A.B. Bergman. (2005). Evaluation of a community-based handgun safe-storage campaign. *Pediatrics* 115(6):e654–661.

Sinauer, N., J.L. Annest, and J.A. Mercy. (1996). Unintentional, nonfatal firearm-related injuries: A preventable public health burden. *Journal of the American Medical Society* 275(22): 1740–1743.

Stennies, G., R. Ikeda, S. Leadbetter, B. Houston, and J. Sacks. (1999). Firearm storage practices and children in the home, United States, 1994. *Archives of Pediatric and Adolescent Medicine* 153:586–590.

Thygerson, A.L. (1992). Safety, 2nd edition. Sudbury, MA: Jones and Bartlett Publishers.

Wiley, C.C. and R. Casey. (1993). Family experiences, attitudes, and household safety practices regarding firearms. *Clinical Pediatrics* 32:71–76.

APPENDIX

Core Competencies for Injury Prevention Professionals

The State and Territorial Injury Prevention Directors Association (STIPDA) partnered with the Society for the Advancement of Violence and Injury Research (SAVIR), formerly the National Association of Injury Control Research Centers (NAICRC), to develop core competencies for professionals working in the field of injury and violence prevention, as well as identify and/or develop ways to learn the skills and knowledge identified in the core competencies. For more information about the core competencies and their development, visit www.injuryed.org.

The essential competencies for injury and/or violence prevention are identified here. Following the general list of competencies is a more detailed list including learning objectives.

1. Ability to describe and explain injury and/or violence as a major social and health problem.
2. Ability to access, interpret, use and present injury and/or violence data.
3. Ability to design and implement injury and/or violence prevention activities.
4. Ability to evaluate injury and/or violence prevention activities.
5. Ability to build and manage an injury and/or violence prevention program.
6. Ability to disseminate information related to injury and/or violence prevention to the community, other professionals, key policy makers, and leaders through diverse communication networks.
7. Ability to stimulate change related to injury and/or violence prevention through policy, enforcement, advocacy and education.
8. Ability to maintain and further develop competency as an injury and/or violence prevention professional.
9. Ability to demonstrate the knowledge, skills and best practices necessary to address at least one specific injury and/or violence topic (e.g., motor vehicle occupant injury, intimate partner violence, fire and burns, suicide, drowning, child injury, etc.) and be able to serve as a resource regarding that area.

Core Competency 1 with Learning Objectives

Ability to describe and explain injury and/or violence as a major social and health problem.

To achieve this core competency, participants will be able to:

a. Define injury and/or violence and describe the concepts of intentionality and mechanism as they relate to injury and/or violence.
b. Describe the biomechanics that underlie how injuries occur.
c. Describe how injury and/or violence compare with other leading causes of morbidity and mortality and with regard to burdens on the population (e.g., incidence, cost, years of potential life lost, etc.).
d. Explain how injuries and/or violence are preventable.
e. Describe an approach to prevention that includes the following steps: (1) problem detection/assessment, (2) identification of risk and protective factors, (3) development of interventions, and (4) evaluation of the effectiveness of interventions.
f. Explain the continuum of injury and/or violence prevention, from primary prevention to acute care and rehabilitation.
g. Explain the importance of collaboration and the role that different agencies, organizations, and disciplines play in prevention.
h. Describe how conceptual models (e.g., Haddon matrix, social ecological model, etc.) are used to portray the multiple factors underlying injury and/or violence.
i. Describe the disparity in the risks of injury and/or violence (e.g., differences by age, gender, race, ethnicity, education, location, access to economic resources, access to health care services, sexual orientation, creed, community norms, and the environment).
j. Describe the influence of a variety of factors (including age, gender, race, ethnicity, education, access to economic resources, sexual orientation, creed, community norms, access to health care services, and the environment) on injury and/or violence prevention.

Core Competency 2 with Learning Objectives

Ability to access, interpret, use and present injury and/or violence data.
To achieve this core competency, participants will be able to:

a. Describe key sources of data at the national, state, and community level and describe their strengths and weaknesses.
b. Describe the strengths and weaknesses of the International Classification of Diseases (ICD) system and its use.
c. Describe the differences between primary ("self-collected") and secondary data ("existing data") and provide examples of appropriate uses of each method.
d. Describe how data can be used to identify disparate populations.
e. Explain how data can be used to identify emerging issues in injury and/or violence.
f. Identify the ethical and legal issues involved in the collection and use of data.
g. Identify how a variety of factors (including age, gender, race, ethnicity, access to economic resources, community norms, etc.) may influence the collection, interpretation, and use of injury and/or violence data.
h. Define quantitative and qualitative forms of data and give examples of their use in constructing and evaluating injury and/or violence prevention programs. Describe the benefits and limitations of each kind of data.
i. Explain the importance of data for use in priority setting, program planning, quality improvement, evaluation, and advocacy in injury, and/or violence prevention.
j. Describe how qualitative and quantitative data can be used in conducting an assets-and-needs assessment of a community of interest.
k. Demonstrate the ability to present data in a clear and understandable manner for different audiences.

Core Competency 3 with Learning Objectives

Ability to design and implement injury and/or violence prevention activities. To achieve this core competency, participants will be able to:

a. Identify and explain the roles of national, state, and local level agencies and organizations that can serve as resources for prevention efforts.
b. Explain the role and benefits of collaboration in prevention efforts.
c. Identify types/examples of current and potential stakeholders/partners and their current prevention activities.
d. Describe how to identify and prioritize injury and violence problems.
e. Describe how to locate and evaluate the best sources of information (or "evidence") available on which to base intervention decisions.
f. Describe various levels where prevention activities can be focused (e.g., individual, institutional, community, public policy).
g. Demonstrate the use of a conceptual model (e.g., Haddon matrix, social ecological model, etc.) for identifying intervention opportunities.
h. Provide examples of interventions that use education/behavior change, legislation/enforcement, and technology/engineering to prevent injuries and/or violence. Describe how they can work together to create a comprehensive program.
i. For a given injury or violence problem, choose and justify an intervention based on (1) relevant data, (2) characteristics of the intended audience, (3) a conceptual model or theory (e.g., social ecological model, stages of change, etc.), and (4) evidence related to "best practice."
j. Design an implementation plan to include a description of the intended audience, goals and objectives, proposed activities, evaluation component, timeline, and resources.
k. Describe and understand how cultural, socioeconomical, political, and physical environment factors may influence a prevention effort.

Core Competency 4 with Learning Objectives

Ability to evaluate injury and/or violence prevention activities.
To achieve this core competency, participants will be able to:

a. Understand the importance of evaluation and why and when evaluation should be done.
b. Understand how evaluation should be integrated into intervention design and implementation.
c. Describe formative, process, impact, and outcome evaluation and describe when and how to use each of these.
d. Describe the use of qualitative and quantitative methods in evaluation, and explain the benefits and limitations of each method.
e. Understand effective means of communicating evaluation results as well as the role of evaluation in identifying the key components of an intervention that are effective, for whom they are effective, and under what conditions they are effective.
f. Identify potential stakeholders/partners and resources to assist in conducting an evaluation.
g. Identify potential barriers to specific types of evaluation and approaches to overcome these.
h. Develop an evaluation plan for an intervention.

Core Competency 5 with Learning Objectives

Ability to build and manage an injury and/or violence prevention program.
To achieve this core competency, participants will be able to:

a. Describe how to establish and maintain an advisory group to assist with the development and monitoring of goals for injury and/or violence prevention within a population (e.g., a community, a state, among children, among Latinos, etc.).

b. Develop a long-range plan for injury and/or violence prevention and identify issues that may impact program goals, implementation, and sustainability.

c. Identify key funding sources for injury and/or violence prevention activities.

d. Prepare a proposal for funding from an external source.

e. Demonstrate the ability to create, justify, and manage a budget.

f. Demonstrate the ability to prioritize the allocation of resources (e.g., personnel, financial, space, time, equipment, etc.) to align with program goals.

g. Develop a plan for hiring, supervising, and promoting the professional development of staff.

h. Demonstrate knowledge of ethical issues that may arise in injury and/or violence prevention practice.

i. Describe ways that injury and/or violence prevention can be integrated into other programs and identify common barriers to integration.

j. Demonstrate the ability to leverage program success to further program growth.

k. Demonstrate the ability to develop and use performance standards to monitor program success.

Core Competency 6 with Learning Objectives

Ability to disseminate information related to injury and/or violence prevention to the community, other professionals, key policy makers, and leaders through diverse communication networks.

To achieve this core competency, participants will be able to:

a. Identify and differentiate the components and methods of designing and delivering effective messages for different audiences.
b. Demonstrate the ability to prepare different types of written documents (e.g., written testimony, public health brief, fact sheet, press release, letter to the editor, policy statement, Web site content, etc.) to effectively communicate information about injury and/or violence.
c. Be able to serve as a resource to the public, media, and policy makers when appropriate and be able to provide referrals to other resources.
d. Demonstrate the ability to be effectively interviewed by both broadcast and print media on an injury and/or violence topic.
e. Participate in the preparation of a professional report or publication that addresses an injury and/or violence prevention finding or theory.

Core Competency 7 with Learning Objectives

Ability to stimulate change related to injury and/or violence prevention through policy, enforcement, advocacy, and education.

To achieve this core competency, participants will be able to:

a. Develop and implement a culturally appropriate marketing plan to promote an injury and/or violence prevention activity (e.g., within an organization, given community, etc.).
b. Describe the differences between policy, education, lobbying, and advocacy as tools to stimulate change in the community.
c. Identify key prevention policies, laws, or regulations that address injury and/or violence.
d. Identify gaps in policies, laws, regulations, and enforcement that, if addressed, could reduce injury and/or violence in the community.
e. Identify potential partners and opponents in influencing policies, laws, regulations, and enforcement and distinguish their roles.
f. Describe the role the media and other communication channels play in public education and how to utilize these channels to shape public opinion about injury and/or violence prevention.
g. Identify information on the cost of injury and/or violence and be able to describe its application in policy making.
h. Demonstrate the ability to work effectively with advocacy/survivor groups (e.g., MADD, National Coalition Against Domestic Violence, etc.) to advance injury and/or violence prevention policies, laws, or regulations.
i. Demonstrate the ability to use research and evaluation to develop culturally appropriate policy, advocacy, and education initiatives.
j. Demonstrate the ability to translate policy into organizational plans and programs.
k. Understand how policy change can have positive or negative effects on injury and/or violence outcomes.

Core Competency 8 with Learning Objectives

Ability to maintain and further develop competency as an injury and/or violence prevention professional.

To achieve this core competency, participants will be able to:

a. Demonstrate the ability to access and use key journal and electronic resources to obtain updated information regarding injury and/or violence prevention.
b. Identify key professional organizations and agencies related to injury and/or violence prevention and describe how these organizations can assist in maintaining and developing skills.
c. Identify a potential mentor/advisor who has experience in injury and/or violence prevention and can assist with professional development.
d. Identify and describe training resources, conferences, and courses that would be appropriate for learning new information on injury and/or violence prevention strategies, research, and best practices.

Core Competency 9 with Learning Objectives

Ability to demonstrate the knowledge, skills, and best practices necessary to address at least one specific injury and/or violence topic (e.g., motor vehicle occupant injury, intimate partner violence, fire and burns, suicide, drowning, child injury, etc.) and be able to serve as a resource regarding that area.

To achieve this core competency, participants will be able to:

a. Describe the causes and characteristics of the specific injury and/or violence topic.
b. Identify major sources of data related to the problem.
c. Identify at-risk populations and stakeholders.
d. Describe major risk and protective factors.
e. Demonstrate the ability to apply varied approaches to prevention, including the use of evidence-based information and/or best practices.

Source: Core Competencies for Injury and Violence Prevention. Developed by the National Training Initiative for Injury and Violence Prevention (NTI), a joint project of the State and Territorial Injury Prevention Directors Association (STIPDA) and the Society for the Advancement of Violence and Injury Research (SAVIR). May 2005. Available at http://www.injuryed.org/competencies.htm.

PHOTO CREDITS

INDEX

Accidents
  See also Unintentional injuries
  use of term, 9, 152
Adolescents
  driving, 172, 179–182
  graduated driver licensing, 172,
    179–182
  risk factors and, 31–32
Advisory boards, 63
Advisory groups/committees, use of,
  116–118
Advocacy
  defined, 134
  media, role of, 138
  members, selecting, 137–138
Advocacy groups
  list of, 140
  working with, 139
African Americans, injury rates for, 34
Age
  bicyclists, injuries to and, 194
  carbon monoxide poisoning and,
    210
  drowning and, 238
  falls and, 219–220
  fires and, 256–257
  motor vehicle injuries and, 155
  pedestrian injuries and, 187–188
  poisoning and, 203–205
  risk factors and, 30–32
Agencies and organizations involved
    in injury prevention, 60, 61–62,
  145–147
Aggressive driving, 169–171
Alaska natives, injury rates for, 34
Alcohol abuse, drowning and, 239
Alcohol-impaired driving
  checkpoints and patrols, as
    deterrence, 159–160
  communication and outreach
    strategies, 163–165

laws, as deterrence, 157–158
  prosecution and adjudication,
    160–161
  repeat offenders, monitoring,
    161–163
American Academy of Clinical
  Toxicology, 208
American Academy of Pediatrics
  (AAP), 208, 250
American Association of Poison
  Control Centers (AAPCC), 201
American Indians, injury rates for, 34
American Public Health Association
  (APHA), 145
American Red Cross, 251
American Society of Safety Engineers
  (ASSE), 145
American Trauma Society (ATS), 146
Anonymity, 48
Assessment (surveillance), 19–20, 65
  asset, 50–51
  needs, 51, 88
Association of Schools of Public
  Health (ASPH), 145, 146
Association of State and Territorial
  Health Officials (ASTHO), 146
Association of Teachers of Preventive
  Medicine (ATPM), 146

Basic Priority Rating System (BPRS),
  67, 69–72
Behavioral Risk Factor Survey System
  (BRFSS), 39, 46
Best practices, 20, 91
Bicyclists, injuries to
  brain injuries, types of, 194
  children, interventions for,
    195–196
  interventions for all, 196–198
  statistics, 193–194
Biomechanics, 9–10

collection errors, 54–56
emerging issues identified with, 47
ethical issues, 48
identifying disparate populations
with, 46–47
International Classification of
Diseases system, 44–45
interpretation errors, 57–58
national sources on, 39–43
presentation errors, 56
presentation methods, 51–54
primary versus secondary, 45–46
quantitative versus qualitative,
49–51
racial and gender differences,
48–49
state and local sources on, 43
statistical analysis, problems with,
54–58
Injury prevention
agencies and organizations
involved in, 60, 61–62
collaboration, 22, 60, 63
defined, 8, 19
factors that affect, 92–93
Haddon matrix, 22, 23, 24–26,
79–82
Haddon strategies, 26–27
primary (pre-event phase), 22,
24–25
program, description of
implementation plan, 87–92
secondary (event phase), 22, 24, 25
social ecological model, 27–29
spectrum of, 78–79
steps, 19–21
tertiary (postevent phase), 22, 24,
25
3Es, 82–84
use of term, 9
Web sites on, 77, 143–145
Institute of Medicine, 201
Insurance Institute for Highway Safety
(IIHS), 61, 135–137
Intentional acts, 4
Intentional injuries
defined, 2
examples of, 2
Internal collision, 154
International Classification of
Diseases (ICD) system, 44–45

International Classification of
External Causes of Injury
(ICECI), 45
Internet
See also Web sites
writing Web site content, 131
Interventions
See also Injury prevention
classification of, 22
develop and implement, 20
evaluation of, 21
Haddon matrix, 22, 23, 24–26,
79–82
Haddon strategies, 26–27
social ecological model, 27–29
3Es, 82–84
Web sites on, 77
Interviews
giving, to the media, 132
in-depth individual, 50, 51, 108,
109, 110
telephone, 110

Journals, list of, 143

Latinos, injury rates for, 34
Laws (legislative)
examples of, 135
identifying gaps in, 135–137
interventions, 82, 83
regarding choking, suffocation,
and strangulation, 235–236
regarding fires, 265–266
Letters, to editors, 130
Life lost, calculating potential, 16, 17,
47, 64–65
Lobbying, defined, 134

Malins, Joseph, 67
Marketing, social, 133–134
Maternal and Child Health Bureau
(MCHB), 61
Media, change/advocacy and role of,
138
Mentors, 148
Mission statements, 88–89
*Morbidity and Mortality Weekly Report
(MMWR)*, 47
Motorcycle safety, 175–179
Motor vehicle injuries
adolescent drivers, 172, 179–182

Lesson Plan
Behavioral Objectives
concept (content
Learning activities